The Truth Is...

Confessions and Tips from an Elementary School Teacher

Rebecca A. Thomas

Written by Rebecca A. Thomas
Cover Art by Mary Gartner
Copyright © 2012

ISBN: 1497595436
ISBN 13: 9781497595439

After twenty-eight years of teaching in the public schools, Rebecca (Becky) Thomas has some stories to tell and confessions to make. She also has tips for new teachers that are almost guaranteed to make the journey through the public school system a little easier. Reading this book will help you realize that in the good times, as well as the difficult, you're not alone in your thoughts and experiences as a teacher. So take a break from grading papers, writing lesson plans, answering emails, and attending workshops and treat yourself to *The Truth Is...Confessions and Tips from an Elementary School Teacher.*

During her years teaching in the public schools Rebecca has received various awards for creativity in the classroom, most significantly the Disney Teacherrific Special Judges Award. She was also nominated by selected students as Orange County Florida's "Most Influential Teacher" and honored at the National Staff Development Conference.

Rebecca writes children's songs and developed a math program — *Academics through Music* — using her songs, related activities, and a 100 square foot math mat. Rebecca taught *Academics through Music* in the Orange County Public Schools, and as a result saw a rise in student test scores. To find out more about the program, use the free K-1 sight word helps, buy center bundles (which include songs), skits, or books, or to find other products and free teaching ideas and activities, go to www.msthomaspresents.com.

Dedication

This book is dedicated to my family and friends who, throughout my years of teaching, supported me by listening to my stories, volunteering in the classroom and on field trips, giving me ideas and counsel, encouraging me when I felt overwhelmed, and consoling me as I experienced the sad changes in education.

To the children, parents of the children, school employees, and community members with whom I worked in my years as a public school teacher, thank you all for letting me be a part of your life as you have been a part of mine.

Thank you, Kori, for your editing skills and for helping me stretch as a writer.

Introduction

Over the years, I've kept notes and journals about my teaching experiences. Although I had forgotten some of the details I've included in this book and was thankful for the written records, the stories are so ingrained in my brain I could never forget them. This book is written, of course, from my perspective. What I share is how I felt in the different situations and the effect the situations had on me. I've tried to be honest about myself and the part I played in the mishaps you'll read about. The names of all people mentioned in this book have been changed. If you know someone with the same name as one of my characters, and the person you know just happens to be like the character with his name, it's purely coincidental — especially if the name is Miss Thomas. For teachers reading this book, I hope that it brings you some laughs, as well as comfort in knowing that you are not alone in your feelings of frustration with your workload and with the restraints put on you as a teacher. If you are not a teacher, I hope this book helps you understand that all of the crazy things concerning teachers that you hear about, read about, and witness with your own eyes are not always what they seem. *The truth is...*

Addendum

Since writing *The Truth Is ...Confessions and Tips from an Elementary School Teacher*, the No Child Left Behind Act has been repealed and the U.S. Congress has passed the Every Student Succeeds Act. According to news reports, this act will take a great deal of power — regarding public education — from the Federal Government and give it to the states. This shifting of power allows states to change the mandate that teachers be evaluated based on student test scores, the result of which would be the return of creative and inspiring teaching. The world of teaching will never be perfect, but it can be great if teachers are allowed to teach using the individual gifts they possess rather than using a government prescribed method. It is my hope that some of the sad changes in education that I wrote about in this book will be erased, and that elementary school teachers will once again be given the freedom that restores to them a passion for their calling. The truth is...nothing could be better for the public schools.

The Beginning of the End

It was Thursday, October 27, 2011, and I was looking forward to Friday the twenty-eighth. The students had the day off, the teachers had a workday, and I was hoping to make some sense out of the stacks of papers on and around my desk. Things had changed so much since I first entered the public schools in 1979 that it was hard to recognize my profession as the one I had become a part of so many years ago.

When I began my career as an elementary school teacher, I had the liberty to create innovative lessons for my students as I taught them the foundations of reading, writing, and arithmetic. So much of teaching now focused on testing that the world of education seemed to have gone from a place of creative thought and exploration, to a robotic delivery of information. I couldn't imagine that anyone who was in the position to decide what would be taught in the public schools, and how it would be taught, meant for things to end up this way. Nevertheless, my love for my job was dying because I could no longer teach the way I loved. The emphasis in the classroom had shifted from teaching so that the students loved to learn, to teaching for data collection. For me, the emphasis had shifted from creating and delivering stimulating lessons, to testing students for data collection, recording and graphing the data, and then being made to use the data to show that the students needed more intense drilling so that when they were tested again, the data would look better.

The weight placed on testing and data collection put a damper on the fun activities we once shared with the students in the classroom. The autumn with Columbus Day, Halloween, and Thanksgiving, the winter with Christmas, Hanukkah, New Year's, Valentine's Day, and Presidents' Day, and the spring with St. Patrick's Day, Easter, and Memorial Day once brought feelings of excitement and happiness to the teachers and children as they busily worked on fun, creative projects while learning about the history of the United States and its traditions. In many of the public schools these activities were now considered frivolous, or even more disturbing, politically incorrect, and so if a teacher presented a lesson and activity related to a popular U.S. tradition, she did so with the fear that she might be reprimanded for it. Everything taught in the classroom had to relate directly to one of the required benchmarks and evidence was to be written in our lesson plans.

Lesson plans — another area that was becoming difficult for me to keep up with. Weekly lesson plans that used to fill two handwritten pages now took fifteen or more typed pages because of the additional required information that had to be included in our daily procedures. My lesson plans were to be written two weeks in advance, but for me, writing lesson plans that far ahead of schedule was a frustration because they often didn't go as planned and had to be rewritten, usually more than once. For those who have never been an elementary school teacher, the following are some of the reasons lesson plans don't go as written: **students' teeth fall out, students wet their pants, students throw up, students tip over in their chairs and get hurt, students get their feet stuck in the rungs of chairs, students have emotional problems and disrupt the class, students have anger problems and scare the class, children with special needs run around the room screaming or sit lethargically when they're supposed to be working, fire drills, tornado drills, lice checks, technology breaks down, toilets plug up, students cut their hair in class, students get bloody noses from picking them, students take things from other students which causes arguments, school pictures don't go as planned, teachers get sick on the job and other teachers have to take their students, one-on-one testing takes longer than planned, bad weather, parents pulling their children out of school early with no notice which disrupts the class, parents bringing their children to school late with no excuse which disrupts**

the class — and these are just a few of the things elementary teachers deal with on a daily basis, and this at the schools where parents care about their children's education.

For me, one of the saddest changes that had come to many of the public schools across the nation was that the students were no longer required to stand for the Pledge of Allegiance or the Star-Spangled Banner, and as teachers, we were not allowed to ask a student why he wasn't standing. Throughout my teaching career, I shared with my students the love I had for the United States and tried to instill in them a sense of patriotism. How could I teach in a system that was now telling the students it was okay not to be patriotic? The conflict I felt within myself was making it harder for me to be a part of something I couldn't whole-heartedly support.

That Thursday afternoon, I stood outside at recess watching my students play. I was tired, but so was everyone I worked with. In a few more hours the students would be dismissed and I would have Friday to recharge my batteries as I worked alone in my classroom. As I mentally prioritized my Friday work list, a wave of exhaustion washed over me and I shared with Mrs. Rodriguez, a first grade teacher standing beside me, what I was experiencing.

"Whoa. I don't know why, but I'm suddenly really tired. It's like I just ate a whole Thanksgiving turkey and I need to lie down," I said. "Maybe I'm hypoglycemic."

"Do you want me to get you some water or juice?" Mrs. Rodriguez asked. I thanked her, but declined the offer telling her I would be all right. As she took her class inside, I felt my body becoming weaker and knew that if I didn't sit down I would fall over. I headed towards a table and bench that was close to the playground equipment. When I reached the bench, I sat down, folded my arms on the table and laid my head on them.

Two of my first grade students saw that something was wrong, ran to me and asked, "Miss Thomas, are you okay?"

"Please get the nurse," I said. After that, I couldn't speak.

The experience that followed is difficult to explain. The nurse came, as did other teachers, administrators, and office personnel, and

I could clearly hear everyone talking, but I was unable to respond. My body was dead weight and devoid of energy.

"Did I have a stroke?" my brain questioned. Like a computer with no feeling, it scanned its information banks and concluded that what I was experiencing did not have the symptoms of a stroke. I was still unable to move and sent out a prayer asking for my energy to return. The principal called the paramedics and I heard Mrs. Rodriguez tell the others present that I thought I might be hypoglycemic. When the paramedics arrived, one of the school staff told them that I was diabetic.

"Diabetic?" I thought, "I'm not diabetic!" My situation felt very similar to how I often felt when I heard on the news, or read in the paper, many non-educators commenting on public education, not understanding the complexity of the issue they were addressing. I felt powerless to correct their misconceptions, just as I was now powerless to tell the paramedic I wasn't diabetic. I was taken by ambulance to a hospital that specialized in heart care and on the ride over I heard the paramedic talking to the medical personnel at the hospital. "She's diabetic," he told them.

My brain was screaming, "I'm not diabetic!" Finally, after twenty minutes of not being able to respond, I felt life slowly flowing back into my body and I forced my eyelids open. Then, with every bit of energy I could muster I said in a slow, deliberate voice, "I'm...not...di...a...be...tic."

"You're not diabetic?!" The paramedic was surprised.

"Noooo..." I yelled in a whisper.

I stayed in the hospital for two days as they ran test after test on my heart. My heart checked out fine, but my blood pressure was low and I was diagnosed with a condition called neurocardiogenic syncope — my blood was not always getting to my brain when it needed to get there, causing me to faint. The doctor said that the condition was often brought on by stress, and then made the comment that teaching was an extremely stressful occupation.

As I lay in my hospital bed, I thought about my teaching profession and the conflict that had developed between my personal feelings regarding effective teaching and the new mandates and regulations we educators had been given. Realistically, I didn't have many options when it came to leaving teaching. If I left the public school system I would have no health insurance. My monthly retirement pension would not even cover my house payment and utilities. My sense of reason would be questioned by those who saw me quitting my job in the midst of a less than certain economy. My heart, however, spoke louder than my fears and I knew it was time to take a leap of faith.

I returned to work on Monday, October 31st — Halloween. Halloween was the perfect day to return to work after giving the school a scare with my fainting incident. Many who had seen me after I fainted thought that I, as well as my teaching career, was dead. That's why when I came back to school on Halloween I saw fear on more than one face that passed me in the hallway.

I had bus duty Halloween afternoon, and as I took attendance for the kindergarten riders, one of the little girls said to me with wide eyes and a serious look, "My brother told me that you're dead."

"I am," I answered with a straight face. "It's Halloween and I'm a ghost. Oooooo!" I continued walking down the line, checking the names of the students who were present, not giving a second thought to my ghost comment.

I finished taking attendance and helped load students onto buses. Ten minutes had passed and a few groups of students were still waiting for their buses. I glanced in the direction of one of the groups and there was the little girl who thought I was dead. Her terror-filled eyes were fixed on me, and I immediately realized that she thought I was really a ghost. I quickly went to her. "I was only joking," I told her. "I'm not a ghost. Feel my hand." She touched my hand and relief filled her eyes.

The next day as I took attendance at bus duty, I came to the same little girl who the day before thought I was dead. This time she told me, "My brother said that you're a half-blood." Wow, two supernatural stories about me in two days! I didn't clear this one up. I was going to need a new source of income after I left teaching and I could see that I just might have a chance to star in a few teacher horror movies.

The day I returned to school from the hospital, my principal came to me and asked how I was doing. I told him that when the school year ended I would be leaving teaching. I would miss the children. I would miss the love and hugs I received on a daily basis. I would miss working with people who wanted to make a difference in the lives of others. But the truth was that in 2011, the teaching profession was no longer what I had gone to college to be a part of.

The morning bell hadn't yet rung so the students were not in the classroom. I walked into my empty room and was instantly filled with conflicting feelings. On one of the walls was our "Genius Town" mural — a depiction of a community showing schools, churches, neighborhoods, businesses, and government buildings. The first graders had made their own construction paper houses, cars, and people who lived in Genius Town, and a parent and I had glued them onto the mural. We had been adding to the mural for three years and every item on it reminded me of a student and evoked a memory. I was filled with homesickness — a homesickness for the happy days of teaching. On the front wall was the common board, the daily schedule, the learning objective for the first lesson of the day along with essential questions and vocabulary words. On the same wall was a data chart showing student test scores of all the never-ending tests these first-graders were given. One glance at this wall reminded me that the decision I had made to leave teaching was the correct one. There wasn't a hint of creativity or thought-provoking information found on this wall, and yet by edict of those in charge, this wall continued to grow, slowly crowding out the other walls in the room.

I sat at my desk and looked over my lesson plans for the day. I had looked over lesson plans thousands of times throughout the years and it felt surreal to me that this part of my daily routine would soon be nonexistent. Thirty-three years had come and gone since I first sat at a teacher's desk in my own classroom, and yet the memory of my first moment as a teacher was as clear to me as the moment I was now experiencing. In my life as a teacher I had myriads of students who had given me countless memories. Yes, I felt homesick for the happy days of teaching, but in reality, they had never left me. I would always be able to pull from my memory the stories of my teaching experiences, and as I have, I'm reminded that every day in teaching *wasn't* happy. *The truth is…*

One

The Truth Is...It Wasn't the Janitor

My first teaching job was in a small Ohio town. I taught sixth grade and it didn't seem that long ago that I had been in sixth grade. I could vividly remember my friends and teachers, my feelings about boys and the ups and downs with my girlfriends. I remembered how alive I felt and how intense every moment was. Now I would be teaching students like the one I remembered being. My youngest brother was fifteen — four years older than these students. Somehow this wasn't how I pictured myself as a teacher. I thought that when a person became a teacher, with the title came great wisdom and knowledge and much to offer one's students in the way of life skills. I hadn't lived that much longer than they had and felt more like an older sister than an instructor.

When the students came to class that first day, some of the girls were taller than I. Being only 5'3", it's not that hard to be taller than I am, but it seemed like the teacher should be taller than the students — at least in elementary school. I was told by seasoned teachers that for the first week or two it was important not to smile. "Let them know who's in charge. If they see that you mean business, they'll stay focused." I tend to smile a lot, so for me not to smile was going to take a lot of conscious effort. The bell rang and I was now officially in charge.

"Good morning, Class." I spoke with authority and the students listened. "As you know, I'm Miss Thomas and I'm happy to be here with you." I continued with my introduction and then took attendance. I was nervous beyond words and hoped it didn't show.

I finished with attendance and then went over the routine procedures for the year. It was now time for math. "I'd like everyone to take out their math books and turn to the first page where you will write your name and then the numbers 79-80." I wrote an example on the board and then sat down and opened the bottom drawer of my desk to get my math book. Because I was so nervous, my adrenaline was flowing at full speed. When I pulled on the heavy metal drawer with all of that extra energy, the drawer came flying off its tracks and landed on my shin, tearing a big hole in my pantyhose. I looked down and noticed blood leaking from a hole I had also gouged in my leg. I grabbed a tissue, dabbed my leg, and then feeling that I needed to show my students that a little blood wasn't going to stop me, I acted like nothing had happened. When I got up to teach, not one student said a word about the blood dripping through the tear in my pantyhose and down my leg. Despite their silence, I doubt that any of the students were unaware that their teacher was either really nervous or psychotic. I might have been both.

Things have changed a lot since 1979 when I first entered the world of elementary education. I couldn't have imagined the day we'd be walking around with a telephone in our purses or pockets and would be able to send messages through the air within a matter of seconds via a computer. In 1979 we typed student tests on typewriters and were happy that the typewriters were electric. We had to be extremely careful when we typed because we were typing on two-ply spirit masters. This was the type of form we had to use when making copies on the ditto machine — the only copier we had at that time. The top sheet of the spirit master was plain and the second sheet was coated with a layer of wax that had been permeated with purple coloring. When we typed on the plain sheet of paper, the force of the typewriter keys hitting the plain paper also bore down on the waxed paper behind it and caused the ink from the waxed paper to make an imprint on the plain paper. Any mistake that was made on the plain paper was duplicated from the waxed paper and imprinted forever. Not only was the process nerve-wracking, it was also messy. Most of us wore purple ink on our clothes, hands, or faces. Having a Xerox copy machine would have been really nice.

Ditto fluid was used in the printing process, and adults and students alike loved the smell of the freshly printed papers. When I was in school, our worksheets were run off on a ditto machine, and now that I was the teacher the smell of ditto copies launched a plethora of school-related memories, mostly positive and happy.

It seems that today's babies are born understanding technology. I don't remember understanding technology when I was born, so when it came to being proficient as a teacher, I had to be taught how to use a filmstrip projector, how to thread and operate a reel-to-reel projector, and how to use a ditto machine. Xerox copy machines were being used by businesses, but they were expensive and the public schools didn't have money for frivolous inventions like the copy machine. Who needed a Cadillac with the works when a Pinto with a steering wheel, accelerator, and brakes would do?

One day, after the students had gone home, I was in my room grading papers when a teacher friend walked in.

"Hey, Becky, do you know how to put duplicating fluid in the ditto machine?" JoAnne asked.

"I do," I answered. "Do you want me to show you how?"

"Sure," she said and so I walked with JoAnne down the hall to the ditto room. On our way, we met up with another friend, Lucy, who joined us on our mission to fill the ditto machine with duplicating fluid. We didn't know where to find the fluid so we asked the custodian, who was coming down the hall with his cleaning cart, where it was.

"It's in the boiler room in a large, rectangular, metal can," Bob told us and then continued down the hallway to clean the restrooms.

The three of us left the janitor and went to the boiler room and found two large rectangular metal cans sitting side by side, looking almost identical. Lucy picked one up and we went to the copy room. JoAnne then took the can, I showed her where to pour the fluid, she did, then ran her dittos, and we all felt pretty proficient.

The next day, while my students were at lunch, JoAnne burst through my classroom door and grabbed the edge of my desk where I was sitting. Her eyes, wide open, bulged as she leaned close to my face and said in an intense whisper, "Do you know what we did?" I had no idea what she was referring to. "We put mop oil in the ditto machine!" We? I hadn't touched that mop oil can.

"How do you know?" I asked.

"Because I was just eating in the teachers' lounge and the other teachers were talking about it and Connie Carter said, 'I can't believe any custodian would be stupid enough to put mop oil in the ditto machine.' I couldn't tell them that *we* did it."

I always thought of myself as being an honest person, but that was when we were talking about things like returning money when I got too much change or admitting I ate the last cookie. I had never been in a situation where my honesty would require me to give up half of my yearly pay. I didn't know how much a new ditto machine cost, but my entire pay for the year, before taxes, was around eighty-five hundred dollars. How could I buy a new ditto machine and not become homeless? If they made the custodian pay for the machine, I would have to say something. But unless that happened…

It was a little uncomfortable around the school for the next few days. There was no way to make copies of work for the students and believe me, some teachers get really upset when they can't copy worksheets for their students. Then, something completely unexpected happened. It was like Santa had made a surprise visit before Christmas, or the stork had delivered a baby to the school and it looked just like a Xerox machine! The teachers hovered around it and explored its many features. No more purple ink. No more ditto fluid. No more counting the copies. No more worrying about mistakes on a spirit master. It was beautiful! I wondered how much it had cost and if they were garnishing the custodian's wages.

The teachers who were so upset about the ditto machine being destroyed were now elated. A new world had opened to us, and education in our school would never be the same. We could copy more work for the students than ever before and never have a purple mark on us! Despite the excitement over the new addition to the school, I felt guilty that the custodian had been blamed for ruining the ditto machine.

Months after the ditto machine episode, I went to a clothing boutique in the town where I taught. One of the school custodians, a cute, petite woman named Gladys, owned the store. I talked with Gladys for a few minutes before I confessed.

"Gladys, you know the ditto machine and the mop oil?"

"Yes," she said, trying to read my eyes.

"Well, Bob didn't put that oil in the machine. It was a couple of other teachers and me. The whole thing was an innocent mistake, but I have felt terrible that Bob got blamed for it."

I never knew if Gladys told anyone that I had been involved with the destruction of the ditto machine. I promised myself that if ever I had enough money to pay for a new ditto machine, I would send a check to the school system where it happened. I never made enough money as a teacher to do so, but my life isn't over yet. The main thing is to tell Bob that I'm sorry he got blamed. If I had been a little older and a little braver (and a little richer) at the time, I would have fessed up. So if you're still with us on this earth, Bob, I'm sorry. But in actuality you became the hero. If someone hadn't put mop oil in the ditto machine, teachers at that school might still be walking around with purple marks!

Tip for New Teachers: Don't try to blame anything on the custodians. Most of them have more power in the school than you do.

Two

The Truth Is...I Wasn't Sure What Kind of a Teacher I Was

When the supervisor of elementary education interviewed me for my first teaching job, she told me that she was afraid I might be a little dictator with the children. A little dictator? Why would she think that? I didn't have the courage to ask her, so I mentally tucked the comment away and tried hard not to be a dictator. Other than making students put chewing gum in their hair if they were caught with it in their mouths (just kidding), my methods of discipline were pretty standard for the seventies — yell and threaten. I hadn't heard anything from the elementary education supervisor who had hired me, and I took that as good news. Then one day she called.

"Hello, this is Sharon Ann Phillips. I would like to observe your class next Tuesday." Sharon Ann feared that I would be a dictator and now she was coming to find out.

For me, one of the hardest things about teaching was knowing whether my methods of instruction were considered creative and effective, lackluster, or in this case, dictatorial. Over the years, some teachers sang my praises and told me what a wonderful teacher I was. Others observed my teaching and didn't say a word about my methods or style, and I guessed it was because they were polite. I finally came to the conclusion that because people learn differently and teach differently, there would probably never be a teacher whose teaching methods were perfect for every student or observer. That conclusion has comforted me over the years as I've thought back on Sharon Ann's visit.

It was April 1st and it was time for Sharon Ann to come. Yes, she came on April 1st but when the appointment was made, she only mentioned the day, not the date, so neither of us connected the day of her observation to April Fools' Day. Sixth grade students, however, would never forget a day like April Fools in the classroom and it wasn't long before their fun began.

To give my students a little credit, there was also a school counselor in the district by the name of Sharon Ann *Philson*. When Sharon Ann *Phillips* walked through the door, I introduced her to the class, never mentioning who Mrs. Phillips was. Sharon Ann inconspicuously sat at the back of the room where she could not only observe my masterful teaching, but where she could also see the students' reactions to it. I really did have a good class that year, so despite my nervousness in having Mrs. Phillips there, I wasn't concerned about the students. We had a good student-teacher relationship —maybe too good.

Mrs. Phillips wanted to observe me teaching reading, one of the most important subjects taught in elementary school. I told the students to take out their reading books. We had a routine that we followed every day and it was usually executed with very little noise. Today, however, there was a low drone in the room as my students whispered to one another. This was adding to the nervousness I already felt. I tried to ignore the whispering, wondering the whole time what Sharon Ann was thinking.

"Class," I said, "please open your books to page one hundred twenty-three." None of them opened their books. "Class," I said again, trying not to sound too dictatorial, "please open your books to page one hundred twenty-three." They stared at me with silly grins on their faces. I became firmer, "Boys and Girls, turn to page one hundred twenty-three *please*." They knew I meant business and reluctantly opened their books. I glared at them as I opened my book, and then slowly looked away to focus on the day's story.

To my horror, when I looked on page one hundred twenty-three, there was a huge beetle sprawled across the first paragraph. "Ahhhhhhhhh!" I screamed as I threw my book into the air.

Thud! The book hit the floor and the beetle slid between desk legs in the front row. Before it could run, the students yelled, "April Fools!"

April Fools! I couldn't believe I hadn't connected the date April 1st with April Fools' Day. Did Sharon Ann realize she had scheduled my observation for April Fools' Day? I looked back at her. Sharon Ann was quite a bit older than I, had short hair and glasses, and was trying to assure me with a tight little smile that she understood that children would be children. Was she thinking I was creative and effective, lackluster, dictatorial, or a pushover?

The beetle lay still under the desk. "Stunned," I thought, until one of the students picked it up and bent its rubber body in half. Fooled by a fake bug. The students had their laugh and settled down, taking turns as they read the story.

A short time passed and I once again felt like I was losing control of the class. Should I scream at the students and forever be labeled "dictator" by Sharon Ann, or should I break down crying and be known as the teacher with no control?

My students were again whispering amongst themselves. I politely told them to get quiet. They didn't. I got firmer and they got noisier. I understood that today wasn't an ordinary day, but did they know what their behavior might be doing to my job? When the classroom clock's minute hand hit the twelve, all of the students fell out of their seats and onto the floor where they lay flat on their backs and laughed uncontrollably. I didn't want to look at Sharon Ann or know what she was thinking, although I was pretty sure she wasn't thinking I was a dictator. Someone with my inability to control sixth graders sure wouldn't be able to control an entire country. This time when I looked back at Sharon Ann she wasn't smiling. In fact, she had gotten up from her chair and was walking towards me. The students were back in their seats, laughing over the good one they had pulled on Miss Thomas. As Sharon Ann and I walked towards the door, I quickly steered her away from my desk where slimy, dirt-covered earthworms were slithering towards my grade book.

Sharon Ann and I stood in the hallway outside of my door. "Well," she said not sounding very amused, "I can see your class has fun, but

I wonder if they're learning anything." Boy, I never could have imagined those words coming out of her mouth the day of my interview.

"They're usually not like this," I tried to explain, but she was too shaken by the experience to listen to what I had to say. "Maybe you could come back another day." I didn't want to be observed again, but I *really* didn't want her to think my students always had that much fun in school. She said she'd be in touch and left the building.

It was time for lunch and the students were all smiles when I walked back into the room. I didn't smile. "Line up," I ordered in an uncharacteristically stern voice. After lunch we had a talk, or maybe it would be more honest to say I let them have it.

"What were you thinking?! That was my supervisor and I'm not sure if I'll even have a job after today. She wondered if you were learning anything. Get your social studies books out and do the pages I have written on the board. And *no* talking." The students quietly got their books out and went to work. I knew in my heart that they were just having fun with me and on any other day it would have made me laugh. Why did my supervisor have to come on April Fools' Day?

I went to the back of the room and graded papers. The room was still except for the occasional turn of a page. As I worked, one of the girls got out of her seat and came to the back. "Miss Thomas," she said softly, "we didn't mean to cause you any trouble. We thought that lady was the school counselor."

Why didn't I tell them who she was? There was something in me that never allowed myself to prep students when I was being observed or visited by a superior. I wanted my visitors to see what my classes were really like. Talk about stupid. My student continued, "If you want, I can call the superintendent and tell him we've learned a lot in your class. I didn't even know where the United States was until this year." Hmmmm... better not tell the superintendent that.

I really did love my students and they were just having a little April Fools' fun. I felt bad that it had backfired and I got upset with them. I wrote Sharon Ann a letter apologizing for the disorder in the classroom, and invited her back for another visit. She answered me, telling me not to worry. She hadn't thought about it being April Fools'

Day when she made the appointment and as she thought over what had happened during her visit, she knew that the students were just being kids. I detected a chuckle in her words.

Over time, I actually began to think that Sharon Ann and I had developed a relationship of mutual respect. It wasn't until I had gone a full week with one hand of fingernails painted and the other not painted that I realized Sharon Ann would never really know or understand me or what my job required. The day I had begun to paint my fingernails at home, I ran out of time to do both hands. I now had ten minutes before the students would arrive and I decided this would be the moment I would paint my naked nails. Since I stayed hours past contract time each day, I didn't think taking sixty seconds to paint my nails would be cheating the taxpayers who paid my salary. I quickly began dabbing a nail when Sharon Ann unexpectedly walked into my room. Very curtly she said, "I wish I had time at my job to do my nails," and walked out. That was the first of many times I felt misunderstood as a teacher. The truth was, I barely had time to breathe in my life, but if someone wanted to think I had nothing better to do at my job than paint my nails, and didn't want to find out the truth, I guess there was nothing I could do about it.

Over the years that I taught, I came to realize that most people don't know what a teacher's job entails, sometimes not even the supervisor or principal over the job. But I also came to realize that it didn't matter as long as I was doing my job and the students were learning — and having a little fun in the process.

Tip for New Teachers: Do not schedule an observation for April 1st — unless you have to prove you're not a dictator. Don't worry about your fingernails being painted. Whether in or out of school, painted fingernails show you have too much time on your hands. If your fingernails look really bad, wear gloves.

Three

The Truth Is...I Didn't Love Every Child

Some of you reading this confession might not be at all surprised. Others of you might think I shouldn't have been a teacher if I didn't love all of my students. The truth is, there were only two children in all of my years of teaching that I tried over and over to love, but the harder I tried, the harder they made it to love them.

As you can imagine, I've taught numberless personalities over the years and tried to relate to each one according to his or her uniqueness. I taught a student with borderline personality disorder. He was tough, but he still brings a smile to my face when I think of him. I taught quite a few children who had been labeled emotionally handicapped due to anger issues, but I still loved them (and stayed a safe distance from them when they became angry). I had students who cheated and stole from me, students who lied to me and called me names, and students who at times disrespected me by using foul language. All of these students I loved, and despite the difficulties they often caused in the classroom, they each gave me at least one fond memory. There were two students, however, who wouldn't let me love them.

One of the unlovable students was in my first class. Carl was a huge, snide sixth grader who had no friends. He was pulled out of class on a daily basis to attend another class where he was being taught acceptable social behavior. I made every effort to show him that I cared about him and his success in school, but he emotionally and mentally pushed me away with every attempt I made. Although he was difficult to deal with, I was able to keep things balanced in the classroom and when he caused a problem with another student, I knew how to take care of it so that nothing more than the exchange of a few unkind words was made.

It was now spring and a new student had moved in. He was as large as Carl, but unlike Carl, he was kind. It was interesting to see these two students in my class, in some ways looking so much alike, but being complete opposites in character and social behavior. Unlike Carl, the new student was involved in sports. Carl didn't get involved in any extracurricular activities other than smoking marijuana with his mother and seven-year-old brother. Baseball season had just started, and despite not playing baseball, Carl wanted to wear a baseball cap in class. One rule that stayed consistent throughout my years of teaching was that no student was allowed to wear a hat while in the school (unless it was "Hat Day").

When I talked to Carl about his hat, I tried to communicate with him so that he didn't feel threatened. I didn't know what had happened in his life that had made him so mean-spirited, but I suspected he had been verbally, emotionally, and physically abused by a father who was no longer in the picture. Also, knowing that his mother used pot as a way to bring her family closer gave me a huge clue as to why Carl was so dysfunctional. So when Carl first wore his cap I smiled and said, "Carl, please take off your hat." He smiled back, but it wasn't a pleasant smile. It was more of a sneer, a threat that if I made him take it off he would get even with me. Like I said, he was huge. He wasn't more than five feet plus a couple of inches tall, but his build was like a bulldog's and he was carrying at least one hundred extra pounds beyond what he should have weighed. He kept the hat on and I dropped the issue.

The next day Carl walked into the classroom wearing his hat. He sat at his desk and stared at me, daring me to tell him to take it off. "Carl, you know you're not allowed to wear a hat in class. You need to take it off." He didn't. At the end of the day I told him that if he wore the hat in school again, I would take it from him and he wouldn't get it back. Although I stood directly in front of him and looked him in the eyes when I spoke, he left the classroom giving me no indication that he had heard a word I said.

The following day Carl came to class with his hat on. I'll have to admit, I felt sick to my stomach because I knew that I would have to follow through on my threat to take his hat and I didn't know how I was going to do that. At the time, I weighed one hundred ten pounds so Carl had at least one hundred pounds on me, and he was mean. Again, when he took his seat, he crossed his arms, fixed his eyes on me and waited to see what I would do.

As I spoke to him, I tried to be firm. "Carl, I told you that if you wore that hat again I would take it. Give it to me, please."

"No," he said in defiance.

"I'm serious, Carl, give me your hat or I'll have to take it off of your head." I was 99.9% sure he wasn't going to give it to me and I was frantically trying to figure out how I could get the hat off of his head without being flattened. He didn't budge. Every pair of sixth grade eyes was on me, and tension, mixed with my fearful thoughts of what Carl might do to me when I tried to take the hat, filled the classroom.

I knew the time had come for me to make good on my threat. I stepped towards the mammoth child and the minute I put my fingers on the rim of his hat, he lunged out of his seat to grab me. I didn't know what he was going to do to me when he got me, but I did know his options were wide open. As I thought about how my teaching career — and life — were coming to an end, the new boy lunged in front of me, and I watched as he threw Carl to the ground and kept him pinned there until another student got the principal.

Although I struggled all year to love Carl, my love for my protector grew effortlessly that day. Because the new boy joined our class towards the end of the year, I didn't get a chance to know him like I did the other students, but I loved him just as much, if not more, because he was willing to take a risk for me. Of course, he was at least twice the size of the other students and I'm pretty sure that years later I saw him playing in the Super Bowl. But despite that, he didn't have to step in. I don't know if he did so because he cared about me or if it was because he, too, had a hard time loving Carl.

Despite Carl's attitude and meanness, I've always hoped that as he grew older he would be able to turn himself around and find some happiness in life. And, in case he recognizes that I'm talking about him, I also hope that he's gotten really weak so that he won't be tempted to find me and finish the job he started in sixth grade.

The second student I tried to love, but couldn't, was in a fifth grade class I taught in Florida. This student wasn't with us when school started and before he came, my class was wonderful. We were able to do all kinds of special projects and the students worked well as a team. Then "Mick" moved in. I will call him Mick because his looks reminded me of a young Mick Jaggar. Although Carl was mean, he was sullen. Mick, on the other hand, constantly interrupted my teaching with sarcastic remarks and defiant comments, challenging everything I taught that encouraged students to become happy humans and good citizens. Like Carl, Mick didn't smile, he sneered and his anti-social behavior pushed every student away from him. Because of his nonstop disruptions, the class was no longer able to work as a team, and one day a group of extremely upset students came to me after school.

"Miss Thomas," David said, "we used to do so many fun projects in class. Ever since Mick came, nothing's fun."

"It's true, Miss Thomas," Stacy added. "He ruins everything."

They were right. There were no more fun learning times because Mick couldn't stand for anyone to be happy. Anything done in a creative or "out of the box" way he made fun of or caused havoc so that every lesson ended with me disciplining him, and the other students having to endure the bad energy in the room. I set up a conference with his father.

When his father and I met, I learned that he and Mick's mother were divorced. The father was a policeman and had custody of Mick. He mentioned that Mick had previously gotten counseling and that the mother was unable to handle him. We discussed ways that we might be able to help Mick and when Mick's dad left, I at least felt I wasn't fighting the battle alone. Not long after our meeting, Mick's father asked me out. I apologized for not being able to accept his invitation, but as Mick's teacher it would be inappropriate for me to date him (unless he was really rich). From that time on, Mick's dad was not supportive. Things grew worse in the classroom until it was virtually impossible for me to teach. I talked with my principal about the situation and she basically told me to just keep trying.

When I talked with the students about laws and why we had them, Mick felt that people should be allowed to walk into any store and take what they wanted. The other students and I tried to explain to Mick why his version of the free market system wouldn't work. He got mad and angrily told us that he should have the right to have what he wanted when he wanted it. That day when the students went to art class, I went to Mick's desk and took his Sony Walkman that he had stashed behind some books. (Those were the days when a teacher wouldn't get in trouble for going into a student's desk without permission.) The students returned from art class and we began math. It was then that Mick made the discovery that his Walkman was missing and started to rant.

"Somebody took my Walkman!" he screamed. The students looked at him and then at each other. Mick was not big like Carl, but the students knew that Mick was a loose cannon and no one dared cross him. I stayed calm and let him rant for a few minutes. "Miss Thomas, someone took my Walkman! It was in my desk and it's gone."

I finally spoke. "So."

"It was mine! That cost a lot of money! I'm gonna kill someone!"

Without flinching I said, "But I thought you said that we should be allowed to take anything we want from anyone we want. I wanted your Walkman, so I took it." All of the students but Mick smiled with surprise.

"That's mine! You have no right to take my stuff!"

"But you said we should have the right to take whatever we want." He wouldn't listen to reason. People like Mick never listen to reason. Somehow in their heads everyone owes them something but they owe nothing to anyone. Mick ignored my words and demanded his property be returned. I'm pretty sure my lesson was lost on Mick, but the rest of the class got it and I could say that they truly learned that day.

The year went on and Mick didn't get any better. I finally kicked him out of my class. The principal and I talked and I told her that unless I was able to teach when Mick was present, he couldn't come back to class. There was no one at home to take care of him, so Mick stayed under the principal's watch for three days. That's all the longer she could take him and so she brought him back to class.

"I won't take him back until he's ready to behave," I reminded her.

My principal smiled and said, "Oh, I'm sure he's ready. Aren't you Mick?" Mick snarled at me and I could see that he had really changed. "He's sorry," my principal went on. "Tell her you're sorry, Mick." He didn't say a word. "Come on, Mick, tell her you're sorry."

I sat patiently and waited for the miracle. "Mick, I have to get back to work," said Mrs. Frank, "so tell Miss Thomas you're sorry."

With animosity he finally blurted out a sarcastic, "Sorry."

"There you go," smiled Mrs. Frank, "I told you he was sorry." Either my principal had never been sincerely apologized to or she couldn't handle one more minute with the agitator. She left Mick with me and as she walked away, she held her shoulders and head higher as a weight had been left behind. I felt my body droop.

Of course Mick hadn't changed. In fact, he pushed the limits of disrespect and antagonism to new levels. The students and I had to do our best with the situation. I had never felt such strong hate from a child. I didn't know what had happened that made him the way he was, but I felt deep in my bones that if he had a gun he would kill me.

One day after school, the P.E. teacher came to my room and talked with me about Mick. "I don't know what's with that kid," he said, "but if he had a gun, I know he would shoot me." So it wasn't just my imagination. Then the art teacher came to me and said the same thing. Obviously there was something wrong with this child, scarily wrong, and yet he stayed in the public classroom. When I tried to talk with his father, the father accused me of being a weak teacher because I couldn't handle his son. And when I talked with my principal, she insisted that Mick needed to stay in my class because he needed my love.

My class and I made it through the year and after school let out for the summer, Mick was sent back to his mother who lived out of state. His policeman father, even with tear gas, pepper spray, and a few other deterrents, couldn't control his son. When school started the next year, Mick was kicked out of all the public school systems in the entire state where his mother lived. He was brought back to Florida and the last I heard he had been kicked out of all of the schools in the greater Central Florida area. I guess I wasn't the only one who couldn't handle him.

Like most teachers, I had visions and aspirations of being a support to students like Carl and Mick. I would be the one who would love the unlovable child when no one else would or could. I would find a way to help mend the broken spirit and help each student rise to his greatest potential. I would be the teacher who made the difference.

I finally faced the truth that not every student accepts love, and when it is offered, these children will throw it back to the giver wrapped in hate. These students are very rare, but they exist and can drain a teacher of the positive energy needed for the other students. After my experience with Mick, I made up my mind that I would never again allow one student to rob from the rest of the class a positive classroom environment. Unfortunately, I also learned that as a teacher my power was very limited and no matter what my resolve, if I wanted a job I would put up with whatever I was given. In the years that followed, despite the countless number of challenges I faced with various students, I never had another child who couldn't be loved.

Tip for New Teachers: If you are given a student who makes it hard to love him, find someone who is especially vocal about teachers pulling their weight in the classroom and ask him to be a volunteer

tutor for your difficult student. This approach might help a person who really doesn't understand what you're dealing with in the classroom look at things in a different light. (Unless, of course, the student is his child — then you're stuck!)

Four

The Truth Is...I Didn't Understand the Importance of Details

As a teacher, I can say that my intentions were always to give the students a memorable learning experience. Every year I tried to think of ways to reach the students so that they would remember the application of an academic skill found in math or science, or a life lesson found in reading passages from such sources as history books or autobiographies. However, it seemed like sometimes other teachers, and maybe parents, misunderstood my intentions because they only saw the outcome and didn't know my whole thought process and the desired effect I was after.

I've never thought of myself as being absent-minded or forgetful, but maybe that's because I don't remember. Once in a while, no, rarely do I pay attention to the smaller details around me and this can sometimes lead to trouble. That's why one day at school when the alarm went off, I took my students outside. After waiting with my class for a few minutes, wondering where everyone else was, I walked my class back inside. As we came through the doorway into the hall, hundreds of eyes peeked up from their tornado drill duck and cover positions and the principal rolled his eyes. Fortunately it was a practice.

It was the beginning of another school year and we were having our first teachers meeting. I sat with the teachers I had befriended the year before who were part of the ditto machine escapade, and listened as the principal went over routine housekeeping policies. My ears pricked up when his tone of voice changed.

"It's not necessary to mention names, but one of you left your classroom windows open and last night the police patrolling the area had to call Bob at 3:00 a.m. to open the school and check things out. Everything was okay, but please, Teachers, remember to close and lock your windows before leaving."

"I'm so glad that for once it's not me he's talking about," I whispered to my friends.

The meeting ended and just as the staff was leaving to work in their rooms, Bob, the custodian, walked by and loudly said, "Don't feel bad that you left your windows open, Becky. I took care of them and everything was all right. It wasn't that big of a deal that I had to get up at three in the morning to come to the school."

I wanted to go straight to my room, open a window, and crawl out of it.

Slowly, I was learning the importance of details and thinking my ideas through to the end before presenting my lessons. As I said, I was slowly learning but hadn't yet mastered the "thinking it through to the end" skill. In math, the students were learning about writing numbers with decimals. I thought it would be a good idea to show them how decimals were used in real life.

"Today I'm going to teach you how to write a check," I announced to the class. I was now teaching fifth grade, and as an adult I often wished that when I went to school I had been taught about taxes, insurance, bank accounts, and writing checks. I would give my students an education that I never got. "When you write a check, you have to be able to write numbers using decimals," I said. I then explained the different parts of a check and showed the students how to fill in the empty lines. I gave each student a few copies of a blank check and they practiced filling them out. The lesson went well and I knew that these students were one step ahead of where I was in the fifth grade — or even the twelfth.

The Monday following the practical application of decimals lesson, a group of students rushed into the classroom and up to my desk, talking so fast I couldn't understand what they were saying. I was only able to catch a word here and there. "Jamie...trouble... check..."

"Whoa!" I stopped them. "Blake, slowly tell me what's going on."

"Jamie Shuckleston went to his neighbor's house after you taught us how to write checks, stole a check from his neighbor and filled it out. He took it to the bank and they cashed it. The neighbor found out and called the police. Jamie's in the juvenile detention center!" Who would ever have thought that a bank teller would cash a check filled out and brought to him by a fifth grader? I guess I was doing a pretty good job as a teacher!

News spread fast. As I walked down the hall to lunch, a teacher coming from lunch made a loud remark. "Heard about your student in the Juvie Center. Why do these things always happen to you?" They didn't always happen to me. Sometimes it was me and my friends.

Jamie wasn't held in the JDC long — only a day. Later that year he pulled a knife on a student in the restroom. Jamie was suspended and I was proud to say I had nothing to do with the knife incident. Of course, he might have bought the knife with the money he got from the check he wrote. That was one detail I didn't want to know.

I learned that thinking through the details of a lesson is an important part of being a good teacher. On the other hand, if I had thought through every detail of everything I did as a teacher, there wouldn't have been time to teach. Sometimes you just have to take a chance!

Tip for New Teachers: If you plan on being spontaneous in the classroom pay no attention to details. In many ways this will make your teaching more interesting. However, details can be important if you want to keep your job.

Five

The Truth Is...I Knew Better

O ver the years, I taught in many different schools and several different school systems. Basically, the same subjects were taught, but cultures were different and so what was socially acceptable varied from school to school. When I taught Vietnamese children, they wanted rice and deer jerky for their Christmas party food. When I taught mostly Mexican children, piñatas were a part of every festivity. For an after-school fundraiser in an all black school where I taught, pickled hard-boiled eggs were sold, and in the school where I first worked, we weren't allowed to do fundraisers.

Things might have changed since I taught there, but at that time it was decided that fundraisers made a bad impression on the taxpayers who might be wondering what we were doing with their tax money if we had to have fundraisers to supplement the students' education. There were teachers who got away with making a little extra money for their classrooms by slipping in a quiet fundraiser on the side. "It's easier to ask forgiveness than permission" was an oft-quoted saying in the school. Although it was tempting to raise some extra funds for my students, it just wasn't in me to go against the rules the administration had laid out. That is, until the pencil sharpener came in the mail.

Teachers often get mail advertising educational products. In today's world, most of the mail comes over the internet. In the eighties, it came by way of the U.S. postal service.

One day after school, I sat at my desk opening my school mail. In my mail was a small box and when I opened it, I found an adorable die-cast Model T Ford pencil sharpener with wheels that turned. I set it on the front of my desk and read the brochure that came with it. The company that made the sharpeners offered many different designs and every design had a moving part. There was a globe, a sewing machine, a typewriter, a piano, and at least twenty other different sharpeners to choose from. I knew that if we were allowed to do fundraisers, this product would bring in some money. I didn't think anymore about it.

The next day when the students came to class, they immediately noticed the little die-cast car sitting on my desk. "Oh, Miss Thomas, that car's so cute! Where'd you get it?" asked Megan.

"It came in the mail," I said. "It's a pencil sharpener."

"A pencil sharpener! I want to buy one!"

I instantly put a stop to that idea. "Sorry, we're not allowed to do fundraisers at school."

"But it wouldn't be a fundraiser. I just want to buy one for myself." Megan looked at me with puppy dog eyes.

"Yeah, me too," chimed in the rest of the students.

They had a point. It really wouldn't be a fundraiser if the students were buying the sharpeners for themselves. I needed to think about that. As the day went on, I came to the conclusion that if the students wanted to buy a sharpener for themselves, that wouldn't be breaking the rules. The sharpeners were a dollar fifty apiece and we earned thirty cents for each sharpener sold. I really didn't think I'd get in trouble for earning eight dollars on pencil sharpener sales to my students. It would be spent on them anyway. At the end of the day I handed each student a pencil sharpener brochure to take home. The next day, more than half of the students came back to class with the brochures, and the brochures had many sharpeners checked indicating that each student wanted many sharpeners.

"What's this?" I asked. "I told you that you could each buy one sharpener!"

"They're all so cute, my parents want to buy some for stocking stuffers," Cindy explained.

"Yeah, mine too!" said Frank.

Kenny added, "My mom wants to buy a bunch to hand out at work."

"Kids, we're not allowed," I reiterated my words from the day before. "There is a no fundraising policy at this school!"

Cindy again spoke up, "But Miss Thomas, we're not selling them to raise money, we're selling them because people really want them. It would help out our parents if they could buy some."

I would give my fifth graders high marks in reasoning and persuading. I thought about what they were saying. Again, they were right; we weren't doing this to raise money. The sharpeners *were* cute and I could understand why their parents wanted them. I was even thinking of ordering a few more for myself just because they were so unique. At the end of the day I told the students that their parents could buy them. The students were excited and I hoped I hadn't stepped into the forbidden world of disobedience to authority. I could feel the slightest anxiety creeping through my nervous system and hoped it wouldn't last. When the students returned with their order forms the next day, my anxiety level tripled.

"What are all of these orders?" Most students had brought back their order forms and most students had sold ten or more sharpeners. That was over two hundred fifty sharpeners!

"My mom showed my neighbor and my neighbor wanted some," said Paul.

"I showed the bus driver and he ordered some," Susan beamed.

"And my grandmother wanted some," Tiffany piped in.

I was in trouble. I could have backed out and changed my mind, but now the parents (and neighbors, grandmas, and bus drivers) were counting on these sharpeners for Christmas giveaways. What would be worse, losing my job or having parents, students, and their neighborhoods mad at me? Maybe my principal would never find out. I talked about the situation with the students.

"Boys and Girls, you know we're not allowed to do fundraisers. But as you said, this really isn't a fundraiser. I don't want to do
anything that we're not supposed to be doing, but we're really not
doing anything wrong because we're just helping your parents and
everyone else you know." I would be getting high marks in rationalizing. After holding a lengthy debate in my mind, the "Goodwill to
all Men!" side won out and I mailed in the pencil sharpener orders.
I told the students that we'd be receiving the sharpeners in about
three weeks and until they came in, I didn't want to hear one word
about them. Hopefully, this would keep anyone else from finding
out. The students made a promise and nothing more was said about
the sharpeners.

A few weeks later I got a call from the office secretary, Mrs. Lee.
"Miss Thomas, there are two boxes here in the office for you." These
boxes could have been book orders or something the school had
ordered for my classroom so I didn't think much of the message.
When I got to the office I was handed two boxes with the words,
"World's Most Unique Pencil Sharpeners" printed on the outside of
them. Could Mrs. Lee see "guilt" written in my eyes? She didn't seem
to suspect anything as I took the boxes, thanked her, and nonchalantly carried the boxes out of the office.

The next day I handed out the sharpeners. They were even cuter
in real life than in the pictures. I got another call from the office.
"Miss Thomas, we have two boxes for you." This time I immediately
felt nervous, but put on a calm façade as I got the boxes from the
office and thanked Mrs. Lee. I wasn't sure how many more boxes
would be coming in, but I was pretty sure someone was soon going
to start asking questions. I continued to pass out the sharpeners and
every day that week I got a call from the office about more boxes.
Still, no one in the office asked any questions and I was starting to
breathe easier.

The week following the delivery of the pencil sharpeners I had
parent/teacher conferences after school. I was in the middle of a
conference when my classroom door flew open and in stormed my

principal, her eyes full of fury. "Miss Thomas, as soon as your conference is over I want to see you in my office!"

She didn't offer an explanation and I couldn't imagine why I was in trouble. She marched out of the room and I jokingly said to the parents, "Uh-oh, wonder what I did." They smiled and as we continued with our meeting, my curiosity was peaking. What could my principal be so upset about? After the conference, I walked down the hall with the parents and when they continued out of the building, I walked to the principal's office.

In all of my years growing up, I had never been sent to the principal's office. I was taught to be respectful to my teachers and the truth was, I loved school. As I walked into the principal's office, my heart sped up and for the first time I felt a tinge of fear as I walked through the door to see *the principal*.

"Hi Mrs. Walters. You wanted to see me?" She didn't ask me to sit down.

"I had two parents in my office furious about some pencil sharpeners you were selling." My heart skipped about fifty beats and my life flashed before me. The last scene in my life review was me waving goodbye to my students as they held up their cute little sharpeners. How could I explain this so that Mrs. Walters understood my intentions were not to raise money?

"Do you not know our fundraising policy?" I wasn't sure how to answer.

"Yes, I know that we're not supposed to raise money for the classroom, but we weren't selling these to make money. The students saw a sample pencil sharpener on my desk that a pencil sharpener company had sent me and it was so cute, they all wanted to buy one."

"There is a policy that the students are to sell nothing. Apparently one of your students sold sharpeners to her bus driver, he got fired and the parents are now stuck with the bill. They barged into my office while I was in the middle of a conference and began blasting me about pencil sharpeners I knew nothing about and then said that they would not pay for the bus driver's pencil sharpeners."

Not only was I in trouble for going against school policy, I was now also stuck with a pencil sharpener bill. I guess they'd have to add it onto the ditto machine tab.

There was nothing I could say that would make things better. I hung my head and apologized. I told her that I would take care of the bill. I used some of the money that we made on the pencil sharpeners to pay for the bus driver's sharpeners. The good news was that when my mom saw the sharpeners that the bus driver didn't buy, she fell in love with them and bought them all. So once again we had a little money to spend on the classroom (even though it was against the school law). I felt so bad about causing Mrs. Walters grief that I called her at home that weekend and broke down crying, telling her how sorry I was and promising her that nothing like that would ever happen again. She didn't know what to say. Then she softened and said, "Well, all right, just be sure it doesn't." Never did I think I would have to go to the principal's office to be reprimanded. What I didn't know then was that there were more principal visits ahead. Fortunately there was a policy against spanking teachers.

I learned that when there was a school policy put in place, I should never try to rationalize any reason for going against it. That was a challenge that would prove difficult for me, but I did my best.

Tip for New Teachers: If you get a sample die-cast pencil sharpener in the mail, do not open it or you will be rationalizing why you need to break school policy. And if you do, don't say I didn't warn you. Bus drivers can still be fired.

Six

The Truth Is...I Thought I Was Rich

For me, Christmas, spring, and summer breaks were always welcome times. I loved the students, but after being with twenty-five or more students day after day, and having schoolwork to do when I wasn't with the students, it was nice to have a break. When I first became a teacher, summer vacation lasted for three months instead of two. During those months off I worked another job to supplement the pay I wouldn't be receiving during the summer. I can't count the number of times people said to me, "You're so lucky that you get the summer off." Yes, we did get the summer off but it wasn't a paid vacation (and it still isn't). That was three months with no pay. That would be the same as a person working for a company and getting three months off each year — with no pay. Now, teachers can have their money divided so they get paid twelve months instead of nine, but that just means instead of working a job during the summer to make up for not getting paid during the months off, many teachers work part-time jobs all year to make up for the smaller paychecks.

Up to this point in my life, most jobs I had paid minimum wage. My first years in teaching paid close to that, but I did get health insurance. So when I was given my summer check for almost seven hundred dollars I was ecstatic! I had never had that much money at one time and although it had to get me through three months, I would be teaching summer school so I knew I'd have a little extra money to pamper myself. I began imagining what I would do with that much money.

I went to my bank and stood in line with other customers, feeling pretty important that I, too, had money to deposit and it was more than four hundred dollars. It was amazing to me how money could make a person feel just a little more important and a little more powerful. I held my head high and waited my turn in line. When I got to the teller, she asked me what I wanted to do with my money. I guess she could see the excitement I felt about my big paycheck and it made me happy that she was interested in knowing how I was going to spend it.

"Well," I started with a beaming smile, "I'm going to buy a bicycle and probably some new summer clothes and I'm pretty sure I'm taking a trip to Maine to see a family friend."

I wondered what the others in line were thinking. Were they jealous? I knew they could hear me and I hoped they were happy for me. I thought for a moment about what else I would do with my money and during the moment of silence the teller said, "That's nice, Honey, but what I meant was, do you want to put your money in savings or checking?"

Tip for New Teachers: Most bank tellers (and the people standing in line behind you) probably aren't interested in how you're going to spend your money — unless it's on them. So keep the line moving and keep your dreams to yourself. P.S. I did go to Maine.

Seven

The Truth Is...I Didn't Let the Students Use God's Name Disrespectfully

This particular confession may cause some controversy among my readers. When teachers, and especially younger teachers, heard that I wouldn't allow students to use God's name in a disrespectful way, some were shocked and told me that I wasn't allowed to prohibit the students from speaking that way. In response I would ask, "Why not?" When they tried to answer my question they realized that their reasoning came from the age-old "separation of church and state" argument. But when you think of it, using that argument is a very good reason not to allow the students to use God's name disrespectfully — it keeps church and state separated. So my rule was, if you used God's name in the classroom it was to be said with respect. Not many students used God's name in the classroom unless it was being used as an expletive so the rule kept a pretty good separation of church and state.

Parents also responded to my rule of not letting the children disrespect the Lord's name. Their response to this often went something like, "Oh my, G--, Miss Thomas, my daughter...oh, I'm sorry, I used the Lord's name disrespectfully. My daughter's been getting after me about that. She told me that you don't let them use His name disrespectfully in the classroom." I never dreamed that my students would get after their parents about this. I just wanted my classroom to be as positive and full of happy children and teacher as possible, and for me, starting with respect for God set the tone. I never once had a parent complain about this classroom rule.

In my first years of teaching, things were uncomplicated and as a teacher I had a great deal of freedom to teach the way I felt the students would learn best. All of the lessons I taught were not academic, and one year in particular I had a class who seemed to use God's name in every sentence. No matter how I reminded them, they just couldn't seem to break the habit. Then one day, off the cuff I said, "If we can get through one day without using the Lord's name, unless we're being respectful with it, we'll take a field trip to the Cleveland Zoo." As I said, there was a great deal of freedom in the public schools at that time (and I have the feeling I never mentioned to my principal the deal I had made with my students).

The students were very excited about the field trip and made every effort to speak without using the word "God" as a slang word. If they slipped and used God's name inappropriately, they would quickly correct themselves, until the day came that none of the students were using God's name in their everyday language. That is, no one but Charlie.

As a fifth grader, the use of God's name was so ingrained in Charlie's everyday speech that him trying to speak without saying "God" in every other sentence would be like trying to take away a chain smoker's cigarettes. As the days went on and Charlie couldn't seem to speak without using the Lord's name, I began to wonder if I had made a big mistake in making the zoo deal with the class. The students were becoming angry with Charlie because they wanted to go on the field trip, and as Charlie felt the pressure build, he used the Lord's name more frequently. I had visions of Charlie's parents calling the principal, or even worse, the superintendent because I had put their child under such stress. I knew that if I made an exception for Charlie using God's name disrespectfully so that we could go to the zoo, the class might be happy, but they would also know I wasn't as committed to my principles as I claimed to be. I would also be telling Charlie that he wasn't as strong as the other students and so in his case, I would make an exception. It might take the pressure off of Charlie for the moment, but I knew how kids teased other kids and coming from an extremely dysfunctional family, Charlie was already emotionally handicapped. What was this doing to him? I said a prayer for Charlie — and for me — that he could get through a day without disrespecting God's name and that his parents wouldn't call the principal on me.

Another day came and things were going along as usual, except for one thing — Charlie had not used God's name as he spoke. I didn't call attention to it because I was afraid of putting a jinx on Charlie. (Can a person be God-fearing and superstitious at the same time?) Each time he spoke I held my breath. I believe the whole class was holding their breath. By this time, the students were carefully monitoring each other's words on a daily basis, and although no one said anything, I knew that every fifth grader in that class was intently listening to Charlie when he spoke. It was time for lunch and there hadn't yet been a slip-up. The afternoon came and our classroom speech was still so reverent we could have held a church service. Finally, the end of the day arrived and I announced to the class that I'd be ordering the bus for our field trip. I can still remember the kids hugging Charlie and Charlie grinning from ear-to-ear. I ordered the bus, sent permission slips home, and we went to the zoo.

For me, those were happy days in the public schools. The days around Christmas were wonderful as the students sang holiday songs and concerts were performed containing a variety of Christmas, Hanukah, and other winter holiday music. The spirit in the schools, even for the scrooges, brought a heightened feeling of happiness to the classrooms. But as time went on, I watched as freedoms and God's connection to them were slowly taken from the public schools. A supreme being is central to the beliefs of the majority of Americans, and that includes public school students. How our school systems can remain some of the best in the world without invoking God's help is a question yet to be answered.

With the removal of anything in the public schools that was related to God was the loss of special occasions and celebrations. First we were forbidden to put up anything that said, "Merry Christmas." Then, in the last school where I taught before retiring, during the winter season we were forbidden to sing any Christmas songs, Hanukah songs, or any other holiday songs. The holiday show, which included songs from all of the religions represented in our school, was changed to a generic non-holiday program because a Wiccan parent complained about references to various religious practices, like giving gifts, spinning the dreidel, and decorating a Christmas tree. One person who believed in witchcraft was allowed to determine the December program for the entire school, and due to fear of repercussions, the only protests heard were behind closed doors. The majority of teachers were protesting, but the public never knew.

This removal of reference to God in the public schools also affected patriotic holidays. God's grace and blessings, that made this country great, were now rarely mentioned in the public schools. I still taught my students the U.S. motto, "In God We Trust" and reminded them that our country is great because ultimately our trust in God is the source of our power and strength. I didn't go beyond that, but even by saying that I felt I was at risk of being called out on the carpet.

During my last year in the public schools, the elementary teachers in my school were told that we were no longer allowed to call the fourteenth of February "Valentine's Day" because of its connection to a saint and a religion. If we exchanged cards on that day, it would be for "Friendship Day." I'm so thankful I didn't grow up in today's public schools because I would have missed out on some of the best memories of my life.

The Pilgrims might have come to America for religious freedom, but because of the fight against religion in our country, we're losing our freedoms. We might all want to say a prayer that this doesn't happen. To all of the teachers unable to speak these words in the classroom I say, "Happy Valentine's Day! Merry Christmas! Happy Hanukkah! Happy Easter! Happy St. Patrick's Day! And happy any other day that is important to you!"

Tip for New Teachers: Get to know God. There may be times in the classroom He will be the only support you have.

Eight

The Truth Is...My Desire to Sing and Perform Was Stronger than My Desire to Teach

Since I could remember, I loved to sing and act. As a four-year-old, I climbed the large maple beside our house and hid amongst its leaves, singing with full volume and vibrato, "Somewhere, over the rainbow!" Two of my cousins, along with my younger sister and I, spent many of our childhood days writing and performing short, discombobulated plays for our mothers who, despite the words "Oh, no, not again," written in their expressions, patiently sat and drank pickle juice "martinis" they were served while suffering through our performances. Somehow, maybe because I was bossy with my cousins and sister, I was always the star of those plays. As I grew older I tried out for real plays and without being bossy, got lead parts.

My high school drama teacher wanted me to go to New York. She had a close friend in one of the soaps and she said he could get me a tryout for the show. I never went, but always wondered if my name would have been in lights if I had given acting an honest try. As a teacher, I often found ways to incorporate acting and singing into my lessons, and wrote and put together a number of school talent shows and plays. These were fun, but they never completely satisfied my yearning to perform on Broadway. That's why, when a fellow teacher who knew of my love for the stage one day brought me an audition ad she had cut from the newspaper, I had to find out if performing professionally was my true destiny.

"I immediately thought of you when I saw this," Nancy said as she handed me the clipping.

I read to myself, "Disney World Auditions for Singers and Dancers." The ad listed the date, time, and place where the auditions would be held. It also gave a Florida phone number to call for any additional information.

I was elated. As soon as school was out for the day, I raced home and called the number on the ad. A woman answered, "This is Disney World Casting, where dreams come true. May I help you?"

Where dreams come true! Her words immediately made me hopeful. "Yes. Hello. I saw the ad in the paper about the auditions in Cincinnati next week. I was wondering if you could tell me more about them. I sing and I just needed to know what I should prepare for the audition."

She had a smile in her voice as she explained, "Bring two vocal numbers with you, one ballad style, the other pop. They'll teach you the dance when you get there."

"Dance?!"

Everyone in this world has abilities and talents. Everyone does something that makes them feel completely at ease. Choreographed dancing is on my "makes me feel completely inept" list. I love to dance, but for some reason I was never good at picking up choreographed dancing. Not only was I not good at picking it up, I got dizzy if I even thought about going around in one circle while dancing, and I couldn't kick either leg more than three feet off the ground.

"Yes, it won't be anything too complicated," she said.

"I don't dance."

"Oh, you'll be fine," she assured me. She worked for Walt Disney — or at least his legacy. He would never hire someone who lied.

I decided I'd make the four hour trip to Cincinnati to find out if performing at Disney World was in my future. The day of the tryouts happened to be the coldest day of the year, so I wore a wool pantsuit, a brown turtleneck, and heeled black boots. My sister-in-law Carrie kept me company on the trip. When we arrived, butterflies filled my stomach but I told Carrie, "As long as there are no kicks or turns in the dance I think I'll be fine." No sooner had I uttered those words than we turned the corner of the flight of steps we were descending and there, in front of us, was a large room full of people dressed in leotards and dance shoes.

"Kick, kick, kick, kick, turn, turn, turn, turn!" commanded the dance instructor. The dancers kicked and spun in harmony and I didn't see any of them with vocal sheet music in hand. How could this be happening?

Carrie looked at me, "What are you going to do?" She was as worried as I was. There are times when the fear within us has to give way to a desire that is stronger than the fear. Even more than I didn't want to dance, I wanted to sing.

"We've come all this way," I said. "Nobody knows me so who cares what they think about my dancing? I'm going to go through with it." I was proud of my courage and wondered who had taken over my body. Was I actually going to try to learn a dance that was comprised mostly of kicks and turns? If I didn't lose my balance from the kicks I was sure to be sick from the turns. One of the people in charge of the auditions informed me that before I could sing, I had to first make the dance cuts. I was trying to remember the name of that lady I spoke with at Disney casting...

I tried to fit in with the others as I kicked in my black winter boots, three feet into the air. The turns were murder and it was all I could do to not fall over after the first one. I couldn't have been in the building more than fifteen minutes when they called my name to audition. For me to learn that dance would have taken hours. As I walked towards the audition room, I glanced back at Carrie and saw a look of fear on her face that validated what I was feeling — I was doomed. I stepped into the audition room and the doors closed behind me. There were fifteen dancers in the room and three judges. The judge in charge, John Mitchell, told us to find an X on the floor and stand on it. The X's were big so I was able to do that part. "We" dancers were spaced about five feet apart.

"When the music starts, you know what to do," John directed.

I had no idea what to do. Did I kick or turn first? The music started and when the group went right, I went left — right into the dancers coming towards me. When the group went left, I ran into the dancers on the other side of me. There was mass confusion in the room and with every move I made I apologized to someone for disrupting his audition. I'm not sure if I did all of the kicks, I just remember that wearing the wool pantsuit made the judges very aware of my inability to kick. What dancer would wear a wool pantsuit to an audition? Between me burning up in my wool snowsuit and being on fire from embarrassment, my face began to perspire. The dance only lasted two minutes, but I felt like I had entered a time warp and was doing "Hell's Never-Ending Dance of Torture." The music finally stopped and all that could be heard was the howling of the judges. Nobody else in the room was laughing. I had to give those dancers credit — not one of them slapped me.

The judges wiped the tears off their faces and John said, "Everyone get back on your X's and do it again." He could barely get the words out as he laughed hysterically.

I knew why they were making us do it again. They were being entertained and I was the entertainer. This was not at all how I had envisioned my audition. I pictured a couple of steps to the right, then to the left, maybe a quick cha cha step and "tah dah," we got to sing!

As the music started up again, my brain went even blanker than before and I yelled out, "I'm not a dancer, I'm a singer!"

The judges spared us from doing the entire dance and told us to stand back on our X's. John then pointed to two other people and me and said, "You made it. The rest of you, thank you very much." I looked around to see if there was someone standing beside me on my X.

None of the dancers talked to me, but they were talking to each other, really loudly. "That was totally unfair! I'm going to demand another tryout!" Wow, what sore losers.

I came out of the tryout room and there sat Carrie with that same look of fear on her face. Was I going to burst into tears? "How did it go?" she asked.

"I made it!" I whispered, avoiding the glares of the dancers who didn't.

She accused me of lying, "You did not!"

"I did. I really did. I think God blinded their eyes so they couldn't see what I was doing. He knew how badly I wanted to make the singing auditions. I have to go back with my songs."

I took the music from Carrie and went back into the tryout room with a completely different energy. Now it was my time to shine! The pianist gave the intro and I began.

"Fish got to swim, birds got to fly, I got to love one man 'til I die, can't help lovin' dat man of mine."

"Thank you very much," John said, which meant, "that's it, you didn't make it." Now I was really confused.

I went to the piano to get my music and the pianist said, "You have a beautiful voice, keep singing."

"Thank you." I took the music and wanted to cry.

It wasn't until the summer that I understood the mystery of my audition. My younger sister lived in Orlando and I decided to pay her a summer visit and personally go to Disney casting while there. At casting I was told that there was a singing group who performed at the American Pavilion at EPCOT and no one in the group was required to dance. They stood still and sang. That was the group for me! I made an appointment to sit in at a rehearsal and when my appointment day came, I got to the rehearsal building a little early. After introducing myself to the receptionist, she offered me a seat on the small couch in front of her desk. A few minutes had passed when a nice-looking, dark-haired man walked through the door. The receptionist introduced him to me and when he shook my hand I realized it was John, the judge from Cincinnati! I acted as though I had never seen him before and as he looked at me he said, "I know you from somewhere. Do I look familiar to you?"

I hated to lie, but I didn't want him to remember me. "No, not really." He continued to stare at me, the whole time searching his memory banks.

"I know that I know you from somewhere," he said and then sat down on the couch next to me. "I'm not leaving until I figure out how I know you." It was no use.

"I know where you saw me. I auditioned in Cincinnati..."

"You're the comic dancer!" he burst out, interrupting my sentence. He laughed and said to the receptionist, "Ask her to dance for you!" He then went on to tell her about my audition. Despite the humiliation, I laughed and then asked him why I made the dance cuts but didn't make the singing cuts.

"We were looking for dancers," he said, "but after watching you dance, we decided that anyone who had the nerve you did, to do what you did, deserved to make the dance cuts." I was glad the real dancers I had sabotaged weren't hearing this.

I got to sit in with the Voices of Liberty, the a cappella singing group at EPCOT, and I now had a new goal — I wanted to be a part of that group. So after five years of teaching I decided to pursue my dream of working in the entertainment world. I moved to Florida and tried out, with at least five hundred other people, and made it to the semi-finals of Voices of Liberty. As I recall, there were about thirty of us who made the semi-finals and there were only six positions open. I felt honored, and when I didn't make the finals, I felt crushed. But I wasn't defeated. Instead of singing, I decided I would pursue my dream of writing songs. I thought, "If I go to a Disney tryout and write my own song, maybe they'll want to hire me to write."

It was 1988 and Mickey Mouse was turning sixty. To celebrate, Disney World was putting together a special Mickey's Birthdayland attraction at the Magic Kingdom. They needed singers and dancers. So at thirty-five years of age I tried out for a show that was written for performers in their teens and early twenties. I wrote a song entitled, "Mickey Mouse's Birthday" and lo and behold, when I entered the tryout room, there was John Mitchell, my buddy from Cincinnati. Again, he was sitting in the judge's seat, but this time after I tried out he wasn't laughing.

"Who wrote that song?" he asked, surprised he hadn't heard that particular song about Mickey Mouse.

"I did," I responded, hoping he would say, "Hey, that's good, I'm going to hire you." He didn't say that, but he did tell me I needed to get it copyrighted before someone stole it. I felt great! I knew I wouldn't make the tryouts, but maybe I really would get a job writing for Disney.

I went to tryouts for the Tokyo Disney Park. Again I wrote a song about Tokyo and Disney, and again John Mitchell was one of the judges. I made the judges laugh with the lyrics in the song and again John asked if I had written the song. I told him that I had and he then said, "Would you like to write for Disney? Disney needs a writer like you." I couldn't believe that the very thing I hoped would happen was happening.

"Yes!" I said, "I'd really like to write for Disney!"

"Go to the music department and tell them I sent you." I left the audition and headed home to make my call to the Disney music department.

That same week I met with the head of the music department, Clifford Reynolds, and told him what John had said.

"I don't know what he's talking about," Clifford said. "We don't need any writers." I left our short interview realizing that this show business stuff was a lot harder than I had imagined it would be.

I needed money to live, so I took a job at a destination management company. This company specialized in taking care of the needs of businesses and corporations when they had meetings in the Central Florida area or when they rewarded their top salespeople with family vacations to Central Florida. It was a start-up company and there were only four people working in the office at the time. I became person number five.

In many ways, the job was glamorous. Because businesses in the area that catered to tourists wanted us to bring our clients to them, we were often given free entrance to the attractions, treated to dinner at the best restaurants, and given tickets to live shows so we could preview what was being offered. We had dinner with clients and developed creative packages they purchased. I was used to getting a teacher's paycheck and teaching elementary math, so when I went from small numbers to extremely large numbers when dealing with the costs of our products, I was a bit intimidated. One of my bosses, Rick, coached me on this, telling me that they were just numbers and not to worry about how large they were. I gradually got used to working with numbers in the hundreds of thousands and became confident enough in what I was doing to write up creative packages for our customers.

One day we received a call from a potential client in California. He had groups of advertising agents from around the country coming to Orlando to participate in a baseball playoff. He needed a package put together that would include entertainment for a poolside party at the Disney Grosvenor Hotel where they'd be staying. My bosses, Rick and Stan, suggested he use a professional comedy group in town for the entertainment. The prospective client didn't want the acts the comedy group had to offer. I had an idea, but when I mentioned it to Rick and Stan they told me that we could only offer products that could be provided.

"We *can* provide this product," I told them, "because I'll write the show!" They both looked at me and chuckled, not giving one second's serious thought to what I had just said. I had written quite a few packages for companies who had bought our services and decided that I would go ahead and write up the package for the California man and include my idea for the poolside show. A few days after sending the proposal, the phone rang.

"This is Florida Fun," I said cheerfully. "Becky speaking. May I help you?"

"Yes." It was the California ad man. "We want this show!" I didn't know whether to be ecstatic or to panic.

Of my two bosses, Rick was willing to take risks. Stan was not a risk-taker. Stan was a numbers man and everything had to be in perfect order before he could relax. He didn't think in a creative way and there was no way he would have let me write and perform a show for a client if he had known that I was doing so, so I didn't tell him. The company I worked for had a lot of events going on at the same time, sometimes involving recording stars, sports teams, and companies with more money than I could imagine, so I was able to work on my little event without being noticed. I did the show writing and practicing at home, so although I eventually told Rick I was performing, he never knew or asked what the show was about.

The company I was performing for had offices throughout the United States and a few other places in the world. There were fifteen teams that would be playing against each other in a baseball play-off and each team came from a different state or country. I would write a separate cheer and song for each team, and I would wear a different outfit for each act. I wrote a script for the MC, tying all of the songs together, and hired a pianist. As the days went by, it was harder and harder to be at work as I constantly worried about what would happen if Stan found out about the show. Would he prohibit me from performing? Would I be fired? Although Rick knew, we never talked about it and the day of the performance, before I left the office, I told him that I would be performing that night at the Disney Grosvenor Hotel. He looked at me and put out a nervous little chuckle, then looked back at the papers he was working on. I sensed that he was fearful for his company's reputation, but he was a risk-taker and he was showing a lot of courage with the risk he was taking in me, not having any idea if I would be able to pull off what our client had bought.

My sister Jayne, as well as my sister-in-law Carrie who had gone with me to Cincinnati, were both going to be at the Grosvenor. I also had a good friend, Anne, coming to help me with my costume changes. Since the show was outdoors, a make-shift dressing room had been set up at the back of the portable stage. I placed all of my props and changes of clothing in the dressing area and then went to meet the MC. He was drunk.

I suppose that wouldn't have been a terrible problem if he hadn't also been mad, but he was mad and it was because the company who hired me had always hired his sister and her husband for shows in the past. The MC didn't want me to do the show.

"I changed the script." He looked at me with defiance, daring me to question what he had done.

"What do you mean you changed the script? What did you do to it?"

"You'll see," he said with a sloppy smile.

The nervousness I was already feeling was now on the brink of nausea. I walked away from the MC and saw my pianist setting up. As I came nearer, she turned to me with worried eyes.

"I need a page turner," she said, her words both apologetic and pleading.

My brain raced frantically as it was now dealing with a drunk MC and the need for a page turner. Out of nowhere, a woman wearing glasses who I didn't recognize gently said, "I'll turn pages." I didn't know who this angel was, but after the show was over and I was able to function, I would pay her for her help.

I had a few minutes to visit with my sister before the show was to start. As I sat at a patio table with Jayne and her daughter Margi, I asked if they had seen Carrie. They hadn't and I couldn't imagine where she might be. Carrie told me she was coming and she was always good for her word. I didn't want her sitting alone. I soon left my sister and niece and found Anne, my costume-change helper, at the back of the stage.

"Anne!" I began talking before I got to her. "The MC is drunk and changed the script I wrote!" I was literally sick to my stomach over what might be in store for me that night and how I might be fired from my job because of it.

"What are you going to do?" Anne asked.

"I'm praying," I said. That's all I could think to do.

The show started and I was ready, dressed in my first outfit. After the MC introduced the show, I came through the curtains and gave my St. Louis cheer:

St. Louis had a world's fair
In nineteen hundred and four,
That Judy Garland brought to fame
In a movie we all adore.
But the world really isn't fair
And when you see us play,
You'll wish you'd lived in nineteen 'o four
So you wouldn't be alive today!

"Woo Hoo!" The audience clapped and cheered and my nerves began to relax. If the MC had changed the script, I couldn't tell. I sang Missouri's song and happily went back to the dressing room to change into my next outfit. The MC said a few words and I went onto the stage and gave my London cheer:

> *London's known for theater,*
> *All the world around,*
> *And this week the stage is set*
> *Where acting will abound.*
> *We'll watch as you act tough,*
> *And we'll watch as you act brave,*
> *But there won't be any acting*
> *When you watch us dig your grave!*

"Right on!" the Londoners shouted. I sang their song and things were going great.

I guess the MC didn't like the idea that the audience liked me, so he switched the order of the program and confused my pianist. She began to play the song that was supposed to be next, not the one that the MC had announced. I gave her a signal to stop and then whispered down to her the name of the song the MC had introduced. Meanwhile, the MC sarcastically slurred to the audience, "Don't you just love professional entertainers?"

So he didn't think I was professional, huh? I yelled out to the audience, "He switched the order of the show!" There was tension in the air and I could envision my sister sliding down in her chair, hoping we didn't look too much alike. We got through the rest of the numbers and it was now time for the grand finale — New York. The man who had hired me told me to save New York for last because if I didn't, and the New Yorkers didn't like what I had written for them, they would most likely leave before the show was over and he didn't want that to happen.

I slipped into the dressing room and changed into a black sequin top. I took off the pants I had worn for the last act and asked Anne to hand me the velveteen pants I was going to wear for the finale. She wouldn't give them to me.

"Anne, quick, I need the pants."

"No! You're going out there without them!" What was she talking about? I had on a leotard and a pair of taupe pantyhose under it, but that was it. I needed my pants. She refused to give them to me, but she did give me my black heels. "Trust me; put these on and get out there."

I heard the MC announcing the New York team, and with no other choice that I could see, walked onto the stage in a short, black sequin top, a leotard, taupe pantyhose, and black heels. I felt naked. There were cat-calls and I was sure I saw some snickering. A million thoughts were crowding my mind and none of them had anything to do with the New York cheer I was reciting:

> We'll give your regards to Broadway,
> If that's what you'd like us to do,
> But the show that we'll put on this week
> Will outshine any Broadway review.

"Did I shave my legs?!" The cheer reciting part of my brain went on automatic while the panic mode part of my brain thought of every humiliating scenario possible. "Are there runs in my pantyhose?!"

> We hope that you've practiced your parts
> And have memorized all of your plays,
> 'Cause we really have a hit on our hands
> That will keep your mind boggled for days!

"Do these pantyhose have that brown lining around the panty part or are they nude?!" If I thought I was sick when I found out the MC was drunk, that paled to how I was feeling now.

Somehow I got through the song and when it was over, left the stage and sat on the back step of the dressing area, my whole body shaking. I heard women's voices. "Whah ris she? (Where is she?)" Three women then came around the back corner outside of the stage and said, "We loved what you did for New Yawk! It was mahvelous!"

I gave them a shaky smile and thanked them. Most of my life I thought that entertaining was what I wanted to do. I was used to performing in safe environments where people had your best interests at hand. If someone in the show got drunk, they were kicked out. If someone in the show wouldn't give you your clothes, well, that had never happened to me before.

After I stopped shaking enough to walk, and I put some pants on, I went to thank my pianist. I was shocked when I saw my sister-in-law sitting beside her. "Carrie!" I felt sick again. She was the woman who had offered to turn pages and I hadn't even recognized her!

"What?" When Carrie asked that question, she looked at me like I had arrived from another galaxy. I felt like I had.

"I didn't know you were the one turning pages."

Now she looked at me like I was some kind of smart aleck. "Why not?"

"I don't know." How could I explain that my nerves had become so distressed, they kept me from recognizing her? She would never believe me. *I* wouldn't have believed me.

I had never been so relieved about a show being over. The next afternoon I met with our client from California and he told me that I was the best entertainment they had ever hired. I wondered if their other entertainers wore pants. He paid me more than he had originally contracted to pay me and as I walked out of the hotel into the fresh air, I vowed that I would never again think about performing on Broadway or anywhere else where someone besides me had control of my clothing. I knew that I would always love to perform, and happily, I also knew where I could find a captive audience who wasn't old enough to drink anything stronger than pickle martinis. I was on my way back to the classroom.

Tip for New Teachers: Statistics say that 50% of new teachers leave the profession within their first five years because of teacher burn-out. If you are thinking of quitting your teaching job ask yourself, "Would I rather go to a job each day that is wearing me out or to a job wearing no pants?" If you're not sure, call me.

Nine

The Truth Is...I Wanted a Trophy for Teaching Harold

As I mentioned in an earlier confession, there were only two children I ever taught that wouldn't allow others to love them. I also mentioned that there were other children who made things difficult, but they were loveable. One of those children was Harold.

Harold was in my fifth grade class when I went back to teaching. After my brief venture in show business, I was now teaching in Florida and Harold had been kicked out of a school in Tampa after trying to burn it down. The day he arrived at our school, he stole a bike from a student. We never knew what was up his sleeves, but one time it was numb chucks, and another time it was live bullets. When I found the bullets, I took Harold and the bullets to the principal's office. I thought for sure he'd get suspended. He didn't. Harold, the secretaries in the office, the principal, and I were close to being maimed as the principal took the bullets and pounded them with angry force on the front counter over and over as she said, "How many times have I told you not to bring things like this to school?!" One hard pound for every word. I didn't know how many times she had told him, but I thought this might be the last time as I waited for the bullets to explode.

Harold came from a rough background, so he needed help learning acceptable social behavior. He saw a school counselor, Ms. Manford, on a weekly basis and he also attended a special program designed to help students who needed extra coaching with social skills. For six weeks he was pulled out of my class for an hour each day to attend this program. I began to get reports from the social skills class counselors that Harold was showing improvement in his behavior. I didn't see any improvement from him in my classroom, so I was glad to hear that somewhere he was doing better.

This program emphasized the need to be positive with troubled children at all times. It was important to give the children encouragement and understanding. As a teacher, I really tried to give Harold these things, but teachers are human and as all honest humans know, it's impossible to be sweet and loving and encouraging and understanding every moment of our waking hours — especially when a child brings weapons to school with intent to do harm. I continued to get glowing reports about Harold from his social skills teachers, so I began to wonder if I was looking too critically at Harold's criminal behavior.

Six weeks were up and Harold's social behavior class ended with the news that he was to receive "the most improved student in the class" trophy. I was happy for him and hoped the trophy was made of styrofoam so that when he hurled it at someone in a fit of rage they wouldn't be hurt. I was invited to attend the awards ceremony that would be held in a classroom down the hall from my room, so I arranged to have coverage for my class.

It was the morning of the awards ceremony and in walked Harold, his eyes dark with anger. He cursed under his breath as he slammed his backpack on his desk.

"Good morning, Harold," I said, "are you okay?" I knew he wasn't, but I thought I'd at least give him the chance to respond. He didn't answer, but he also didn't yell at me or stand on a desk and jump on anyone so I knew I had a chance of getting him calmed down before the awards ceremony, which would be starting in twenty minutes.

"Would you like to see Ms. Manford?" I asked.

"Yes." Harold's quick response in the affirmative told me that he really wasn't doing well, but I hung onto the reports from his social skills teachers that Harold was a changed boy and his anger issues had lessoned a great deal. This was the test.

Harold left the classroom and headed to the counselor's office, which connected to the room where Harold's social skills class was held, and where graduation from the class would be. About eight minutes after Harold left, another student of mine, Stacy, left to go to her special reading class. She was a big girl, tall and heavy, and had a way of annoying other students, Harold being the student she annoyed the most.

Fifteen minutes had passed since Harold left the room and I hoped that Ms. Manford was able to get Harold to let go of his anger so that he would be happy when he got his trophy. At that moment, the head counselor of the social skills program, Mr. Smart, came into my classroom.

"Where's Harold?" he asked.

"He went to see Ms. Manford over fifteen minutes ago. I thought he'd be with you by now." I was surprised that Harold wasn't with Mr. Smart because Harold knew that he was to be with him ten minutes before the guests arrived. Mr. Smart left my room and as soon as my coverage arrived, I also left my room, looking for Harold. There was commotion by the school counselor's office and I speed-walked down the hall to find out why Ms. Manford was standing outside of her office looking shaken.

"What happened? Where's Harold?" Mrs. Frost, a third grade teacher with a student in the social skills class pulled me aside.

"Harold's in his social skills class. Apparently (big) Stacy was on her way to her reading pullout class and when she walked by Ms. Manford's room, she stopped to make faces at Harold through the window. When Harold saw her, he took off after her. Ms. Manford grabbed Harold so that he wouldn't hurt Stacy (although I think Stacy could have taken him on). Harold turned around and threw Ms. Manford to the ground. Then he got on top of her and pounded on her with his fists."

The guidance counselor was not a small woman, and Harold was a small boy, but he was a small boy with lots of muscles that were filled with anger adrenaline and I think he could have taken on just about anyone at that moment — except Stacy — and won. When the social skills counselor had left my room and found Harold in Ms. Manford's office, Harold was trying to beat her up.

I would never wish bad things on anyone, and I was sad that the counselor was a victim of Harold's anger, but the one positive thing that I saw might come from this was that the social skills counselors could see that Harold's behavior really hadn't changed the way they said it had since he entered their behavioral program. I knew Harold would be disappointed when he didn't get the trophy for most improved, but I never felt he deserved it in the first place. He certainly hadn't improved in my classroom and it seemed that should have been the measure for the program's success.

I left to find Stacy so I could talk with her about what had happened. By the time the whole ordeal was dealt with, I missed the thirty minute awards program. Under the circumstances, I felt it was best that I wasn't in the room with Harold during the presentation of awards. I didn't want to see him blow up when he didn't receive the trophy.

I went back to the classroom and a few minutes later Harold arrived.

"Look at what I got!" Harold proudly held up a trophy that said he was the most improved student in the program. Had the other students robbed banks before the awards ceremony?

As far back as I could remember, bad behavior in school was rewarded with detention, suspension, restitution — whatever was called for. We were now in the age of, "We don't want to hurt anyone's feelings and besides, Harold comes from a difficult home life;

he needs to feel like a winner." That wouldn't be the last time I would see bad behavior ignored in the public schools, but on a positive note, it was the only time I saw someone get a trophy for it!

Tip for New Teachers: If you have common sense, don't try to figure out the reward system that you might have to implement in your classroom. Unless a lot changes over the next few years, at some point you will have to give every child in your class an award — just make sure some of them are made of styrofoam.

Ten

The Truth Is...I Will Forever be Thankful for the Forgiveness I Received from Parents and Students

As you can see, this confession is on the serious side. I learned in my early years as a teacher that I would make mistakes and that the biggest mistake would be to deny I had made them. I'm a pretty happy and tolerant person by nature, but when it comes to disrespect, I have no tolerance. Disrespect from students always pushed an automatic "look out" button in me and so students were rarely disrespectful to me more than once. Unfortunately, I sometimes misunderstood a student or situation and accused a student of being disrespectful when he wasn't. The worst part about those times was that the accused students didn't say a word to me while I lectured them, and they took my scolding as though they deserved it. When I found out that they were innocent, I felt worse than stupid, I felt heartbroken that I had made such a terrible mistake, and I'll admit that I got teary in front of those students as I apologized and asked for their forgiveness.

All of my students were extremely forgiving of my faults. I suppose there might be some of my former students reading this who are thinking, "Miss Thomas never apologized to me." That's because you were guilty.

There were times that I, as a teacher, made mistakes in judgment of my own behavior, like the time I brought a can of those pop-out silk-covered springs to school for an April Fools' joke. I was teaching first grade and I had a group of wonderful children. This was towards the end of my career when we were no longer allowed to have fun in the classroom. I decided that for one minute, one day, we would have some fun.

The springs were in a fake brand potato chip can. It was snack time and I asked my class if they'd like a potato chip. Of course they all said, "Yes!" Usually, a mischievous little boy sat at the first desk closest to me. He was the perfect person to play this prank on. Unfortunately, he had gone to get a drink and without thinking through the disposition of the student next to him, Ruby, a shy, beautiful girl, I gave her the can.

"Here, Ruby, take a potato chip and then pass the can to Eugene." Ruby smiled shyly as she grabbed hold of the lid and pried it off.

Boing! A six foot silky cloth-covered spring jumped out of the can, hit her in the face, and bounced across the classroom floor.

"Ahhhh!" Ruby screamed as she flew back from her desk. The class broke out in uproarious laughter and the idea I had of using this joke as a perfect example of potential and kinetic energy backfired on me as Ruby's potential energy from being scared turned into kinetic energy as she began to sob.

I felt terrible. I had upset Ruby and I wasn't sure if her parents would think it was a funny joke. What if they were like the parents who barged into my principal's office about the pencil sharpeners? The year I taught Ruby was the year I retired. I could just see my picture in the paper — cloth-covered springs flying through the air and a caption under the picture, "Teacher Springs into Jail for Retirement."

I consoled Ruby and wrote a note to her parents explaining what had happened. The next day I asked Ruby what her parents had said about the incident.

"My dad said it was okay because it was just a joke," explained Ruby. "My mom said, 'She's going to pay!' "

The worst mistake I ever made as a teacher happened the year I had Harold in my class. Every year in the district where I taught, the fifth graders competed in the "Modern Woodmen Speech Contest." This competition gave the students an opportunity to practice their writing and oration skills. The rules were strict and the contest started in the classroom. Each student in each fifth grade class wrote a three to five minute speech on an assigned topic. Then, each fifth grade teacher listened to her students' speeches and picked the top three orators. Those three orators then competed against the top orators in the other fifth grade classes, the winner of which went on to compete at the county level.

The day of my class's competition had come, and as with every competition, some students did better than others. There was one, however, who did too well. Her name was Christine and when she stood and gave her speech, I was impressed at how well written it was, and how natural, comfortable, and dynamic she was as a speaker. Christine's was far and above the best speech in the class, but as a teacher I took into account all aspects of a student's work, and I didn't feel it was fair for her to win when it was obvious her parents had written the speech. I felt bad for disqualifying Christine, but I couldn't be true to myself as a stickler for fairness and let her compete, so I chose the three next best speeches and left it at that. Christine never complained or even talked with me about not being picked. I'm sure that she must have known that her speech was the best, but I wondered if she also knew that having her parents write the speech was really not fair.

The three students who had been chosen to represent our class practiced and prepared for the school-wide competition. The teacher who had previously taught two of Christine's sisters approached me about her presentation.

"How did Christine do with her speech?" he asked.

"She did pretty well, but I picked three others who I thought were better." I hated to outright accuse anyone of cheating, so I didn't tell Mr. Bates the real reason I hadn't picked Christine.

Mr. Bates told me more about the oration contest and its connection to Christine's family. "Over the past few years I had both of her sisters in my class and they both won the school competition for giving the best speeches. Their names are on the plaques on the wall at the front entrance of the school."

I felt a tinge of remorse about not picking Christine and I knew that this must be hard for her, but lots of lessons in this life are hard and that's often how we grow the most.

The school competition finally came and one student was picked to represent the school at the next level. His speech was good, but Christine's was better and I'm sure her name would have been on a plaque by her sisters' plaques if I had chosen her. I felt a certain sadness inside knowing how well Christine would have done, but I still felt strongly that I had made the right decision and let it go.

A few months after the oration contest I gave my students an in-class assignment. They were given thirty minutes to write a talk on a specified topic, and after the allotted time was up, they presented their talks to the class. The words and structure of the talks were all typical of fifth graders. Some were a little better than others, but none of them were polished. And then Christine stood. She began her talk with as much confidence and ease as she had when she presented for the Modern Woodmen competition. But what was more surprising — and horrifying to me — was that the content of her talk was every bit as good as the one she had given for the competition. I knew at that moment that her parents hadn't written her speech and I was sick about what I had done.

There are times in life when we make mistakes and no one knows but us. When this happens, we have to decide whether admitting to such a mistake would be of benefit to those involved. I've learned that sometimes in life it is better not to say anything. I thought long and hard about whether I should talk with Christine and her parents about what I had done. I wanted to do what was best in every way. As I anguished over this dilemma, I decided that it would be harder on Christine if she knew that she could have had the chance for her name to be on the wall with her sisters, but had never been given the opportunity to prove herself. I wasn't afraid of what her parents would think or say, because they were outstanding people, but as a young teacher, I was afraid it might be too hard on Christine and so I didn't say anything.

Years later I received in the mail an announcement for Christine's high school graduation. She had moved to Utah and as I read a letter her parents had included about Christine's accomplishments, I saw that despite her not making the cuts for the fifth grade speech competition, she went on to shine with her talents. I felt it was time to tell Christine the truth about the competition.

I sent her a letter about the worst mistake I had made in teaching. I let her know how proud I was of her and her accomplishments, and how I had anguished over whether or not I should have told her about the terrible mistake I had made concerning her speech. I was glad that I could finally share with Christine that she really was the best fifth grade orator in our school that year. Her parents and I talked and they were as kind, loving, and gracious as I knew they'd be. They told me that Christine was happy when she read the letter I had sent and that the incident in fifth grade had had no negative effect on her life.

Christine taught me a lesson about how to react when you don't get something you want, even when you've worked hard for it; she didn't let it hold her back. She went on to be successful as a student, an employee, and as a wife and mother. Teachers aren't always the ones teaching in the classroom. Thank you, Christine, for showing me how to be gracious when life isn't fair. I still have a ways to go in that department, but I have a good role model to follow.

Tip for New Teachers: You will make mistakes in your job. Mistakes are part of being human. Be honest with yourself when you make these mistakes, and you will know how to handle them. And be forgiving to other people when they make mistakes — you just might need that same forgiveness someday.

Eleven

The Truth Is...My Belief in the Power of Visualization Wasn't as Strong as My Students' Belief in It

In the late eighties, a typical elementary school classroom consisted of mainstream students, gifted students, students with learning disabilities, students who didn't speak English, students with speech, hearing, sight, or other impairments, students with emotional disabilities, and students who were able to learn, but for whom learning was so difficult, they might burst out in a fit of tears or rage over not being able to understand a concept. Some students had been abused physically and verbally, and knowing the statistics, some had surely been sexually abused.

My class was really no different from most classes in the public schools at that time. It was getting harder and harder to know how to reach the students who couldn't be taught in the "mainstream" way. Unless an educator went to school to become a special needs teacher, she was often unequipped to deal with the children she was hired to teach. Personally, I hadn't been trained to use any special techniques. I just knew that there were many students who were struggling and I was always looking for new ways to reach them. That's what led me to teach my students about visualizing.

There were a few situations going on in my classroom that year — one was Harold. Another situation was the need for the three gifted students in my classroom to be challenged. Then there was Manny, the boy who burst out in a fit of rage when he couldn't understand a math concept. Instead of using the problem-solving techniques he had been taught, he would immediately get upset and completely shut down. Once he did that, nobody could teach him.

It was on one of those days when Manny got upset that I decided to step outside the box and introduce my class to visualization.

"Class," I began, "I'd like you to put your pencils down and look at me."

I waited quietly as they gave me questioning looks and then, one by one, set their pencils on their desks.

"Now, I want you to close your eyes and take a deep breath through your nose. Hold your breath until I tell you to exhale." Getting the entire class to do this in a quiet and serious manner was not easy. The boys, of course, had to see who could make the most noise as they inhaled through their noses. Once the class quit breathing, eyes began to open.

"Close your eyes," I said once again, and then gave the students whose eyes were still open, and making faces at each other, the demon teacher look. Soon, all eyes were closed.

"Now, slowly and quietly exhale through your mouth. Don't open your eyes. Just slowly exhale." The students were becoming calmer, but I knew that this simple exercise was taking most of the children out of their comfort zones.

Together we repeated this series of steps a few more times, and then I told the students to continue this exercise on their own while I talked to them.

"It's important to take time to dream," I explained, "to clear your mind and to see in your mind's eye what you want to be. Your imagination is very powerful and whatever you can visualize you can accomplish if you take the time and energy to do so." All students were now quietly, rhythmically taking in deep breaths of air and with closed eyes, listening and visualizing. "I want you to remember this phrase, 'You can be what your mind can see.'"

Some people, when meditation and visualization are mentioned, immediately become fearful. I guess they think of out-of-body experiences and levitation. I had no experience with those phenomena, and hoped all of my students would stay in their bodies, but I had used deep breathing and visualization techniques in my own life and knew of their benefits.

When I felt the students were comfortable with what they were doing, I told them to listen while I read to them the math problem we had been working on.

"Keep your eyes closed," I said. "Try to picture what the problem is saying. 'Mr. Brown has twenty-five rows of corn.' Don't open your eyes, but raise your hand if you can see rows of corn in your mind. Don't worry if you can't see twenty-five rows; raise your hands if you can see corn growing in a field." All hands went up. I continued to read. "'In each row, there are ten corn plants.'" Although none of the students opened their eyes, some began to fidget and I could sense frustration coming from others. I knew that the numbers were probably now overwhelming their ability to visualize so I stopped at that point.

"Okay, everyone, open your eyes for a moment." As the students opened their eyes I asked, "Who could see the corn in your mind?" Again, everyone raised his hand. "How many could see rows of corn? Do you all know what a row of corn looks like?" A bilingual student was having trouble understanding, so I had one of the students draw a row of corn on the board.

"Who can tell me how many rows of corn Mr. Brown planted?"

"Twenty-five," called out more than one student.

"Exactly. So we have a field with twenty-five rows of corn growing in it. Does everyone understand that?" All heads nodded in the affirmative. "Now, close your eyes again and try to see those rows of corn in your mind. Can you picture two corn plants in each of those twenty-five rows?" Again, heads nodded in the affirmative. "Without opening your eyes, raise your hand if you can tell me how many corn plants there are if you have twenty-five rows of corn with two plants in each row." Two-thirds of the class raised their hands and I then asked them to call out the answer.

"Fifty," was the answer given by every student with his hand up.

"Very good," I responded. "Raise your hand if you can tell us how you got that answer." I called on Megan.

"You multiply two times twenty-five."

"Who can remember how many corn plants Mr. Brown actually planted in each row?"

I called on Steven and he answered, "Ten."

"And how do we figure out how many plants there are in Mr. Brown's field?"

"We multiply!" answered the class in unison.

"Open your eyes," I said and then asked them to write down the steps to the problem and solve it. "If, as you read a problem, you can't see every step in your mind, it's okay to draw the steps as you go along. We all have different abilities and for some of us, visualizing will take more practice."

For the rest of the year, whenever possible, we worked with visualization tapes that had us walking along a beach, hearing seagulls call as waves lapped against the shore. It really was a nice fifteen minutes with the class and once they got comfortable with silence and with their eyes being shut, I believe the students enjoyed it as much as I did.

Although I didn't see every child using visualization while working in class, there were many students who did use it and one of those students was Manny.

It was a typical afternoon in math class. The day's math concept was hard and to arrive at the solution to the problem, multiple steps of computation were required. Manny got to his breaking point and exploded, smashing his hand down on the desk. "I don't get this!" he yelled. I began to walk towards him to see how I could help, when he suddenly put his hand out signaling that he wanted me to stay back. He then closed his eyes, began to breathe deeply and became calm. In less than a minute a visible change came over him. He smiled, opened his eyes and said, "I get it," and wrote down the correct answer to the problem.

That experience with Manny made my year. To watch a student who struggled with math, implement, and then succeed with a technique I believed in and taught him, even though I had never heard it mentioned in an education class, was truly rewarding.

The end of the school year was approaching and field day was coming. As an elementary school child, I loved field day. And as an adult, I still felt like a kid when field day came. At the school where I now taught, the first-place winner in each event received a blue ribbon. My students were not excited about field day.

"Miss Thomas, Mrs. Fredrick's class is going to cream us. Those kids are huge!" William exclaimed. It was true, Mrs. Fredrick got the athletes that year and I got the visualizers. I wanted to motivate my students but I didn't want to lie to them about being able to beat the Goliaths in the room next door.

"Class," I began, not knowing how to encourage them, "you can beat them. You just have to believe you can beat them. You have to see it in your mind. You know how to visualize. Before each race, I want you to visualize crossing that finish line before anyone else. I want you to see the blue of the ribbon, feel its silkiness in your hand, and internalize how good it feels to win!" Even I was beginning to think that maybe we could win a race or two. The students' confidence was building and they were now smiling, actually looking anxious to get out to the field for the competition. No matter what happened, at least they wanted to try.

All of the students had signed up for one or more of the events. We walked to the first race and I gave a student who, due to his size I'll call *Pee Wee*, a pep talk. "You can do this!" I assured him. "Close your eyes. I want you to see yourself reaching that finish line before anyone else. As you're running, don't look back, don't look to the sides, just picture yourself looking straight ahead, going over that line first!" I finished my visualization speech and Pee Wee kept his eyes closed for a few seconds. When he opened them, he walked to the starting line with a serious look of determination on his face.

The announcer spoke. "On your marks. Get set. Go!" The group of fifth grade competitors took off, and lo and behold, Pee Wee took the lead! He ran ahead of the Goliaths and the Usain Bolts and crossed the finish line before all of the more athletic runners.

He received his blue ribbon and came running to me.

"Miss Thomas! I did it! I won!" He held up his ribbon and was immediately surrounded by the entire class who hugged and congratulated him.

It was time for the next competition. *Pee Wee Number Two* was in this race. Many of the students in my class I could have called Pee Wee that year because they were small. And those that weren't small weren't very athletic.

Again, I went through the pep talk and had my student visualize winning the competition and receiving the blue ribbon. She did what I told her and she won the ribbon! It was an amazing day. Competition after competition my students won blue ribbons. Even I, who believed in the power of visualization, was astounded at how well my students were able to visualize winning results, feel what they envisioned, and then make it a reality.

The ultimate contest was the tug of war. I knew that Mrs. Fredrick's class was a lot stronger than mine and I had no hopes of my class beating hers in that competition. My students, however, were completely convinced that there was more power in their visualizing than there was in the muscles of Mrs. Fredrick's students, and so before the referee blew the whistle to *pull*, the students from my class closed their eyes and pictured themselves dragging the other team over the loser's line.

I'm really not sure how energy of the mind and spirit works, but it does and I witnessed it that day as my class of nonathletic visualizers defeated Mrs. Fredrick's future Olympians in tug of war. I don't know if it mattered much to Mrs. Fredrick's students that my class beat them. I do know that it meant everything to my students that they had won. They knew that Mrs. Fredrick's students were stronger and faster and more athletic on a daily basis, but for one day my class proved that greater physical strength didn't always guarantee a win in athletic events. My class won more than twelve blue ribbons that day — the majority of all classes — because they believed in their minds that they could. I'm not sure that I had the will to visualize that many wins for my students.

I still treasure the memory of the look on my students' faces as they basked in the limelight of victory. I don't know if any of them ever won another athletic competition in their lives, but somehow I don't think that mattered to them. What mattered was that they had won a contest they previously thought they could never win and it was all because they could see it in their minds as reality. After all, you can be what your mind can see. It's time to start visualizing!

Tip for New Teachers: Deep breathing exercises are an excellent way to calm an over-active class. Visualizing is a great way to get students motivated. Hypnosis might be the only way to get approval for these methods in today's system of teaching.

Twelve

The Truth Is...I Wanted a Different

Answer

The school year was coming to a close and our principal held a meeting to inform the teachers that, due to boundary changes, our school population would be declining. The three teachers newest to the county would have to find jobs in other schools. I was one of those teachers and so I once again looked for a job. Because I hadn't given up my dream of making money as a writer, I took a part-time teaching job in a neighborhood school and spent the other part of my time as a freelance writer. What I learned during that period was what the word "free" in freelance meant.

"We want you to write for us, but we can't pay you. You can use our name on your resume," or, "We'd like you to write a song for our program," and when I did, the whole program was changed so that my song could no longer be used and I wasn't paid.

It was around Thanksgiving when my principal told me that the funding for my part-time teaching position would end at Christmas break. I began to search for a full-time teaching job.

I interviewed for, and took, a fourth grade position that proved to be one of the greatest challenges of my teaching career. Most of the students in the class came from extremely unstable, and in some cases, horrific home lives, and trying to get them to focus on learning was for me, a learning process. The interview for that job was one of the strangest interviews I can remember. I asked all of the questions and the principal defended this particular teaching position in a way that made me ask more questions. Three teachers had already left this fourth grade class and I wanted to know if the students were chasing them away. The principal told me that these were good children, they just needed someone who would be committed to them. Because I needed a job and was offered the fourth grade position on the spot, I took it and started the following Monday.

I soon came to understand why teachers didn't last long with this class. First of all, to take some of the blame from the students, the room itself had the worst acoustics I had ever encountered. Everything reverberated and the smallest noise was amplified twice its normal volume. On top of that, the books and teaching items were old. Personally, I have never had a problem with religion and its history being taught in the public schools. After all, religion was the driving force of the Pilgrims' voyage and settlement in America, and religion was instrumental in the writing of the greatest constitution in the world. But even I was surprised to see the words Easter, resurrection, and crucifixion on our April spelling list. These books must have been published before Madeline O'Hare got vocal about religion in the public schools. I didn't mind the spelling list, I was just surprised and knew that the books were old and wouldn't pass "inspection" if a government schoolbook inspector ever came around. So with it being difficult to communicate well due to the acoustics, and having outdated material to work with, this job started with challenges. Then, when the students were added to the mix, I almost became the fourth teacher to leave them.

I don't remember any of the students smiling my first day with them — at least not at me. I'm sure they had a secret communication system going, sending each other messages like, "Don't look at or listen to the teacher, don't be respectful, and don't act like you want to learn anything."

These students wandered around the room, talking and ignoring any directions I gave them. Because the room echoed so badly, I wondered if they could understand me. That question was answered when I hollered, "You have to the count of three to be in your seats or you'll miss recess. One! Two! Two and a half!" Before I said, "Three!" the entire room of bodies ran to their seats, some of the boys literally sliding down the aisle like they were sliding into home base. So I now knew that it wasn't that they couldn't understand me, they were just ignoring me.

That day I tried every method, tactic, and rant I could think of to get those students to listen to me. Nothing worked. They calmed down here and there, but the whole day was a fight and I wanted out. I felt like they all hated me and it was only my first day. I hadn't been there long enough to give them reasons to hate me, other than my constant warnings about the pending consequences of their disrespect. My warnings didn't seem to faze them and I left school that day determined to find another job. I felt little hope of being able to reach these students and didn't know if I had the will to try.

I prayed that night that God would bring me a different job. The next day I woke up and I was still a teacher at the same school. I drove to work feeling nervous, knowing what was awaiting me. This day didn't go any better than the day before. I had never had an entire group of students so cold and disinterested in me as their teacher. I began to doubt my ability, as an educator and as a human being, to connect with other humans. That night I said another prayer about finding a different job. I was feeling more desperate and was hoping that God would feel that desperation and have pity on me.

The third day at the school I had a glimmer of hope. As I drove up to the school parking lot, one of my students was walking along the sidewalk. When she saw me, a huge smile appeared on her face and she began to skip towards the school. That student actually seemed happy to see me! I felt a noticeable release from the job anxiety I had been feeling. When the students came through the classroom door, however, the anxiety came back. Their actions and attitudes were the same as the previous two days. Even the girl who I had felt sure was glad to see me acted cold towards me. That night I said the strongest and most heartfelt prayer I had in me. After crying and begging the Lord for another job, I became calm and then the answer came. It wasn't the answer I wanted and I didn't know how I was going to do what the Lord told me to do, but there was not a shadow of a doubt about what I had been told. "Love them." I asked God how I was to do this. There were no other answers.

What I've learned about prayers in my life is that God will answer prayers, but He often doesn't give us a lot of detail. It's up to us to take what He gives us and use our intelligence, creativity, and determination to make our way. I wracked my brain trying to come up with ways to love these children who were so unwilling to acknowledge me as a human, let alone a teacher.

When the students came into the classroom the next day, I quietly studied them, wondering what was going on inside of each unresponsive soul. What made them want to be so detached from me? How could I possibly get them to share with me any part of who they were when they treated me as though I was a nonentity? Things weren't going any better that day until the students lined up for lunch. They were noisy and rude and wouldn't listen to my instructions. As one of the girls walked past me to get in line, I noticed she had a pretty raspberry-colored bow in her hair. I really liked it and told her so. For the first time since entering that school, I received a smile from a student in my class — while in the classroom — and I felt her heart open the slightest amount. I was able to smile back and send a little of my love into her heart before she closed it again. I now knew how I could get the students to open up to me. It would take time, but I believed with all of my heart that it would work.

The days were long and hard, but millimeter by millimeter I began to make progress.

"Nick, you're really good at throwing a ball!"

"Patty, your handwriting is beautiful."

"Denise, I love the way you read with expression." I was constantly looking for things on which I could compliment the students. My goal was to give five sincere compliments a day, not to every student, but a sum total of five compliments to all of the class. My compliments had to be genuine or the students would know. I felt that the only way they would open up to me would be if I connected with them in a sincere, nonthreatening way. Most of these students were suspicious and untrusting. I was given no background on the children, so I didn't know the cause of their behavior. My attempts to win their trust was working in subtle ways, but they continued to be noisy and often disrespectful. I knew that before these students would respect me, I needed to respect myself and I felt that I wasn't doing so as I continued to teach all of the students, despite the rudeness of many.

I pondered the options I had in addressing my dilemma. The first idea that came to mind was kicking out of class all of the children who wouldn't listen. That would leave me with about three students. I liked the idea, but didn't think the parents would support it. I could punish all of the noisy children by taking away their recess. The problem with that solution was that I, too, would be punished as I tried to keep them quiet while they had their heads down in the classroom. I finally came up with an idea that, because of human nature and the desire to be included, I believed would work.

One day, I stood in front of the class and began my lesson. Three students listened, so I addressed them. I asked them to bring their chairs close to where I was, and the little group and I began our reading work. I didn't use my teacher voice with them. They were close to me and so I talked with them as I would when conversing with friends over lunch. The rest of the class was rowdy and clowning around. Then, some of the noisy students noticed my little group and me doing something that they weren't a part of. No matter how much they didn't want to do school work, even worse, they didn't want to be left out.

"Hey, what are you doing?" interrupted a student.

I nonchalantly looked at the student and quietly said, "I'm teaching reading." I didn't say anything more before I turned back to my group. Although I acted as if I didn't notice, I could see students, one by one, quietly taking their seats and opening their reading books. Like a horse whisperer, I tried to read them by watching their body language. What were they thinking? What were they feeling? I knew that none of them wanted to be excluded. Here and there I saw a student give a quick glance to other students, looking to see if his classmates were serious about listening. They were and I continued on with the lesson as though nothing unusual was happening.

I waited for students to raise their hands to answer questions I asked, but if no hands were raised, I gently coaxed the class into conversation by looking at a student, and in a nonthreatening way using his name and asking his opinion about the subject. If I felt the slightest tension or fear coming from the student, I would pull back and let him know that it was okay if he didn't want to share his thoughts, but if he did, I would love to hear them. More times than not, the student would say something, and what was said would often give me some understanding of what was going on inside of that student.

Like I said, the going was slow and most days started out noisy and chaotic, but the students were beginning to bond with me. Gradually they were willing to talk to me on an individual basis. They asked questions about my life and in turn gave me a little information about theirs. Slowly I began to put the broken pieces of their lives together and my mind developed a picture that shed light on their behavior.

I had a fiery redhead in my class who was wild and unpredictable. Her name was Jamie and I never knew what she would say or how she would react under any given circumstance. She had a good heart, but it was very guarded and didn't seem to trust anyone. One day she stayed after school and without warning, spilled out the story of her father and how he had robbed her family.

"My father is a drug addict," Jamie began, her words full of anger. "He doesn't live with us, but one night me and my mom and brother and sister were sleeping and my father broke into the house." Jamie's eyes filled with tears. "He stole everything he could pawn. Then he came into my room. I was hiding under the covers." Jamie gritted her teeth and sobbed, "He grabbed my piggy bank and smashed it on the floor. He took all my money I had saved!" She wiped her blotchy, red face and left the classroom. I sat in my chair, overcome with sadness, and wondered why I was so fortunate to have grown up in a wonderful family. Somehow I had to help Jamie see that despite her father's terrorizing actions, there was still goodness to be found in life.

Another student in my class, Shannon, was extremely quiet, and had a sweetness that drew me to him. He rarely spoke, and when he did, I felt honored that he wanted to share a little of himself with me. I could feel that this student was ever-so-slowly letting me into his world. I would often find him looking at me and when his eyes met mine, he would give me a soft smile that melted my heart. I knew that he, too, must have a story. He did, but he wasn't like redheaded Jamie who was willing to tell me her worst nightmare.

It was another teacher who told me about Shannon. I was told that the teachers before me could not control Shannon. He was sarcastic and out of control and was the main reason the last teacher had left. I was dumbfounded when I heard this, as he was just the opposite with me. Shannon had a younger brother and at some point their parents had split. He and his brother lived with their mother, and one night as the boys slept, their father kidnapped them, put bags over their heads, and drove them from Orlando to Chicago. The boys had been traumatized and were having a hard time feeling safe at home or at school. I wanted to rock those boys in my arms and let them know that they were safe with me. I gave Shannon extra doses of kindness which he willingly accepted.

Although my teaching to only those who would listen worked for a short time, the novelty wore off and the class continued to have many noisy days. No matter how loudly I yelled at them to be quiet (yes, I at times tried to be noisier than they were to get them quiet), I was often the invisible teacher. I thought about why my firm, stern, loud voice wasn't having any effect on them, and then it occurred to me that most of these children probably lived in homes where yelling was a normal part of their lives. They had learned to shut it out and that's what they were doing to me. I finally decided to try a new approach; I would whisper.

This particular day started like all of the others. The students were noisy, preoccupied with talking, and ignoring me. Then things changed. I didn't yell to get their attention; I whispered. At first, no one noticed. They didn't notice my whispering and they didn't notice me. Then a few children began to give me strange looks, wondering what their eccentric teacher was up to. They sat down and strained to hear if anything was coming out of my moving lips. It was. I was actually teaching science, but no one had yet figured that out. As a few students paid attention to me, the noise level in the room went down ever so slightly. The minute difference in noise level caused the other students to pause and look around to find out what was making the room quieter. Eventually, every student sat and strained to hear what I was saying. When I knew I had everyone's attention, I explained to them why I was talking so softly.

"Every day that I've come in here I've tried to yell over your noise. There were times you got quiet, but it didn't happen very often and didn't last. I began to think that maybe you needed me to be softer with you. Maybe you needed me to be quieter so that you would want to be quieter. So I will not yell to get your attention. I will quietly talk to you and you will have to be quiet to hear me."

They did. It wasn't perfect, but they truly began to change. And I began to change. My love for them grew deeper as they became more willing to try. We talked about respect and about kindness. We talked about trust and belief in oneself. One day, as the students worked, the room was so quiet I was afraid to breathe. I didn't want anything to disrupt the sound of thinking minds as pencils moved across paper. I sat at my desk and looked up from the papers I was grading. I knew I was witnessing a miracle. Shannon, who sat right in front of my desk, also looked up and whispered to me, "Do you notice anything?" I gave him an inquisitive look. "It's quiet." I smiled, and he smiled back at me and then continued with his work. I fell asleep happy that night.

Tip for New Teachers: Sometimes, no method you are familiar with works when teaching. Trust that there are always answers. If you can't find them in a book, look in your heart.

Thirteen

The Truth Is...I Wanted to be Able to Brag About My Bowling Score

ield day was coming up. This school did field day in a way different from any schools in which I'd worked. The students rotated from activity to activity and points were kept for each event won by a class. At the end of all the activities, the points were tallied and the winning class was announced.

I talked with my class about field day and told my students that my main concern was how they treated the students against whom they would be competing. We practiced how to be humble winners and losers and how to show good sportsmanship. These students now listened when I taught and wanted to succeed in being good sports. When field day came, my students were well-mannered and respectful. I don't remember how many activities they won that day — I don't think very many — but I do remember the pride they had when over the loud speaker came the announcement of the team who had the most points, which wasn't ours, and then the team who won the good sportsmanship award and it *was* ours.

"Yay!" The students broke out in wild cheering and I told them how wonderful they were. Four months previous I couldn't have imagined this moment.

Booooommmm! As the class cheered, claps of thunder shook the room. We looked out the windows to see rain pouring from the heavens. Who cared? My once disrespectful students had won the best sportsmanship award!

It was time for dismissal and I stood at the door congratulating my students as they left. Some were dismissed to their parents, while others walked under the overhang that protected them from the rain and climbed onto the buses waiting at the end of the sidewalk. I went back into the room and sat at my desk, rethinking the day and feeling amazed at how far these students had come in four months. As I sat there, the door suddenly opened and Jamie, my fiery redhead, darted into the room soaking wet and barefoot. She ran to me, threw a card with no envelope on my desk, quickly hugged me and then ran out the door. I was surprised and chuckled as I picked up the card. I opened it and written inside the card were the words, "We couldn't have won the sportsmanship award without you. Thank you, Miss Thomas. I love you." I cried.

One day, an announcement came over the loud speaker that all students who lived in the Bella Palmeras apartment complex were to report to the media center. About a third of my class left. When they came back, they were loudly laughing and kidding around. I couldn't imagine what was going on. When I asked them, one of the especially loud boys said, "Someone was killed at our apartments and someone else is being held hostage!" and then he laughed. What had these children seen and lived through to make them so unaffected by the worst of human behavior? I saw no fear in any of them. Did they really have no fear, or had they just gotten really good at hiding it? That was one answer I never got before leaving that school.

Although the majority of the students in my classroom had unstable family lives, a few didn't. There was one boy in particular, Sam, who came from a loving family, but he would get extremely frustrated when he couldn't understand his schoolwork and would let everyone know how frustrated he was. I worked with him the best I knew how, but I often felt inadequate in being able to reach him. Like many teachers, when a student was not understanding something being taught, I couldn't leave my concern about it at school. I took it home with me and mulled over ways I could better reach the student.

Sam struggled in math and often shut down when he couldn't understand. Visualization wasn't an option this year — the student trust level was too low and my time with them that year was too short. I tried different approaches with Sam's math instruction, but math was not easy for him and none of my approaches seemed to be working.

In this school, the fourth grade classes had an annual bowling field trip. Even though I had never been a good bowler — I had broken one hundred only once or twice — I was looking forward to this outing with my students.

When we got to the bowling alley, I began my usual bad bowling. My students were divided into teams of four and I was on one of the teams. Sam was on a team that bowled in the lane next to mine. As I rolled my ball down the lane, Sam watched me.

"Miss Thomas, when you let go of the ball, your arm is turning so that it's curving the ball's path. Try to keep your arm straight," he instructed.

It was obvious that he knew more about bowling than I did, even though he was only in fourth grade, and when I did what he said, my ball actually stayed out of the gutter and I knocked down quite a few pins. He gave me more advice on how to knock down the remaining pins. I followed it and got a spare. By the end of the first game I had broken one hundred. We bowled a second game and I was improving. Sam gave me many tips and I tried my best to use them. Strike! Strike! Strike! Maybe I had a new career. Three strikes in a row! A turkey was flashing on the screen for all to see. I was so close to two hundred points it was inevitable that by the end of the game I would break two hundred.

Sam was amazing and I had learned more from him than just how to be a better bowler. The first thing I learned was that with good coaching, I could do things I never dreamed of (or even thought to dream of). Second, I learned that good coaches can take mediocrity to championship levels. Third, I learned that I didn't have to worry about Sam and his academics; he was doing just fine with math that day. He was motivated and interested and was able to put the math he knew to practical use.

I never knew I could be so excited about bowling. Students and teachers were slapping me on the back and I'll have to admit, even I was impressed by my score. Just as I picked up the ball to break two hundred, all of the overhead scores vanished as the power was turned off. Through the quiet bowling alley came the voice of the manager.

"Thanks for coming. We hope you had a good time and will come back soon." Was he kidding?

I called out, "I was just about to break two hundred!"

"You can come back another day," he casually answered as he put away bowling shoes.

I've hardly bowled since that day. Who wants to go back to mediocrity? Without Sam, I'm a bowling nobody. Just recently I went bowling and did break one hundred after playing a few games. I also stepped beyond the black line that separates the bowling lane from the area where you're supposed to keep your feet. I never knew they oiled those lanes. I slipped and skidded on the oiled floor and then twisted around before actually hitting the hard wood with my left arm, hip, and leg. I didn't see a turkey that day — I was the turkey. I missed Sam.

Tip for New Teachers: Although you're the teacher and your job is to encourage the students to become the best they can be, you, too, should always want to be the best you can be and there just might be a student or two who will show you how.

Fourteen

The Truth Is...I Was More Afraid of My Students Seeing My White Legs than I Was of Losing My Pantyhose

T here was only a month left of school. The students were working on a project for social studies and needed crayons, glue, scissors, and a few other odds and ends. There was a supply closet in the room and on normal days, when the students needed something from the closet, they were allowed to get it. Today was different. I was experiencing difficulty in a personal manner and so I insisted on going into the closet anytime someone needed something. Not only would I go into the closet, but I would shut the door and adjust my pantyhose that were trying to get away.

I believe that a whole city library could be filled with volumes of stories written by teachers about embarrassing wardrobe malfunctions at school. For some reason my new pantyhose were not staying up around my waist, and so the entire day I was preoccupied with the thought of them dropping below my skirt to my ankles while in the middle of teaching. I could have taken them off when the students were at lunch, but I carry childhood trauma about my ghost-white legs and so I was willing to take the risk of losing my stockings before I took the risk of students making fun of my white legs. Every chance I got, when the students weren't looking, I grabbed the elastic waistband that was getting close to my knees and pulled it up as high as I could. Having to concentrate on my renegade pantyhose while teaching proved to be exhausting.

During the social studies project, I used every opportunity I could get to go into the closet and adjust my pantyhose. I'm sure the students must have suspected something in my peculiar behavior. On any other day I didn't pay attention when they retrieved crayons or glue from the closet. Today, however, the moment I saw a student walking towards the closet, I beat him to the door and asked what he wanted.

"I'm getting some crayons," a student would tell me.

"I'll get them," I'd say and then walk into the closet, shut the door and before getting the crayons, grab the waist of my pantyhose and pull it back to where it belonged. I would then step out and hand the crayons to the student with the strange look on his face.

"I need scissors, Miss Thomas," another student would say.

Again, I would step into the closet, shut the door and repeat my actions, this time grabbing scissors after adjusting my pantyhose. I was able to pull up my pantyhose in the closet about fifteen times that day, which I think might have saved my dignity, although I'm sure my sanity was questioned more than fifteen times that day.

Only once did a student try to open the door while I was in the closet. I had hiked up my skirt so I could grab the waist of my pantyhose, when the doorknob suddenly turned and the door began to open. I pulled the door shut on my side and screamed, "I'm getting the glue! Don't come in here!" There were no cell phones at that time, and no phones in the classrooms, so despite my erratic behavior no one called 9-1-1.

The day was over and the students were being dismissed. My pantyhose waist was around my thighs and making its way to my knees. I smiled and said goodbye to my students, trying not to sound too anxious for them to leave. I had about ninety seconds before my pantyhose would be on the floor.

Everyone was gone except for redheaded Jamie. She loved to hang around and I usually let her, but today she had to go. Of all students, if my pantyhose fell to the ground she would be the one to make sure that everyone in the school knew about it. I said goodbye to her three or four times but she wouldn't go. My pantyhose waist was slowly walking down my legs to my ankles. Once it got past my knees, the trip would be quick.

"Jamie, you need to go now." My voice was firm. She smiled. "I'm not kidding." I was desperate. I figured I had ten seconds left. "You have to the count of three to go through that door or I'm giving you detention." Detention for wanting to stay at school? "One! Two!" She was still looking at me and smiling. "Three!"

I didn't mean to sound so scary, but I felt the waist pass my knees and my fear translated into anger. Jamie shot through the door just as my pantyhose hit the floor. I shut the door, and totally spent, removed my shoes and the mischievous pantyhose. I then went next door to share my day with Mrs. Schofield, another fourth grade teacher whose room connected to mine.

Mrs. Schofield was close to retirement and had a lot of stories to share about teaching. After I told her about my pantyhose, she told me the story of her turtleneck.

When she first began her teaching career, she taught ninth grade biology. Mrs. Schofield was well-built, and I could imagine that in her younger years she was a knock-out. She was in the middle of teaching her class when she became very warm and decided to take her sweater off. She was now wearing just her turtleneck shirt. She turned back to the board and as she wrote, she began to feel strange, like she was missing something. She looked down and to her utter horror, realized that the turtleneck she was wearing was a "dickie," a mock turtleneck that consisted of a turtleneck collar and a short square piece of material that hung below the neck about five inches. She was standing in front of her class in her underwear! She turned around, grabbed her sweater and shouted, "Why didn't you tell me?!" A few boys looked down and smiled, but no one said a word.

My pantyhose story suddenly seemed pretty tame. I told Mrs. Schofield that I was certain her story about teaching in her underwear was a favorite that had been told and retold many times by the students who were in her class that day.

"Don't you know it!" she agreed.

Tip for New Teachers: Embarrassing things will happen to you in the classroom. No matter how bad they might seem at the time, you will eventually be able to laugh at the situation. In some cases it might not be until you hear the story told at your funeral.

Fifteen

The Truth Is...I, Too, Wondered How God Could Be Unchanging and Be the Same God of the Old and New Testament

When I first began teaching this fourth grade class, time dragged and I wondered how I would survive the endless torment I felt as the seconds slowly ticked by while in the classroom each day. Now, the end of the year was near and I no longer thought about the passage of time, except that it was suddenly passing quickly. I stood in the kitchen of the duplex I was renting, washing dishes and thinking over the school year. I believe that most humans experience moments of inspiration when they're still and quiet and not expecting them. That's what happened to me as I rinsed the suds off of the dish in my hand, thinking about the change that my students had experienced that year.

For many years I had wondered about the God of the Old Testament and the God of the New Testament. The scriptures say that He is an unchanging God, but it sure seemed like He had changed a lot from the time the earth was covered with a flood to the time that Christ had come to earth to preach love and peace. I wasn't thinking about this seeming contradiction when I received insight into it. I was thinking about my class and the change that had come over them. I was thinking back to how they behaved when I first came, and how and why their behavior had changed, and how and why my approach to teaching them had changed. And then it hit me. God has always loved His children — that's us — He just can't always get through to us with His highest level of love. Not because He doesn't always love us that way, but because we won't accept that level of love until we're ready.

When I first came to my fourth grade class that year, I was ready to teach those students with as much energy and love as I had in me. They wanted nothing to do with me or with what I had to offer them. And so it is with us and our relationship with God. I realized that God has always wanted to give the people of this earth all of the love that He has, but so often we are unwilling to accept it. So He has to work with us in ways to get our attention and to help us understand who He is, who we are, and what our potential is as His children. There were many times that year, and in the years since, that I had to be extremely stern and strict with my class. I didn't want to be that way, but because the students chose to be disrespectful and unruly, I had to teach and guide them with a necessary strictness that I didn't enjoy any more than they did.

As I stood in front of the kitchen sink, I realized that God hadn't changed from the Old to the New Testament — His children had changed and were finally ready to learn His higher law of love. As an educator, I was always learning, and that night I felt I had traveled light-years.

Tip for New Teachers: Never feel that a difficult teaching experience is a waste of your time or expertise. Many times you learn more through the difficult assignments than you do through the less demanding ones. Truthfully, though, I don't know of any "easy" teaching assignments anymore. I guess today's educators are destined to learn a lot.

Sixteen

The Truth Is...I Never Could Have Imagined that Sam Would Understand Shakespeare

The year had come to an end and I loved my class. As we spoke openly and frankly one day, I asked them why they were so mean to me when I had first come to the school. One of the students began, "Three teachers had left us and so we got together and decided that the next teacher that came would not walk out on us unless we pushed her out."

Jamie then explained, "We agreed that we would be mean and rude and disrespectful and so if the new teacher left, we could say that it was because of what we were doing to her, not because she didn't like us."

I was shocked. They were so young and had already experienced enough rejection and fear in life that they knew how to use what they had experienced to hurt others before others hurt them.

"It almost worked," I said, "I almost gave up."

"We're so glad you didn't," answered Shannon. And so was I.

Eight years after teaching that fourth grade class, I received an invitation from Sam, my bowling coach, to attend a special event honoring teachers. Sam was now a senior in high school and had given me the honor of being his favorite teacher in school. I was humbled and a little surprised. I could remember the times I got frustrated when Sam couldn't get the math I was teaching and felt bad that I didn't have more patience with him.

There were many times throughout the years when I wondered if I expected too much of my students. I wondered if my high expectations caused me to exhibit frustration when the students didn't meet my standards. On the other hand, there were times I felt I wasn't strict enough with the quality of their work. Sometimes I was happy just to get an assignment turned in by some students, even when the content of the assignment was poorly written or the writing barely legible. I guess that despite all of my faults as a human and as a teacher, most of my students knew, above all else, that I loved them.

Sam had grown up to be a wonderful person. He was kind, respectful, and a gentleman. He presented me with a red rose and took my arm as he walked me to my seat. As we sat through the program, my mind frequently went back to my experience with Sam's class. I was now witnessing the true miracle from the prayer I had offered to God, asking Him to find me a different job. I think if I had kept up my pleadings and decided I didn't want to love the students that year, I would have found another job. But I was given a higher calling, and I've learned that when we are given a higher calling and answer it, the resulting blessings are greater. How could I ask for more than what I was being given that night? I was being given love and honor by a child that I once didn't know I could love.

After the program, Sam shared with me that he was involved with theater and that he loved doing Shakespeare. Shakespeare? That was the last thing I expected to hear from Sam. I might have understood math in school, but Shakespeare was not easy for me to read. Not only could Sam teach me how to bowl, maybe he could also help me with Shakespeare. I could see greater miracles ahead!

Tip for New Teachers: It may be years before you see the results of your hard work and dedication, but if you are able to make it

through these days of paperwork, data collection, and testing, I believe the day will come when teaching will once again become a profession of concern for the child and his or her welfare, and you will experience, like I have, the miracle of the higher calling of teaching.

Seventeen

The Truth Is...My Students Could Spell Better than I Could

My year with Sam, Shannon, and Jamie had come to an end and Karen Wallace, the principal at the neighborhood school where I had previously taught, called and offered me a full-time ESOL job. ESOL stands for "English for Speakers of Other Languages." My job would be to teach English to Vietnamese students. Even though I had no experience teaching students who didn't speak English, there were numerous advantages to this new opportunity. Karen's school was twenty-five minutes closer to my home than the school where I had just worked, but more importantly, I really liked working with Karen. She encouraged me to teach the way I felt I could best reach the students, and she believed in discipline. The consequences my current principal gave students for unacceptable behavior were nowhere near what I thought the consequences should be.

For example, towards the end of the school year, I had picked up my students from the cafeteria and walked them past the cafeteria windows to our classroom. As we passed the cafeteria, Angel, a new student in my class, spit on the window where fifth graders were seated eating their lunches.

"Angel," I commanded, "step out of line!"

My class stopped and I briskly walked to Angel. "I can't believe you would do something so crude. I'm sure you just ruined the appetites of all the students sitting at the tables eating their lunches." I pointed at the window where he spit. "You will be washing that window after school tomorrow!"

The principal happened by at that moment. "What's going on, Miss Thomas?"

"Angel just spit on the cafeteria window and I told him that he'd be staying after school tomorrow to wash it."

The principal immediately undermined me in front of Angel and the rest of my class. "No, he will not wash the window. That's way too harsh. He will say he's sorry. Angel, say you're sorry."

"Sorry," Angel said to the air. That was that. Angel, and the rest of the class, learned that day that they could be rude and offensive and the principal would enforce no consequence for such behavior. Karen Wallace, like I, thought punishment should be equal to the crime. Karen liked my teaching style, my way of disciplining, and her school was close to my home. I accepted the ESOL job.

My Vietnamese students had come to America under some very difficult circumstances and were here with their families, or extended families, in hopes of making better lives for themselves. The only curriculum material I had for the three groups I'd be teaching — third, fourth, and fifth graders — was a thin workbook with some pictures to color and English words under the pictures to help the students learn simple vocabulary. I would have to come up with the majority of the curriculum. I accepted the job and hoped I could figure out what I was doing.

When I had taught at this school the previous year, I often saw the Vietnamese students but I had no connection to them, so I didn't know them. Because I didn't know them, they basically all looked the same to me. I wondered how anyone could tell one child apart from another. Then I began teaching them and everything changed. Quickly each child became his or her own person and they looked nothing alike. I found that what I had first experienced in not being able to tell the students apart was also common among people in other cultures I worked with. They, too, had a hard time distinguishing people from one another who were not of their culture. I can't count the number of times someone of another culture confused me with another white person who looked nothing like me in facial features, size, or hair color. When this first happened to me, I was shocked that anyone could mix me up with the person that they had (except when it was Marilyn Monroe). As it happened more frequently, I quit taking it personally, knowing that all cultures I had worked with did this. I guess at first glance, most people from a specific culture different from our own do look the same. Getting to know people as individuals quickly changes that perception. I know it changed mine as I got to know my Vietnamese students.

Taking this job stirred feelings within me that took me back to my teens when what I heard and read about Vietnam was frightening. America was engaged in the Vietnam War, causing me anxiety as I wondered which of my two older brothers would be drafted and sent to fight in this nightmarish conflict. Many American soldiers who went to Vietnam never came back, and those who did, did not come back the same people.

Now I would be teaching Vietnamese children who had come to America to escape the communist takeover of their country when the war was lost and our soldiers were brought home. These students were full of life and promise. It wasn't their fault that many of our American soldiers died while fighting a war that these students never knew and yet by being Vietnamese were connected to. As I greeted my seemingly happy, young students on that first day of school, I thought about these Vietnamese students having little to no idea how the Vietnam War had affected Americans. And I wondered what kind of effect, if any, the war had had on them.

After introducing myself, each child told me his or her name and I didn't have a clue how I was going to get through the year. It would take me all year just to learn their names. Over time, although I never got the pronunciation perfect, the students recognized who I was talking to when I said a name. They tried to teach me some

Vietnamese, and I knew I was pronouncing the words exactly the way they were, but the students just laughed at my attempts and said, "No, Miss Thomas, dat not it!"

Because I had so little material to work with, I decided that the best way to teach my students English was to give them hands-on assignments and teach them vocabulary that related to what we were doing. Our classroom was in a portable and in the middle of a sandy patch of land with no landscaping. I decided that we would plant, from seed, flowers next to the portable to spruce up our "home," as well as plant a small vegetable garden on some empty land close to the portable. I thought this would be a good way to teach basic words as we worked together on the plants.

The day of planting was warm and sunny. I stood before my fourth grade class and explained the project. "Boys and Girls, today we're going to plant a garden. I brought flower and vegetable seeds to plant, as well as dowel rods and thin rope to create a fence around our garden. I also brought in a few garden tools to help us with the planting." The students who understood were excited and anxious to get going. I wasn't a great gardener, but growing up we had a family vegetable garden so I at least knew that the seed went in the ground and that you covered it with dirt.

I opened the portable door and the students happily walked down the ramp onto the sandy ground. I stood in the middle of the students with the dowel rods, rope, and seeds in my hands. "Okay, Class," I began, and then pointed to four different spots on the land by the portable. "We will put the dowel rods there, there, here and..." Before I could finish with my instructions, Van, one of the students who spoke only Vietnamese and who had come from very poor circumstances, grabbed the rope and dowel rods from me and started barking orders in Vietnamese to the other students. Within a few minutes the class had put up the fence and were beginning to plant the seeds. I stood speechless as I watched a boy who I had felt a certain pity for, take control of the class in a way I never could have and get the students to plant and fence-in a garden in record time. These students knew a lot more about gardening than I did. Their lives in Vietnam depended on it.

When all of the seeds were planted and watered, I told the students that if the popcorn seeds actually grew corn so that we could pop it, I would call a photographer at the Orlando Sentinel newspaper and ask him to come take pictures of our garden. The challenge began.

Along with the flowers and the garden, we planted twenty different herbs and the students learned their names. When we got to the herb "Vietnamese Citronella," the children became very excited and said, "Miss Thomas, we know this! We love! Eat on eggs!" Their faces lit up and they enthusiastically spoke to one another in Vietnamese as they had a moment of connection to their homeland. One of my advanced students spoke to me in English, explaining how they used the herb.

"We put on goose egg. Just before the baby goose hatch, we cook in egg. After bird cook, we crack egg open and put citronella on it. It really good!" I hoped there wouldn't be any of those treats at our classroom Christmas party.

One day a huge cockroach ran across the floor of the portable. The boy who had taken over the planting of the garden began to speak rapidly in Vietnamese, pointing to the roach. A few students said to me, "He say he eat those in Vietnam." The students then shared with me that they had eaten dogs, cats, mice, and cockroaches in Vietnam. Some also said that they had drunk urine as a way to get well when they were sick. I felt like I was going to be sick. I found that these children were very detail-oriented and that they were excellent at drawing. This seemed to be a trait of the Vietnamese culture. I also found that communication was a never-ending frustration for me, and for the children as well.

One day I had the fifth graders working on book reports. Tam, one of the students who spoke no English, was having great trouble with this assignment. I picked up the book he was reporting on, thinking I could find some key words to help him with his report. When I saw the title of his book, I knew that this assignment was way over his head — he was doing his report on the Merriam-Webster dictionary. I laughed, and although he had no idea what I was laughing about, he, too, began to laugh.

Although Tam spoke no English, he could spell any word I gave him. That was true for all of my students. I gave the students weekly spelling words and even the academically lowest of my students scored high grades on their spelling tests. I ran out of typical elementary-level words and began to give them more challenging words. I couldn't stump them. I gave them words that I didn't know, and they spelled them correctly. I wondered if their ability to remember the spelling of words was part of their gift for detail or if was because they were disciplined and studied hard. I was used to the students who were born and raised in the United States and was taken aback by the difference in the discipline of the U.S. students and these Vietnamese students. The Vietnamese parents made their children do their work and never complained about them being given too much. (The amount of homework now given students of all ages has increased so much since that time, even the Vietnamese parents might be complaining.) I learned that to the Vietnamese, education, or enlightenment, was of utmost importance and that a teacher was second only to God in the way he was shown respect and honor.

As I taught English to these students, I began to realize how difficult our language is. There are countless rules for the English language that often don't apply when trying to use them to make sense of a word. English has many homonyms — words that sound and are spelled the same but have different meanings — and learning the meaning of homonyms proved to be especially challenging for my Vietnamese students. For instance, while learning how to tell time the students thought that a quarter after meant twenty-five minutes past the hour and that five minutes past the hour was a nickel after.

Another challenge in learning the English language is understanding idioms. One day as I talked with my students about a field trip we would be taking, riding the city bus to get there, I said, "We'll catch the bus at 9:15 in the morning."

The room became silent and I felt an energy of fear mixed with wonder coming from the children. I couldn't imagine what had made them feel this way, until Huong asked with trepidation, "How we catch bus, Miss Thomas? It big." There were many more idioms I would be explaining to them that year; English is full of them.

One Friday, as a reward for the children doing so well with their lessons that week, we went outside and had a picnic under the one little shade tree on the playground. The cafeteria ladies packed a lunch for each of my students and I brought in some blankets. It was good to be with the students in a setting where we could socialize and laugh. One boy who had arrived from Vietnam a few months previous was smiling as he spoke in Vietnamese. A student next to me said, "Miss Thomas, Minh say this best day of his life!" Another child agreed that it *was* the best day. I had to be more aware of, and more grateful for, each day that just might be the best day of someone's life who hadn't grown up with what we Americans lived with on a daily basis.

As we ate our lunches, Duc brought his milk to me. "I no want dis Miss Thom, it come from cow."

"Yes, that's where milk comes from," I said.

"I only like milk from cat," Duc said as he handed me his milk carton.

"From a cat?" I thought I heard him wrong.

"Yes, Miss Thomas," Thi responded, "he say cat! C-A-T, cat!"

"How do you get milk from a cat?" I couldn't imagine.

Thi looked at me like I should have studied a little harder in college. "You know, a cat have kittens and you drink milk from cat." I always suspected that these students were laughing at me behind my back.

As is typical of many students, some of my Vietnamese students tested the boundaries and tried my patience. Because of the language barrier, I often felt ineffective with my discipline. One day, the students were completely out of control, talking a million words a second in Vietnamese. When I tried to get their attention in English, they ignored me, so I began mimicking their language in hopes it would stop them. One of my students, Binh, burst out laughing. I was proud of myself for getting his attention.

"You speak Chinese!" he said.

"Really?" I felt excited and surprised.

"Yes!" he laughed, "you say bad words!" I never again used that method for quieting my class.

Tips for New Teachers: To have empathy for a student who is learning English, try to learn her language. That has helped me become more empathetic towards my ESOL students than anything else I've tried.

Eighteen

The Truth Is...I Had No Idea What the Vietnamese Refugees in America Had Been Through

All of these students were truly beautiful people, but there was one student who had a lasting impact on me. Tuyen Lam was that student. She always had a smile on her face and lit up any room she was in. She was smart, respectful, and a hard worker. As I got to know the students, they shared their stories with me. Tuyen's story was like that from a book.

"My parents own a jewelry store in Vietnam," she told me. "They want to leave Vietnam after communist come, but every time they try, something happen. One day my parent say that my sister, Kim, and I will go on trip with my aunt and uncle. It would be vacation. They tell me that they sew a pocket inside a pair of my pants and that they put a diamond in the pocket. They say I can sell diamond if I need money. I was excited that night when my aunt and uncle come for me and my sister — she was nine."

"How old were you?" I asked.

"I was six and I had to run through jungle with my sister and relatives and other people I didn't know. It turn out we were escaping from Vietnam and I was little and so I couldn't run as fast as others. My shoe came off and when I stop to get it, a man point gun at me and tell me if I can't keep up, he shoot me. I was scared, but my aunt and uncle help me." Tuyen's eyes showed fear as she retold the story of her escape to freedom.

"When we get to boat that take us to Malaysia," Tuyen continued, "we lie under tarp with cargo so that we were hidden." Tuyen's and Kim's parents had paid the boat owner one thousand dollars to smuggle their daughters out of the country. They traveled four days on the boat with one hundred nine other people before arriving in Malaysia.

"When we on boat, we had only rice to eat that we cook in ocean water. We run out of drinking water and the men who own boat say that if there is not drinking water for adults, the children will be thrown in ocean. That night, all Christians on boat pray to God. It rain and we were saved."

Tuyen continued her story, saying that they arrived in Malaysia where they stayed for two years. They then took a boat to the Philippines where they stayed in a refugee camp for six months before making the last leg of their journey to the United States.

When Tuyen, Kim, and her relatives arrived in America, they lived with other relatives who gave them support as they adjusted to their new lives in Orlando, Florida. Tuyen had not seen her parents since that night five years ago when she had run through the jungle to escape communism.

I had always known that living in the United States was a great blessing, but listening to Tuyen's story, and the stories of the other students, drove home to me with even greater force how fortunate we were to be in the U.S. and how important it was to fight to keep the freedoms we had in this country.

I didn't know what my students knew about the Vietnam War and America's involvement in it, but I hoped that as the students grew older they would understand what they had been given, and at what cost. The USA needed people like these students to refresh the memory of so many of us born in this country, who have known nothing but freedom, how valuable a gift we have. A gift so valuable that those born without it, or those who once had it and lost it, would risk their lives for it. In so many ways, these young students had already lived a lifetime of experiences that most American adults would never live — and that included me.

One day, when I was walking my students from the main building to our portable, we stopped at a sidewalk close to the office and waited for a few students who had not yet joined us. Beside us was another group of ESOL students. They were all Spanish-speaking and their culture was very different from that of the Vietnamese. My Vietnamese boys held hands at times and it meant nothing more than that they were great buddies. These Spanish-speaking boys, however, had no tolerance for the Vietnamese boys' display of friendship.

"You boys love each other," they taunted as they pulled their eyes up into a slanted position.

Without warning, my mother hen instinct came out. "You'd better stop that right now!" I warned the Spanish-speaking students. "If I ever again catch you making fun of my students, you'll be going with me to see Mrs. Wallace." The students loved Mrs. Wallace, but they didn't want to visit her for misbehavior. The Hispanic boys looked away and I knew that they understood my reprimanding.

When my class and I got to the portable, my students were extremely upset. They were hurt by the way the others had made fun of them and a few students were crying. At that moment, an idea came to me and I told my students to find a spot in the classroom where they could sit alone. I then went to my cupboard and got out a sixteen-piece Santa puzzle. I kept it hidden from the students and quickly pulled the pieces off of the cardboard frame. I then walked around the room and gave each student a piece of the puzzle, a plain piece of paper, a ruler, and a pencil.

"First of all," I said, "I don't want you to show anyone your piece of the puzzle. You are to work alone and keep your piece hidden from view. Now, using the ruler, I want you to divide your paper into four equal boxes."

I waited while the students measured and drew, as always, doing a meticulous job. Once they were finished I told them, "Now, number the boxes and in the first box, draw a picture of what you think the whole puzzle looks like." Students with nothing recognizable on their pieces groaned, while those who had something identifiable began to eagerly draw what they thought the puzzle picture was.

After giving them a few minutes to finish, I paired them up. "This time I want you to share your puzzle piece with your partner and then, in the second box, draw what you think the puzzle picture is."

After five minutes the students were put into groups of three and were instructed to once again share and draw. They regrouped one last time, so now there were four students in a group, and drew their last picture. I then had the students come to the back of the room with their puzzle pieces and their pictures.

We sat on the floor in a circle and I asked them to fold their papers so that we could only see the first picture they had drawn. Once they did this, they placed their pictures on the floor. Of course, none of the pictures looked the same.

"Kim, why doesn't your picture look like Phuoc's picture?" I asked.

"Because we only have one piece of puzzle," Kim said.

"But some of your pictures are closer to the actual picture than others. Why?"

"Because some people have better piece of puzzle. They have more information," Anh answered.

"Now show picture number two." The students unfolded their papers, displaying box one and box two. Understandably, their second pictures were a more accurate rendition of the puzzle picture than the first. We continued unfolding pictures until we got to box number four where the pictures were closest to the actual puzzle picture. Once we looked at all of the pictures, I put the puzzle frame on the floor and had each student place his or her piece in the frame. Although the pictures they had drawn were close to the actual picture, none were exact.

"Why did you leave out details that are in the actual puzzle picture?" I asked.

The students were a little frustrated with me. They had actually done an excellent job with their drawings and yet I didn't seem to be satisfied with their efforts. "Because we didn't have all pieces," answered Chung in an agitated tone.

"Exactly," I said, "and that's what happens to us as humans every day. We see someone or meet someone new and only have one tiny puzzle piece to his or her life. We create a whole picture about that person based on one puzzle piece and as long as that's the only piece we have, we are never completely accurate about who that person is. If we take time to get to know the person, more of the puzzle pieces will be revealed and we will get a clearer picture of who that person is. Lots of times in this life, people only rely on the one puzzle piece they have of a person. That's what happened today with the children who were making fun of you. They only saw one small piece of your puzzle and if they really knew *you*, they would see a completely different picture. Sometimes we have to be the ones to reach out to people who are unkind to us and offer them some of our puzzle pieces so that they will want to get to know who we really are."

"But they mean. They hurt feelings." Huong was visibly upset.

"I know. That's what makes this experience of getting to know people different from ourselves so hard. But someone has to be brave and do it, so why not you?"

It was time for the students to leave. I hoped that what they were taught that day would help them. A bigger idea was taking shape in my mind. I would need to go to the mall.

Tip for New Teachers: Although we all make first impression judgments when we meet our students, those impressions will change as more of the puzzle pieces are revealed. Don't stop looking for the hidden pieces. Finding just one of those pieces can make all the difference in a student-teacher relationship.

Nineteen

The Truth Is...I, Too, Probably Would Have Thought They Cheated

The puzzle experience I had with my class that day was something I wanted to share with the whole school. I was learning a great deal from my students and their lives, and I wanted others to have the same opportunity. Before starting my project, I talked with my principal.

"Mrs. Wallace, I have an idea that I'd like to present to the school. I'm calling it 'Solving the World Puzzle.' " I went on to explain my idea to Mrs. Wallace and, being the great principal that she was, okayed it without hesitation.

I left school, went to a store in the mall that sold posters, and picked out a poster of a character the students would recognize — Snoopy dressed as the Red Baron. I bought two identical posters. That night I typed up a treatment of my project and the next day I was on the morning announcements introducing "Solving the World Puzzle."

"Good morning students and staff. My name is Miss Thomas and I would like to share with you an activity I'm excited about. It's called 'Solving the World Puzzle.' As you know, there are many problems in the world and this activity will help us better understand how to solve these problems through communication and sharing. Every class that wants to participate will get a puzzle piece. Your puzzle piece will fit with all of the other puzzle pieces given to classes in the school and when put together, will create a poster with a picture on it. Every class will also be given a poster-size sheet of paper on which they will draw what they think the poster picture is. The poster picture will become clearer as you share information with other participating classes. This is a contest, and the class who draws a picture most like the original poster picture will get an ice-cream party. This morning each class will receive an 'Intent to Participate' form. If your class wants to participate, please fill out the form and return it to me by this afternoon. Tomorrow, each participating class will receive its puzzle piece and a week from today, that's March 11th, each class will turn in its picture. The pictures will be displayed in the cafeteria, along with an untouched poster identical to the one cut into puzzle pieces. Without knowing which drawing belongs to what class, a panel of judges will decide which picture looks most like the original poster. I hope that all classes will want to be a part of this 'Solving the World Puzzle' project."

By the end of the afternoon I had received "Intent to Participate" forms from classes representing three hundred fifty students. This was a small school and almost every student would be participating. There are times in teaching, at least in the teaching we once did, that something magical happens and our students learn more than we ever could have anticipated. This was one of those times.

The next day, the exchange of information and drawing began. My students were allowed to draw and share information with other classes only when their work was done. I didn't know how students in the other classes were doing, but my students, and especially the fifth grade students who had the advantage of being older and "wiser," were amazing in their ability to reconstruct the puzzle pieces that were shared with them. They drew them on separate pieces of paper, and ultimately took all of the pieces they had drawn, cut them out and put them together to make what they believed to be the original picture.

Each day on the morning announcements, students gave updates on "Solving the World Puzzle." At times, these updates included interviews with children from participating classes.

"Claudia and Phillip," I began, "you came to my class yesterday to get puzzle information from my students. Did my students help you?"

"Yes," Claudia said, "they were really nice."

"And their puzzle piece gave us a lot of information," Phillip added.

"Do you think your puzzle piece helped them?" I asked.

"Yes," Claudia said. Phillip shook his head in agreement with Claudia.

"The more we share, the clearer the picture," I said. "Someday I'd like my students to share their stories about their escape from communism with our student body. I think that would give us all a clearer picture of how fortunate we are to live in the United States. It will also let everyone know how brave and strong my students are."

Claudia and Phillip smiled

Of all the participating classes, only one decided it would let no one see its puzzle piece. This class was willing to describe it, but that proved to be of very little value to the other classes. Because this class wouldn't share its piece, the other classes wouldn't share their pieces with that class. In the end, the class unwilling to share its puzzle piece was the only class who had no picture to display. My Vietnamese students said, "Miss Thomas, it like communism. They don't want to share with rest of the world and it hurt the people in that country." These students knew exactly what they were talking about.

The day finally came when all pictures would be turned in. On this day, a Summit on Puzzle Piece Relations was held in the school library. Two delegates from each participating "country" was sent to the summit, bringing their class's picture with them, and then shared with the other delegates what their class had learned through the activity. After the summit, the classes' poster drawings were collected and hung in the cafeteria for all to see. The original poster was also hung in the cafeteria so that the students could see which class's drawing had come closest to it. To my delight, and then to my chagrin, my fifth grade class had drawn an unbelievably close depiction of the actual poster.

At first I was thrilled that their untiring and meticulous work had produced such a close portrayal of the original. Then it occurred to me that everyone in the school probably thought I had cheated and had shown my class the original, or at least had told them what it was. After all, I was the only one in the school who not only knew what the original was, but had a duplicate poster of it. My fears were confirmed as I walked through the cafeteria and heard students everywhere saying, "They cheated. You know they cheated. There's no way they could have gotten that close without cheating."

The truth was, I was extra careful about not giving my students any help with the project, even though I knew there were a few teachers who had guided their students. That was okay because they didn't know what the actual picture was. I did, and so I stayed away from my students as they worked on the World Puzzle. Now, as I looked at my fifth grade students' artwork hanging on the wall and saw how in size, color, and image it looked almost like a carbon copy of the untouched poster also hanging on the wall, I knew that if these hadn't been my students and I hadn't been with them every moment in the classroom while they worked on their drawing, I, too, would have thought they cheated.

It didn't matter what I said, the students who were accusing mine of cheating would not believe me. I understood their doubts. The work my students had done was fantastic, but it really was their work and they had done it all on their own. I was sad that when my students should have been given praise by their peers, they were accused of being dishonest. The students in this school had learned a lot by participating in the World Puzzle activity, but it was obvious they hadn't learned enough. They needed to keep looking for those missing puzzle pieces.

Tip for New Teachers: Don't be discouraged if you come up with a teaching idea that you know will be effective in reaching students, but not every student learns as much as you'd hoped. We're all on different levels and we can only learn what we're ready to learn. You never know if your great idea will turn on a light bulb later in a student's life. You might not be there to see it, but maybe you'll notice that the world's a little brighter because of it.

Twenty

The Truth Is...I Really Didn't Think the Corn Would Pop

After planting our seeds at the beginning of the year, the garden was used for many teaching activities. The students made predictions about the plants, trampled over the plants, threw garden dirt into my eyes, and one of the boys, Danh, sprayed me with the garden hose. Ants ate the first corn seeds we planted. The rain washed out our first group of seedlings and we planted the next group of seeds in large pots that we kept in the classroom in hopes of avoiding all previous problems. I also brought in some sprouting potatoes from my refrigerator and stuck them in the ground, crossing my fingers that we would get baby potatoes.

As I mentioned earlier, gardening wasn't my thing and gardening in Florida was extra difficult. The dirt was actually sand with very little nutrient content. Despite the rain, the scorching sun dried out the plants unless they were manually watered every day. The bugs and other pests were relentless. Regardless of these challenges, we held onto the hope that we would get something to grow.

Planting seeds in pots and then transferring them to the garden when they were strong plants seemed to be working. By the end of November, blossoms on the plants had turned into tiny fruits and our doubts had turned into feelings of accomplishment. We used the garden as part of our Thanksgiving reenactment.

The students made paper fish and "planted" them with the corn. Some of the girls and boys made Pilgrim hats and others made Indian headdresses. We sat outside and ate cornbread, pretending we were the original Pilgrims and Indians at Plymouth, Massachusetts. Despite the cornbread being so dry it stuck to our throats, the students liked it.

As I sat with my Pilgrims and Indians, I felt very blessed to be with them and to be learning from them. I looked at each child and felt a deeper understanding of how important every human being is. I looked at the garden and noticed that some plants had been broken and trampled over. Hmmm...I wondered which of my darling little Thanksgiving cherubs had done that.

Thanksgiving was past and we were on our way to Christmas. The students planned their Christmas party and wanted chips, drink, shrimp, egg rolls, dried beef, and dried Bambi for refreshments. Interesting. The day of the party the fifth grade class was wild. I stepped out of the classroom onto the ramp of the portable for a minute to show a student where to get ice. When I stepped back into the room, Phuoc was crying because Huy had hit him. I sent Huy to the office but he was sent back for the party. He and Thang then shook up the pop and I caught them just before they opened it. I couldn't wait for vacation to begin.

When the second semester began, a late Christmas present awaited my classes. Upon arrival at the portable, they were surprised by flowers in bloom, tassels of silk on the corn, full grown beans hanging from plants, and tomatoes ripe and ready to pick! The garden was a success!

We thought it would be fun to cook the garden food and invite Mrs. Wallace to a "dinner theater" performance by the students. I brought in a fake fur coat and long gloves for her to wear. Always a good sport, she played the part of a wealthy theater-goer, ate the food we cooked from our garden, and laughed at the show (it was supposed to be funny). There was candlelight, a lace tablecloth, and music. Our wonderful garden continued to serve the class and their learning. It was now time to test the popcorn.

I reminded the students of my promise about calling the Orlando Sentinel. "Okay, Class," I said, "I told you that if our popcorn actually popped I'd call the Orlando Sentinel newspaper and ask for a photographer to take a picture of you by the popcorn plants. It's time to see what happens."

We tested the popcorn the old fashioned way. I plugged our single burner cooker into an outlet, covered the bottom of a small pan with vegetable oil and then placed the popcorn kernels in the pan. We set the pan on the burner and put a lid on it, waiting with anticipation for the moment of truth. Listening to the oil sizzle, I knew that if the popcorn was going to pop, it would happen at any moment.

Plink! Plink! Plink! The popcorn hit the lid of the metal pan, the kids cheered, and I called the Sentinel.

I talked with a photographer at the Orlando Sentinel, Margaret Stapleton, and she said that she would be happy to come take a picture of our garden project. Ms. Stapleton came during my fourth grade class time and Tuyen was in that class. Ms. Stapleton took a great picture of the students laughing as they stood by the corn, holding the garden hose, water streaming out of its nozzle, and then she asked the students about the garden, their ESOL class, and their lives.

Like myself, Margaret Stapleton was surprised and touched by the stories she heard, and was especially taken by Tuyen's story. She wanted to do a running story for the Sentinel so that others in the community could read about Tuyen's life. As soon as Ms. Stapleton got permission from Tuyen, the principal, and Tuyen's extended family, she began the story. The public would be given some important puzzle pieces to Tuyen's life.

Teaching Tip for New Teachers: Sometimes when you try something in teaching that isn't guaranteed, it actually works! Don't get used to it.

Twenty-One

The Truth Is...I Didn't Want My Students to Leave

As the year came closer to its end, the students' English was improving and we were better able to communicate. One day, two of my third graders weren't getting along and one of the boys kicked the other. After dealing with the situation I asked them, "Why do you think God made us different?"

I was hoping they would say, "So we would learn to get along."

Instead Long replied, "So when we want to kill someone, we know which one to kill." I would need more than a year to teach that student.

I was asked to sing at the fifth grade end of the year banquet. All of my fifth graders would be going to middle school and so I wrote a song for them. I really didn't want the year to end, but as with all things in this life, nothing stays the same and the children were becoming adolescents. They would be moving on and I would be moving back to the regular classroom. I had many wonderful, loving students throughout the years that I taught, but the overall attitude of the Vietnamese society towards education and towards their teachers was something I would not experience in the regular classroom. Most parents of the students I taught throughout my career were realistic about their children and did have regard for both education and their children's teachers. I just wished that, like the Vietnamese, they could all be that way.

The last week of school was upon us and it was the day of the fifth grade banquet. The students looked so grown up — the girls in their Sunday best dresses and the boys in their suits and ties. I was introduced as the fifth grade ESOL teacher and guest performer. I looked out over the faces of the fifth graders and smiled when I saw my students. The pianist played the introduction and then I sang:

I'd like to say hello,
But it's time to say goodbye,
So I'll say it quick and leave before you see me cry.
I wish that you could stay,
But in my heart I know
That you're on the road to growing up,
And it's time to let you go.
I understand that there's a whole world before you,
A whole life to live,
A whole lot of friends you're going to make.
I understand that there's a whole lot of learning,
A whole lot to give and a whole lot you're going to want to take.
But please remember as you travel on the road you take to growing up,
There is someone who will always care for you,
Who once knew you when you still believed in fairy tales,
And is hoping all your dreams for life come true.
I understand all about that road you're on to growing up.
I understand, 'cause you see, I've traveled that road, too!
I understand all the fun that you'll have as you travel on your way,
All the fun that you'll have as you're becoming you.
I know you want to grow up; you want to get there fast,
But I wish somehow I could find a way
To make your childhood last.
'Cause the road that you're on to growing up
Is not a two-way street.

And the things you can do while you're still a child
You never can repeat.
So take some time to climb some trees,
And skin your knees,
And remember me, please,
On the road to growing up!
And please remember, to remember, I will always remember you!

And I have.

Tip for New Teachers: Every class you have will be different and you will love your classes in different ways. Even if you were to stay with a class you thought you loved the most, they would change and you would change so that a magical year would not hold that same magic as time went on. Be happy with what you experience and then go on to your next experience. Each experience will help you become someone you don't yet know. And what you finally become will be the greatest magic of all.

Twenty-Two

The Truth Is...I Gave a Lesson

on Swearing

An exciting thing happened to Tuyen that summer. On the front page of the June twenty-fourth Orlando Sentinel was the headline, "Vietnamese Family Together at Last." Tuyen's parents had finally made it to the USA, and after five years of separation, were reunited with their daughters. Under the headline was a picture of their reunion — a smiling Tuyen being embraced by her overjoyed father, the rest of her family standing behind her, weary but happy.

Something exciting also happened to me. Walt Disney World had a program called "Teacherrific." This program gave cash awards to teachers who implemented original creative classroom ideas that benefitted students in educational ways. A colleague had encouraged me to submit my "Solving the World Puzzle" project idea. I filled out the application forms, sent them in, and soon received an invitation to attend the Teacherrific ceremony at the Disney Contemporary Hotel.

As with all things Disney, the program was wonderful and, whether I received a Teacheriffic Award or not, I felt honored to be there. The teachers attending were served breakfast, entertained, and made to feel like royalty. When it came time for the MC to announce the Teacheriffic winners, I was awarded five hundred dollars! Oh happy day!

I had now taught for five years in the same Florida county, and due to redistricting, declining student enrollment in some schools, and growing student enrollment in others, I once again had to move to a different school. As most educators know, when a new teacher comes in, the teachers that are already there often stack the deck when it comes to giving the new teacher the most difficult students. I had no way to prove that this was the case when I started teaching that fall, but everyone else believed it was. As always, I had some good students in my class, but I also had some of the most controversial students I would ever teach. These children knew way too much about things they shouldn't have known about and they weren't quiet about what they knew. The few innocent children who started with me that year were not so innocent when the year was over.

I had a student, Tommy, who had a gift of being able to interpret the Constitution of the United States. That year when we read the Constitution as a class, every time I paused to ask the students what a particular phrase meant, Tommy gave clear and concise explanations. I told him that I felt he had a future in constitutional law. There was only one problem; he loved to fight and I knew that if he didn't overcome his anger tendencies, the law he could interpret would put him in jail.

When we talked about our future goals, Tommy said that he wanted to be a drug dealer.

"A drug dealer?!" I couldn't believe that he was not only entertaining the idea of doing something illegal for a career, but that he was telling his class and teacher about it. "Why would you want to be a drug dealer? Drugs hurt people and you'd either end up in jail or dead." There was no nice way to tell him what the outcome of a profession in drug dealing would be.

"My uncle's a drug dealer," Tommy explained, "and he's really rich and drives really nice cars."

Now what? It was true that there were people, probably more than I'd like to believe, who were involved with drug dealing and doing very well as far as the material things of this world were concerned. If I disputed that, I would be lying. But the one problem that was never brought up with reasoning like Tommy's — and others like him — was that they were only looking at this time on earth. I knew that I was about to say something that some would argue was not what a public school teacher should be saying in the classroom, but I could see no other way to address Tommy's logic.

"Sometimes people do seem to get away with doing things that are against the law. Sometimes it seems like people who are dishonest, or people who hurt others, end up with more money or things than the people who are trying to do things the right way. At some point in our existence, whether in this life or the next, we will all be held responsible for our actions — good or bad. No one will get away with doing hurtful things to others. Eventually those hurtful things will catch up to us." Not many years after that classroom conversation, Tommy ended up in jail for assault and battery. I could only hope that while he was in jail he would come up with some better career choice than drug dealing.

One day another student, Rosemarie, told me that her cousin, who was eighteen, was having her third abortion. I was shocked that a ten-year-old was privy to this information and that she was sharing it with me — really loudly. Immediately, my innocent students wanted to know what an abortion was. My typical response to those kinds of questions was, "Talk to your parents."

Before I could get my typical answer out, another very streetwise student, Samantha Eggelstone, answered, "It's when you kill a baby before it's born." This caused my innocent students to gasp (along with their teacher). Samantha, who enlightened the class that day, dressed up as Marilyn Monroe for Halloween and sang to the whole school, "Happy Birthday, Mr. President" on the school stage, sounding very much like Marilyn in the original version. It was good to know that Samantha knew some American history.

One of my students, Jake, was a thief and stole my Sony Walkman from my desk. After spending a few days talking to my students about character and trust and saying, "Do you love your parents, because stealing something would be very hurtful to them," Jake came to me after school and burst out crying as he handed me my Walkman. I was glad he loved his parents more than he loved stealing and I told him how proud I was of him. That didn't cure him, but I knew there was hope.

I have always believed that students should be accountable for their disrespectful behavior, so if a student said something inappropriate in the classroom, I gave him a warning. If he didn't heed the warning, I stopped teaching, called one of his parents and had the student tell his parent what he had just said. This always worked. The parent was upset at her child, the student was mortified that he had to say the crude word to his parent, and I could teach. I used this method of discipline with my controversial class, and it worked, but they needed even more than this. They took innocent words and made them crude, not actually articulating what they were thinking, but snickering at unstated connotations. I decided I would beat them at their own game.

"Class," I announced, "today we're going to have Swearing Class 101." The students squirmed in their seats, some looking at their neighbors, others looking down as they chuckled, while others looked up in surprise. "Words are made up of letters that don't really mean anything until we give meaning to them. Most swear words aren't bad until we load them with negative energy and hateful thoughts. What does the word *damn* mean?"

The students were more uncomfortable than I'd ever seen them and one brave student said in a voice augmented by nerves, "It's something beavers build."

"No, actually, that's d - a - m. I'm talking about the word that is spelled d - a - m - n." I wrote it on the board. "What does that mean?"

"It's a bad word," Francis answered.

"But why? Is the Bible a bad book?" I asked.

All of the students immediately responded, "No!" They sounded relieved that their teacher hadn't gone completely off her rocker.

"The word *damn* is in the Bible so I guess it probably wasn't meant to be a swear word. The word means separation from God, or to condemn someone. Now, that's a bad thing, but the word itself isn't bad. People made it bad by using it with negative, angry energy. What about the word *hell*?"

The look on my students' faces told me that they thought that their teacher was on a quest to be fired. "What is hell?"

"It's where the devil lives," Shantel said.

"Right. God lives in heaven and Satan lives in hell. It's just a place the devil lives. The word is in the Bible and the Bible is a good book that gives us information. The word hell is simply a bad place. So are the words jail and dungeon, but they're not swear words. People just decided to take the word hell, put negative, angry energy with it, and use it to make people feel bad." The students were feeling more relaxed and were taking in their swearing 101 lesson. I went on to explain other words that were found in the book *Where the Red Fern Grows* that I read to my classes every year. The "swear" words in the book at one time had a legitimate use, unrelated to crudeness or anger, and that's how they were used in the book. I told the students the origin of the words and how people had taken these words and made them into something unacceptable.

After giving the lesson on swearing, I could feel an energy shift in the room. The students seemed to lose their interest in the swear words they once thought were "cool" because now they knew what they really meant.

The day after my lesson, Evelyn, one of the administrative staff, saw me on campus and laughed as she said, "Samantha Eggelstone told me that yesterday you taught the class how to swear." Before I could say anything, Evelyn continued, laughing as she spoke, "I'm not sure how she got that out of your lesson, but we all know Samantha and all I could think was, 'Boy she knows how to twist things!'"

"Actually, I didn't teach them how to swear — they already knew how to do that — I taught them what the words meant."

Before I could explain my reason for teaching the students cuss word definitions, Evelyn's eyes took on a shocked look as she exclaimed, "What?! You actually did a lesson on curse words?!"

"It's not like it sounds. I wanted them to quit using bad words so I decided I'd teach them what the words meant so that using them wouldn't seem so cool." Evelyn looked at me in disbelief and walked away shaking her head. My tactic might not have been kosher, but my students cleaned up their language after that *and* they learned correct word definitions.

Tip for New Teachers: Only teach your students the original meaning of swear words if you're in a school where students swear. Otherwise, you might be teaching them to swear and that is definitely not part of the Common Core Standards.

Twenty-Three

The Truth Is...I Was More Frightened than the Children

The county where I taught was looking for ways to save money and so we were now trying year-round school. Some teachers liked the idea, others, like myself, didn't. We taught for twelve weeks, were off three weeks and then came back for twelve weeks. We were on rotations, meaning groups of teachers were off at different times. Maybe the reason I didn't like this schedule was because I was the rover. That meant that I didn't have an official classroom. My students and I used the room of whichever teacher was on her three week break. All of my materials were moved on a cart from room to room which really limited the amount of materials I could use. I don't know if this system affected the children's learning in either a negative or positive way, but I do know that the year I was a rover, the students learned a lesson in science that they would never forget.

I was constantly trying to think of unique ways to teach students the skills they needed to know. Most of the time that was a good thing, but I often told the students my ideas before I was sure they could be carried out and once I verbalized what I was thinking, I had to follow through. That's how the day of the rock candy came to be.

In science, we talked about crystal formations, and of course one of the first things that comes to mind when teaching about crystals in elementary school is making rock candy. No sooner did I see the sugar crystals in my mind than the words, "Why don't we make rock candy?" came out of my mouth. Every day after that, for the next month, the students asked me when we were going to make rock candy. I always tried to keep my promises and told them that we would make it, I just wasn't sure when.

It was a beautiful day in November, the day before Thanksgiving holiday. My students had music for their special area class and it was also the day of the third grade Thanksgiving presentation. I decided that this would be the day we'd make rock candy.

"Line up for music," I instructed my class. In walked Chris, a child who went to "special" classes because his emotional upsets kept other children from learning. Although he was officially registered in my class, he only participated with my class for music, art, P.E., and special programs. Chris had a tendency to irritate other children on a minute-to-minute basis. He picked fights, called kids names, kicked kids, and when someone actually fought back, told his parents that the other child had started it. Chris's parents always believed him and spent many days at the school trying to "make things right" for their child. They had a propensity to clobber him at home, but no one was going to do this to their child at school — especially not a child that he had hit first.

A holiday feeling was in the air and the children happily got in line for music. Even Chris and his agitating ways weren't going to ruin the festive mood I was in.

"Miss Thomas, Chris just kicked me," Billy complained.

"It's almost Thanksgiving. Try not to kick him back."

"Miss Thomas, Chris called me a name. You wouldn't like what he called me," Freddie tattled.

"Then don't tell me. I wouldn't want to be unhappy the day before Thanksgiving break."

I took them out the door into the bright sunshine and smiled as I dismissed them to their music teacher. Now, alone in the classroom, I could set up the rock candy experiment.

I read the directions: *Mix four cups of sugar with two cups of water in a medium-sized pan.*

"Wow!" I thought, "That's a lot of sugar for not much water."

I continued to read: *Stir until dissolved. Boil for five minutes and remove from burner. Pour into glass jar. Tie a string to a pencil and then rest the pencil horizontally across the top of the jar so that the string hangs and is immersed in the liquid. Set on window sill and allow water to evaporate. Watch crystals form on string.*

I had everything ready and waited until just before I was to pick up the class to put the mixture on to boil. Music class was out at 2:10. The Thanksgiving program started at 2:30. If I put the mixture on right before I picked up my students, it would have time to boil, we could pour it into the jar, and then leave for the Thanksgiving program. It was 2:09. I turned the single burner unit on high, placed the pan with the rock candy mixture on the burner, and left to pick up my class from music thirty seconds away.

As soon as I saw my students I proudly announced, "I put the rock candy mixture on to boil. In a few minutes we'll be able to put it into the jar and start making candy!"

"Yippee!" The class was thrilled that they were finally going to make their rock candy.

We walked into the classroom and immediately a voice from the office came over the intercom. "Miss Thomas, you are to take your class to the auditorium for the third grade program." Without telling them to, the children lined up at the door and surprised that we were being called so early to go to the auditorium, we all forgot about the rock candy and quickly left.

Fifty minutes later the program was over and it was great! It was a wonderful celebration of gratitude for this country, our freedoms, and our bounty. I walked with my students back to the classroom and as we passed other teachers with their classes I remarked, "Wasn't that a great production?!" A strong feeling of goodwill bubbled within me.

I was at the end of the class line, making sure all of my students were accounted for, when I noticed a commotion coming from the front of the line. Chris seemed to be causing the stir. I hurried to Chris and was puzzled when I saw a look of fear on his face. Before I could ask what was wrong, I was encircled by long wisps of smoke coming out of the closed classroom door. "Oh my goodness! The rock candy!" I exclaimed.

"FIRE!" Chris screamed.

"There's no fire!" I yelled.

"Oh *please* don't let there be a fire!" I prayed in my head. I imagined flames licking the walls of the classroom, the brand new computers turned to ash, and my job literally up in smoke.

By this time, all of the children who were returning to their classes from the wonderful Thanksgiving program broke loose from their straight, quiet lines and ran wildly across the school grounds to see the fire that Chris was screaming about.

"Get back here!" commanded their teachers.

"Ha! Ha! Ha!" laughed the children who ignored their teachers. They wanted to see a classroom burn down.

I grabbed Chris by the shoulders and moved him out of the way. "STAY CALM!" I screamed at the class and held my breath as I opened the door. I was immediately engulfed by smoke. The smoke was so thick, nothing was visible. I slowly felt my way to the front of the room where I found a carbon volcano in the pan, seconds away from bursting into flames. Filled with relief beyond words, I unplugged the burner and heard a faint voice.

"Miss Thomas," *cough, sputter, hack, hack,* "I can hardly breathe!"

"Me neither!"

"It's awful! I can't see anything!"

"Where's my desk?"

I turned around and saw the phantom bodies of my students crawling across the floor. They were surrounded by smoke as they made their way to their desks. Using the last bit of oxygen in the room I croaked, "What are you kids doing in here?!"

"We have to get our homework."

It was almost worth having the school burn down to finally see my class serious about their homework. I turned towards the ghostly figures and yelled, "Get out of here! It's Thanksgiving vacation. You know perfectly well there's no homework! Do you want to die of smoke inhalation?!"

I don't know who opened the other door, but by this time, smoke was billowing out of both classroom doors and filling the entire campus. The teacher whose class I was using happened to be subbing that day. She stepped out of the classroom where she was teaching and sweetly called to me. "Is everything okay, Miss Thomas?"

"Sure. Just making a little rock candy," I assured her as I walked away in a cloud of smoke, holding the pan with the smoldering volcano.

I don't remember the class leaving for home that day. I trusted they all got out of the classroom alive because I didn't hear from any parents. After vacation, the principal, Karen Wallace who had also moved to this school, put the "volcano" on display in the cafeteria so that everyone could see it, told the school that the good thing about Miss Thomas was that "she tried," and talked about putting smoke alarms on the rover's cart. It was months before the classroom didn't smell of smoke, and longer before the school let me forget the project. The best thing that came out of the experience was a great recipe for volcanoes. Read below for a guaranteed *A* on your child's next science project.

REAL LIFE VOLCANO RECIPE

Materials needed:
1 small pan
4 cups sugar
2 cups water
Hot plate or burner
Fire extinguisher

Directions:

Mix water and sugar in pan until dissolved. Turn burner on high. Place mixture in pan on burner. Do not watch, stir, mess with, or think about for fifty minutes. Check on after fifty minutes (or sooner if you hear the crackling of flames). Remove carbon volcano from burner. Camouflage pan and send to school.

Tip for New Teachers: I'm not sure I need to give you a tip in this category. When I left teaching, we were no longer allowed to use burners, toaster ovens, candles, or anything that in any way related to fire. Despite my one experience in almost burning down the school, I taught many, many lessons where heat or fire were involved, they were carried through without incident, and the students learned from those lessons. So the question is, is it more important to have the students engaged and learning while at the same time taking a chance of burning down the school, or to have the students simply read out of a science book and take a chance that they're not learning? Now *that* could be dangerous!

Twenty-Four

The Truth Is...Sometimes When I Was Stern on the Outside I Was Laughing on the Inside

I f a person is considering elementary education for a career, one quality he has to possess is a sense of humor. Without it, he won't make it past the first week. Throughout my twenty-eight years of teaching, humor has outweighed in importance all other qualities that I have. It has bonded me with students and helped the students trust my love for them as they have seen me laugh when I might otherwise have been screaming at them.

It was Fire Safety Day and there was a fire safety presentation in the multipurpose room. I brought my class to the presentation, seated them on the floor with the other classes, and then sat on a metal foldout chair behind the class, next to my intern who had been assigned to me for nine weeks. I got settled and then noticed that three of my girls, who were best friends and loved to talk, were sitting towards the front of the room, close to the stage, and of course, talking. The principal was on the stage ready to introduce the guest speaker, and so I quickly and quietly got out of my chair and walked to where the three girls were sitting. I tapped one of them on the shoulder and when she turned her head around, whispered to her and the others that they were not to talk during the program or I would separate them. They shook their heads in the affirmative, letting me know that they understood.

I was no longer teaching my controversial class and these three girls were good kids. However, anyone who's had a best friend in elementary school knows how hard it is not to talk when you're sitting next to that friend. Just to be sure they stayed quiet, I slowly walked backwards to my seat, glancing over my right shoulder to spot my chair, and then looking back at the girls to make sure they weren't talking. They were also sneaking peeks at me, wanting to know when I wasn't looking so that they could talk.

I kept a stern look on my face, trying to scare them into obedience. Meanwhile, the thighs of my legs stopped against my chair so I sat down, still keeping an eye on the girls. Something was wrong with my chair. It felt unstable, round and soft. Strangely, my skirt was sliding up and over the seat of the chair. Confused by what was happening to my skirt, I stood to fix it and then sat down again, leaning back to get comfortable. Suddenly, my arms flew into the air as my legs came up off the floor, my limbs desperately trying to balance my body before it did a back flip off the chair with no seatback. I pulled my weight forward and stood, steadying myself, and then turned to look at my chair. What I saw instead was a confused, scared look on the face of a student. I had been sitting on her head. Her name was Kristie and she was an extremely shy student. She hadn't made a sound when her world became dark and heavy. I apologized profusely, quickly eyeing her neck to make sure it wasn't broken. When I made it to my real seat, I looked at my intern who had covered her mouth, trying hard to stifle a laugh.

"It's okay, I know what that must have looked like," I whispered.

I then looked at the three buddies sitting next to each other and they were all looking at me, their lips closed tight, caging the laughter that was dying to be freed.

Our guest speaker had begun his presentation, so I once again quietly walked to the three girls, gave them a stern look and motioned for them to follow me. They did, and when we finally got outside into the fresh air, I looked at their worried faces and said, "Okay, now you can laugh."

"Oh, Miss Thomas! That was the funniest thing we have ever seen!" The girls' laughter and the vision of what my sitting on Kristie's head must have looked like made me burst out laughing, too.

"Poor Kristie!" I said. "I can only imagine what was going through her head when I sat on it."

When the girls and I regained our composure, we went back to the multipurpose room, serious and ready to listen. I wondered if Kristie heard one word during that assembly. And I wondered if she ever told her parents that her teacher had sat on her head. I know in my family growing up, that would have been great dinnertime conversation. I don't know if she told her parents, but I do know they didn't call the principal and no one threatened to sue me. Thank heavens there wasn't a "No Teacher's Left Behind" law — I might have been in trouble!

Tip for New Teachers: Many students will learn more from your reaction to a crazy situation than just about anything you teach them. Laugh. It's the best antidote I've found, even for sitting on a student's head!

Twenty-Five

The Truth Is...I Didn't Take Time to Understand the System

Although all schools are trying to do the same thing, educate students, the way schools are run varies depending on where you live in the country. I went to college in Utah and was surprised when the high schools shut down for a day of hunting. In Ohio there were built-in snow days and I'll admit that on snowy school days when the phone rang early, I crossed my fingers hoping the schools were closed. When I taught in Florida, I was sad to think there would be no snow days. There was a hurricane day here and there, but we had to make those days up at the end of the year and that was not something to look forward to. In the Florida county where I worked, schools got out an hour early on Wednesdays and I was excited about that. Then I found out that it was the students who got out early; the teachers had to go to meetings and workshops. I would *always* choose teaching over going to meetings.

As I looked over the school calendar, I was surprised and happy to see a student holiday at the end of the month. I decided that on this unexpected holiday I would go to the beach.

I got up early that day, excited to be on the road to Cocoa. The trip took eighty minutes and was worth every minute it took to get there. It was a perfect October day and the water and air were still warm. There's nothing that makes me feel freer from life's responsibilities than being at the ocean. After a wonderfully relaxing day, it was hard to head back home.

The next school day I arrived at the same time as Shana, the teacher whose room I had almost burned down. We both got out of our cars and the first thing Shana asked was, "Were you sick yesterday?"

"No," I said cheerfully, "I went to the beach! It was so beautiful and relaxing."

Shana gave me a funny look and said, "You know that yesterday was a workday."

"Workday?! I thought we had the day off!" I felt sudden panic knowing I had played hooky.

"No, just the students had the day off. We were supposed to be working on report cards." How did I miss that memo? Not only was I in trouble for skipping school, I was also in trouble for not doing my report cards. I immediately went to Mrs. Wallace and explained to her what I had done. She told me not to worry about it. Little did I know she'd later make me pay.

Living in the Central Florida area offered unique experiences for our students. One was the privilege of seeing the space shuttle streak through the sky after its launch from the space center. Those were exciting times as the entire school made its way outside to witness one of man's greatest accomplishments being displayed right in our own backyard.

One morning, a week after we had watched the shuttle climb through the atmosphere on its way to orbit the earth, I was on my way to school when a traffic light turned red. I immediately put on my brakes and heard two loud exploding sounds. My heart sank. It seemed that no sooner had I put money out for one thing that needed to be fixed, that something else went wrong. I had owned a car long enough to know that very few car problems cost less than five hundred dollars to fix. I heard two noises when I hit the brakes. "That will be a thousand dollars," I thought.

I pulled into the school parking lot and began to look my car over for possible problems. I was wearing a straight skirt, nylons, and heels and I knew that crawling under my car was probably not what a professional female teacher should be doing. However, most elementary teachers are curious by nature, so I got down and began to look under the back of my car. It was dark and I couldn't tell if anything was falling apart. That's when I heard Shana's voice.

"Becky, are you all right?"

I pulled my head out from under the car and looked up at her. "About five minutes ago I put my brakes on and heard two loud noises. I don't know what it was, but I know it's going to cost at least a thousand dollars to fix."

"You say there were two noises?" she repeated.

"Yes."

"And you heard them about five minutes ago?"

"Yes."

"Do you think they could have been the sonic booms from the space shuttle that just reentered the earth's atmosphere?"

First I almost burned down Shana's classroom. Then I told her I skipped work and went to the beach. Now she knew that I was incompetent in science.

Word got around fast and at the end of the morning announcements Karen Wallace said, "We are so happy that Miss Thomas made a safe landing into the parking lot today." My new name was "Boom Boom" and that week above my classroom door was hung a large wooden sign that read, "Boom Boom's Boutique." It had been retrieved from a dumpster and I was now its proud owner. I loved working at a school where we felt close enough to kid one another. I just couldn't wait for it to be someone else's turn to kid!

Tip for New Teachers: If you get a job teaching in a school other than the one you attended growing up, ask lots of questions. No two schools do things exactly the same and knowing this might save you from looking like the uneducated one at your school.

Twenty-Six

The Truth Is...I Didn't Want a Class Pet

G rowing up, our family had lots of pets. They consisted of large dogs, cats, raccoons, possums, skunks, birds, chicks, wild rabbits, and anything else that could be found in the Ohio countryside. We lived on five acres of land surrounded by hundreds of undeveloped wooded acres and so we were always finding something alive and wild to bring home.

My mother was extremely tolerant when it came to her children bringing these creatures into her house. But now, as a teacher, I didn't want pets in my classroom where I could use them as a teaching tool. It wasn't that I didn't love animals, because I did, it was the distraction it would cause and the smells and the mess that I would have to constantly remind the students to take care of. I loved the idea of having a pet "show and tell" day when the parents brought in the pets, the students showed them, and then the parents took the pets back home. My other classes had done this and it was always a great time. When I mentioned this idea to my fourth graders, they insisted on a class pet.

"Please, Miss Thomas, we'll take care of him."

"We promise we'll do our work and won't be distracted."

"And we'll pay for his food." They had good arguments and I finally decided they could have a pet mouse. It was a cute little thing and they named him Ziggy.

At first, Ziggy seemed to be doing well. I personally didn't know the habits of mice so I wasn't a good one to diagnose his health. I did know, however, that when his hair started falling out it wasn't a good sign. Every day the hairless patches grew bigger until I told the class that we'd have to take him to the vet. I wasn't sure who was going to pay for the bill, but there was no question about taking the mouse in.

The next day my students took up a collection to pay for Ziggy's medical bill. They came up with eighty-six cents and I knew I'd have to throw in my week's lunch money. After school that day, two of my students came with Ziggy and me to the vet. I let them take Ziggy into the Vet's office while I parked the car. When I made it into the building, they had already talked with the receptionist and told her that the mouse's name was Ziggy Thomas (it must have looked like me) and that they had eighty-six cents to pay the bill. She said that the doctor would see the mouse as soon as possible.

Ziggy was diagnosed with having a nervous disorder. I think it was called "being caged up in a fourth grade classroomitis." The doctor only charged eighty-six cents for the diagnosis and Ziggy died the next week. We had a little funeral for him and a few tears were shed. That was the end of classroom pets for me — until the day Chase Jump came to campus.

Karen Wallace loved animals, especially dogs. She had a Golden Retriever that she would sometimes bring to work. While school was in session, it would sleep by the secretary's desk in the office area. One week, another type of dog showed up on campus and it didn't appear to belong to anyone. It was a German Shepherd and some of the students loved it, while others were petrified of it. It was full of life and chased the students around the playground area when they came to school in the morning and when they went out for recess. Unlike Mrs. Wallace, our assistant principal, Ms. Waverly, hated dogs because she was scared to death of them, and threatened to call the pound to have the shepherd taken away and put down. That's how I ended up with the dog.

One afternoon, while my students were at lunch, Karen came to my room and asked me to come with her. She walked me to the cafeteria and took me around to the back entrance. There, right outside the door, was the stray shepherd, lying down and panting so that he looked like he was smiling. Karen quietly asked, "Do you want this dog? Ms. Waverly says that she's going to call the pound if she sees it on campus again. I can't let this dog go to the pound."

What was I going to do with a dog? I spent most of my life at school and I was house-sitting for some friends for two years. The owners had a "no pets in the house" rule and they lived in downtown Orlando where I was sure I couldn't keep a shepherd tied up outside at night. Despite not wanting a classroom pet, I couldn't stand to think of anything bad happening to an animal. Karen looked at me with sadder eyes than a Basset Hound. I gave in.

"Okay, I'll give it a try."

"We can't keep him by the cafeteria," Karen said. "Why don't you take him to your class for the day?" To my class?! How was that going to work?

"Come on, Boy." The dog followed me down the hallway and into my classroom. "Stay," I said. "I have to get the boys and girls from lunch. We'll be right back. Be a good boy." The dog panted, wagged his tail, and surprisingly, he sat down. When I got to the lunchroom, the students were lined up by the cafeteria door.

"Class," I said, "I want you to follow me outside and when we get to the hallway by our room, I want you to line up at the wall by the door. I need to talk to you about something."

The class quietly walked to the room, their faces full of curiosity. Brian, the line leader, stopped by the door and the rest of the students stopped behind him.

"We have an unusual situation in the classroom," I explained. "For this to work, you're going to have to follow the rules I give you."

"We will, Miss Thomas!" promised more than one student. They had no idea what rules they were committing to follow, but they were excited to follow them. Anything different, especially when there was an element of mystery to it, was better than a regular day at school.

"You all know about the dog that's been running around campus." The entire class nodded their heads in the affirmative. "Mrs. Wallace asked me to keep it in our classroom for the day."

"Yippee!" squealed the girls as they jumped up and down, grabbing each other's arms with joy.

"Yes! Yes! Yes!" shouted the boys, as excited as the girls.

"In order for this to work, you're going to have to stay focused on the lessons I'm teaching. No running around in the classroom. No talking to the dog when you're working or when I'm teaching. No trying to get the dog to come to you. I'll keep the dog by my desk. Do you think you can follow these rules?"

The class answered in unison, "Yes, Miss Thomas!"

"Okay, when I open the door, I want you to walk in quietly and take your seats." I opened the door and the dog was so happy to see the class, he forgot he was at school. He chased them around the room and the students went crazy.

"Ahhhhh! Miss Thomas, he's jumping on me!" screamed Monica.

The dog left Monica and jumped up on Scotty, knocking him down.

"Class, settle down! Here, Boy! Here, Boy! Sit! Sit! Get down! Get down from that desk!" I had never seen a dog jump like this dog. He was everywhere at the same time — on the desks, on the kids, on me. I had forgotten to explain the rules to the dog.

"Boys and Girls, please sit down!" I yelled. "If you sit down, I can settle the dog down." The children did their best to get to their seats, although the dog made it as hard as he could for them to do so.

"Here, Boy! Come on, Boy!" I called to the dog. Although I didn't expect it, he came to me. I got him to lie down by my desk and amazingly, the students got into their seats, took out their math books, and I was able to teach. Things were under control for ten minutes when the dog decided he needed to use the restroom. The unfortunate part was that he didn't ask to be let out.

"Eewwww!" The students pinched their nostrils with their fingers.

"All right," I said with exasperation, "everyone go to the picnic table in the courtyard. Leave the classroom door open so I can see you." The students left the room and piled onto the picnic table. They watched through the open classroom door while I had the undignified task of cleaning up after the dog.

I took the dog home with me that day. He was wild. The students named him Chase Jump because that's what he did. We called him Chase. Karen had given me a collar and a long leash for the dog, so before going to bed that night, I attached the leash to the collar and then tied the leash to a tree so that Chase had some freedom to walk around. No sooner had I gotten into bed than I heard howling.

Ahewwww! Ahewwww! I had to get that dog quiet before someone called the police. I went downstairs and outside in my pajamas and there was Chase on the roof of my Honda Accord, a wolf howling at the moon.

"Get down from there!" I commanded in a whisper.

Ahewwww! I pulled on the leash and he walked across the roof and down the hatchback window. How in the world did he get on top of my car?

"Down!" I tugged and he jumped down and then jumped on me.

"Chase! Down!" I was trying my best not to wake up the neighbors. I got my keys and moved my car. I then went back to bed and the next morning Chase was gone.

My neighbor appeared with him, explaining that she had found him wandering around in her yard that morning. I couldn't do this.

"Sorry, Chase," I looked at the dog and felt really bad. "I can't keep you here. You're going to have to go back to school."

After feeding him, I reluctantly put him into the back seat of the car and began my drive to work. We hadn't gotten too far when I heard a familiar, disturbing sound coming from the dog. I glanced in the rearview mirror and saw a look on his face that I had seen on humans' faces right before they throw up.

"No, Chase, no!" There was nowhere to pull off. The dog looked pale, if a dog can look pale, and he then got rid of his breakfast.

I pulled into the school parking lot and some of my students who were standing outside of the school screamed with excitement when they saw Chase looking at them through the back window. He seemed to be feeling really well now. "He's back! He's back!" squealed Veronica.

I got out of the car and warned the kids, "Don't go to the car. He got sick in the back seat and I have to clean it up."

"Oh, I've never seen dog throw-up before!" Veronica exclaimed, her eyes dancing.

"You don't want to see it," I warned her.

"Yes, I do. Please, Miss Thomas. Please let me see it! I'll clean it up."

Some lessons in life can only be learned by experience. "Okay," I said, "go ahead." I've never seen a child's smile change so quickly into a look of horror. Veronica's gag reflex worked really well and her face was hidden as she walked away from the car, her arms folded across her stomach and her head down. I guessed I'd be cleaning up after the dog this time, too.

I took the dog with me to see Karen and explained everything. She understood my predicament and we both felt terrible about the dog's fate. I agreed to take the dog to my room that morning so Karen would have some time to think of a possible last minute solution before the assistant principal called the pound.

While waiting for inspiration, I got a call from the office. There was someone at the school who wanted to talk with me. A few minutes later a woman and her little daughter came into my classroom. She was the owner of Chase. The dog had gotten loose from her yard and she didn't know where he had gone. I explained to her how the dog had almost ended up at the pound and if the assistant principal caught him on the school property again, the dog would be gone. I could tell Chase's owner really loved her dog, so I wanted her to understand how serious this was.

"I was wondering something." I hesitated when I said this. Chase did have a great personality and I knew the students would miss him. "Do you think that once in a while I could bring my class by your house to say hello to Chase?"

Chase's owner smiled and welcomed the idea. "Yes, that would be fine." She and her daughter then took Chase by the collar and led him out of the room.

The class was sad that Chase was gone, but they didn't need to be. At different times that year we saw Chase running around the school, a few times chasing Ms. Waverly who was holding a large stick thinking she could scare or beat him with it. He thought it was a game and went after her to grab it. She never touched him with it, because after all, his name was Chase Jump and that's what he did.

Tip for New Teachers: I have no tips about classroom pets because, as you can see, I was not successful in that area. Maybe you have some tips for me. I'd love to hear them!

Twenty-Seven

The Truth Is...I Really Wanted to Cry

It was now January and we had just returned from Christmas break. My youngest brother, Jack, who lived in Vermont, worked at a bookstore and had sent me a Christmas box full of books for my classroom. As I shared them with the students, one of the books was especially unique and intriguing. In fact, it really wasn't a book, it was a foldout museum. I unwrapped the cellophane cover and read the instructions so that we could put it together.

The students and I were fascinated as museum pieces, combined with other museum pieces, turned into rooms and we soon had a miniature museum for a classroom display. As we looked at the details of each room, an idea popped into my head. "Why don't we make a classroom museum?" All eyes were on me as I expounded on the idea. "We could turn the classroom into a museum. Different areas could showcase different subjects. For instance, the wall facing the courtyard could be an American pioneer section. We could have a separate section for autographs and another for coins, and a place for unusual rocks!" I think I was more excited than the kids, although they began to catch the vision and added their ideas. I wrote up plans for our museum that night.

This fourth grade class had its challenges, as all classes do. Kyle had a speech handicap and wouldn't read out loud or participate in class discussions. He was pulled out of my class for speech therapy twice a week where he received individualized attention. He had two friends who were low-achievers and showed no motivation in class. One of my students, Gene, had a learning disability and was labeled dyslexic. He was a sweet and sensitive child, and he tried hard to read and write, but had little success. A new student, Liza, had moved from Israel to Florida, and the only way I could communicate with her was with the limited Spanish I knew. Her mother was from Spain and so Liza knew Spanish, but her written language, as well as the language she read, was Hebrew. The balance of the class was a typical combination of students with strengths and weaknesses. I felt that the classroom museum would give all of the students an opportunity to participate, no matter what their limitations.

The days ahead were filled with work, learning, and fun. We decided that our exhibits would be: *Antiques, Unusual Collections, Autographs of Famous People, Interesting Things about the School Staff and Relatives of the Staff, Teacher Memorabilia,* and *Items from around the World.* The students were divided into small groups, and each day after school I took a different group to the place where I was house-sitting, and then to antique shops.

The house I was taking care of was beautiful and one-of-a-kind. Kathy, the wife of the couple who owned it, had a flare for decorating and was able to take unusual objects, or sometimes items that were headed for the trash, and make them into attractive wall hangings or tables or just about anything she could think of. Many of the items were antiques and I knew they'd be perfect for the museum. Kathy and her husband were in South America for two years and those were the days before email. It took a while for mail to get back and forth from the states to South America. I sent Kathy a letter asking if we could display antiques from her house in our museum, and hoped the letter would get to her before we were bringing the antiques back to her house from the museum.

When a group of students came home with me, I gave each student an antique from the house. The students studied the objects and then made an educated guess about what they thought the objects were used for. After their predictions were written, we made a trip to nearby antique shops where the students shared their borrowed antiques with the store owner and asked him to explain what the items were. The students then wrote up a summary of what they had learned.

The school where I taught had been around for quite a while and I decided that if we were going to invite the public to the museum, we would have to do some sprucing up. I talked with Karen and asked if my students and I could paint the cupboards in the room. She gave her permission and I asked Gene to be my art assistant. He couldn't read, but he could draw and put colors together.

I chose the colors I thought would work and showed them to Gene. He gently shared with me the colors he thought would work better. Using his art expertise, we painted the cupboards a dark blue and the trim tan. It was the most confident I had ever seen Gene and it made me wonder why schools weren't set up so that students could learn to read, write, and do math in conjunction with their gifts, rather than learning subjects in a compartmentalized way.

Kyle, my student with speech problems, along with his two friends, Greg and Stanley, took a great interest in the museum coin collection. They asked if they could be the ones to explain the coins to the visitors. I tried not to show my excitement as I agreed that they could be in charge of the coins.

By this time, Liza was beginning to understand a little English. She asked if she could be one of the tour guides for the American Pioneer and Antique display. To me, that would be the hardest display for the children to present because it contained so many objects and each had a history of its own. I was hesitant to let her explain the exhibit to our visitors because of her limited English, but she assured me that she could do it so I gave her the okay.

It was getting closer to the day of the *World of Wonders Museum* and all kinds of interesting items were being loaned from teachers and community members to use for our displays. My principal brought in a two piece white suit that her mother had worn the day she and Karen's dad were married. Like so many brides at that time, Karen's mom was married when her husband came home on furlough during World War II. One of the teachers brought in an unusual-looking antique mousetrap. His grandfather had invented it and this teacher claimed that his grandfather was the *real* inventor of the mousetrap before his idea was stolen. Another teacher brought in a beautiful painting that had been done by her grandfather. This teacher told us that her grandfather had a whole wing dedicated to his artwork in the Corcoran Gallery of Art in Washington, D.C. I had a picture of my grandfather with his cello, and I set my violin, on which I could play "Mary Had a Little Lamb," beside the picture. Grandpa was a cellist and percussionist in the Cleveland Orchestra and played under the baton of George Szell, once one of the finest conductors in the world. Students and teachers alike began to learn things about each other that they wouldn't have learned from a regular day in the classroom.

Our autograph section was growing, and we had a good time looking at the famous people teachers and community members had met. There were autographs from U.S. presidents, famous base-ball players, movie stars, singers, and other celebrities. I worked in a Hilton Hotel coffee shop when I was seventeen and it just so happened to be the hotel where many well-known performers of the day stayed. I met Ella Fitzgerald, Peter, Paul and Mary, Sergio Mendez and Brasil '66, Arlo Guthrie, and the cast from "Laugh-In" — to name a few. I also met Leonard Bernstein, one of the most famous conductors and song writers in the world, and got his autograph. Of the celebrity autographs I got that summer, I treasured his the most. At some point in my life, the end of his last name got sepa-rated from the rest of his name. Despite that, it still said Leonard B, he had personally written it, I met him, and it was my most valuable keepsake.

The *World of Wonders Museum* day was right around the corner and we needed to take care of last minute details. I loaded a bag with cleaning supplies from home and put it in my car. I also carefully put my autographs in an envelope where they would be safe and set them on the seat beside me. I had other things to carry in from my car when I got to school so I left the cleaning supplies and autographs on the front seat of my car. At that time, teachers allowed trustwor-thy, upper grade elementary students to get things from their cars if necessary. I asked Kristie, the girl whose head I had sat on, and one of my responsible boys to get the bag from the car.

"There's an envelope on the front seat of the car," I said. "I don't want you to bring that in, just the bag."

The children had barely walked outside when it began to sprinkle. By the time they got back to the classroom, they were damp but proud. "We put the envelope in the bag so that it wouldn't get wet," Kristie said as they handed me the cleaning supplies.

"You brought the envelope? I only wanted the bag." I didn't want anything to happen to my precious autographs, especially Leonard B's.

"Oh, sorry," Kristie said. She really was, but not as sorry as I was when I took the autographs out. Or should I say, when I took Leonard B's autograph out. The top of the 409 cleaning solution had come loose and had done exactly what it claimed it would do — clean. It cleaned the autograph right off the paper.

"Not Leonard Bernstein," I said, almost in tears. And then I had to make a split-second decision about how I was going to react to what seemed, at the time, a tragedy. Should I let all my frustration and sorrow out on these children who were being responsible by putting the autographs in the bag, or should I downplay the incident so that they wouldn't have to live with the guilt I was really close to loading on them?

As the brain will do at unexpected times, mine retrieved a scene from my teenage years when my mother found her favorite antique thumbprint bowl that had been passed down through her family from the eighteen hundreds, broken in a number of pieces and lying on the coffee table in the living room. Someone in the family had broken it and left it there for her to discover. When she saw it, she stood for a moment filled with disappointment and then sadly said, "Not my thumbprint bowl." She then quickly changed her attitude and said, "Oh well, someday all things on this earth will be gone," picked up the pieces and threw them in the trash. She never said another word about it. I was standing beside Mom when she found the pieces and I was impressed at her reaction. What an example she was, and at that moment, she was also my strength.

"It's okay," I said, trying to sound sincere. "You were trying to help and you did the right thing by putting the envelope in the bag." I had sat on Kristie's head and she hadn't said a word. How could I be upset with her for trying to help me?

Just writing about this makes me want to cry. I looked up Leonard Bernstein's autograph on eBay. In some cases his autograph is selling for five hundred dollars. Of course, mine only had the name "Leonard B" on it so it might not have been worth anything — except to me. I didn't have the heart to throw away the blank paper. It's framed and still hanging on a wall in my house. And who knows, maybe I'll find *ernstein* in an unexpected place someday and can put that in the frame. Now that would be a conversation piece!

Tip for New Teachers: There will be a time(s) in your teaching career that something you treasure in your classroom will be destroyed by a student. If it was an accident, let it go. The student's well-being is worth more than anything material. On the other hand, if the student was out of control and being disrespectful of your property, make him pay!

Twenty-Eight

The Truth Is...I Had Never Been in an X-Rated Place Before

In one day, the *World of Wonders Museum* would be open to the public. My students made a video entitled *Museum Manners* which was broadcast for the student body the day before their "field trip" to our museum. When I arrived home after school that day, there was a letter in the mail from Kathy telling me I was welcome to use her antiques for the museum. I was thankful she gave us her approval, considering a whole section in our museum was comprised of her things, and the recently non-English-speaking Liza now knew more American history words in English than most of the students in the school.

When museum day arrived, the students were at their posts anxious to give their presentations. The badge-wearing student security guards were on alert for suspicious-looking characters. The classroom runners were ready for errands, and an actual freelance newspaper writer was there prepared to report on the *World of Wonders Museum*. It was time to open the museum doors to the public!

It turned out to be a great day. Liza did an amazing job at the American Pioneer display. Kyle, who rarely spoke, was able to tell our guests about the coins, and I had never seen Greg or Stanley, who were working with Kyle, so animated. Gene, my dyslexic student, was beaming as visitors commented on his paint job that made the cupboards look like new, and I was as happy as an elementary school teacher could be, modeling Karen's mother's World War II bridal suit and thinking of how all of this had come together through teamwork, individual ideas and talent, and the foldout museum my brother had sent from Vermont. As soon as possible, I was going to fill out another entry for Disney's Teacherrific Award.

When I did fill it out, my typing fingers couldn't keep up with all I had to say about the museum and its effect on my students' learning. There were so many positive, unexpected outcomes it was hard to fit all that I wanted to share on the limited space the application provided. I was bursting with excitement and felt sure our museum idea would win some sort of Disney Teacherrific Award. Seventy-five educator entries would win one thousand dollars, twelve entries would win twenty-five hundred dollars, ten entries would win five thousand dollars, and one entry would win ten thousand dollars.

I sent my entry in and at the beginning of the following school year attended the Teacherrific Awards Program at the Disney Contemporary Resort Convention Center. I brought a teacher friend, Sheryl, from school. We ate and were entertained and then the awards ceremony began.

The one thousand dollar winners were called first. The convention center was packed and loud applause followed the announcement of each name. As time went by and my name wasn't called, I began to feel that maybe I had won one of the big prizes. My stomach filled with butterflies, but before I would let myself believe I had won more than one thousand dollars, I squelched the feelings so that if I was wrong, I wouldn't be disappointed. Name after name was called until seventy-five winners were announced — and I wasn't one of them.

Once again, Disney entertainers filled the stage with singing and dancing before the next group of winners was announced. Feeling nervous, I left the convention room and walked the halls for a few minutes. I saw a teacher I had previously worked with, and as we conversed I congratulated him on winning a one thousand dollar award. He made a comment about me not winning and jokingly said, "Maybe you'll win a bigger award," and then laughed.

I went back to the banquet room and settled in as the performers finished their last song. The MC stood and explained the next category of winners. "It is now time to present our Top Program Award. This award will be granted to twelve program entries which, in the opinion of the Awards Committee, deserve special recognition. Each winning entry will be awarded twenty-five hundred dollars." I swallowed a few times, steadied my nervous leg with my hand, and looked as unaffected as I could. Again, the names were called and with each announcement, my heart beat faster. The entries they had submitted to win this prize were excellent. I felt in my heart that my class's project was just as good, but my name hadn't been called.

They were now ready to announce the Special Judges Award. "The Special Judges Award will be granted to ten program entries which, in the opinion of the Awards Committee, have made significant contributions to the educational curriculum, and surpassed goals and expectations." I felt that our class museum had done that, but could I really hope to win five thousand dollars? For a teacher receiving a less than glamorous salary, winning five thousand dollars was almost unfathomable. Again, the MC announced each winner and this time my name was one of them! I wanted to cry and laugh and find that teacher who thought it was a joke that I might win a big prize. I steadied myself, walked to the stage and put out my trembling hand to accept the five thousand dollar check. It was a happy moment!

When they announced the winner of the ten thousand dollar prize and what the teacher had done to win the prize, I was happy to have come in second place. He was a middle school teacher and his students and he had made a simulated space station where the students stayed for thirty hours straight, their actions being monitored by a Mission Control that had been set up in the school cafeteria. Russian officials read about the project on the internet and invited eight of the student project participants to visit the headquarters of the Russian space agency outside of Moscow. And I thought taking my students to antique shops was highfalutin.

Sheryl congratulated me with hugs and smiles and went with me to deposit my check in the credit union deposit box twenty-five miles away. We arrived at the credit union, but before depositing the check I turned to Sheryl and said, "Wait, I want to make a copy of this so I'll have it as a memory."

"Where are we going to copy it?" she asked.

"I'll bet one of those shops across the street has a copy machine. Let's go see."

We ran across the street and pushed on the heavy metal door which led into a world I'm not sure I know how to describe. Everywhere were leather outfits, or collars, or whips decorated with spikes. I don't go to X-rated movies, but somehow I felt like we were in one. My friend and I tried to act nonchalant when a large, muscular, bald salesman dressed in a leather outfit asked, "Can I help you?"

"Yes," I answered, "I was wondering if you have a copy machine we could use." I'm sure that must have been a daily request — especially from two women dressed in teacher clothes. He said he didn't and then told us that the store next to theirs had one. We thanked him, and tried not to trip over our feet as we anxiously exited. We walked next door with poker faces. We knew the leather guy could see us through the window and we didn't want him to think we had been shaken by walking into the devil's den.

We hastily opened the door to the store with the copy machine and as soon as we entered, I felt like we were in act two of the movie. Pictures of nude men were everywhere. There were turnstiles filled with nude male postcards and on the walls were posters of NM. Before we could make our escape, a salesman approached us. Fortunately he had clothes on.

"May I help you?"

I tried to keep cool as I spoke. "Yes, do you have a copy machine that we could use to make a copy of a check?"

"Yes," he answered, "I can make a copy for you." He was very nice, even though he worked in a nude men picture shop, and I offered to pay him for the copy. He told us it was no problem and to keep the money.

As we stood waiting for him to return from his office, Sheryl whispered, "What kind of places are you taking me to?"

"I have no idea where we are!" I whispered back, trying to look in her eyes and not at the pictures on the walls. The salesman returned and handed us the check and the copy he had made.

"Thank you so much," I said and then felt compelled to explain why we were there. "I was just awarded five thousand dollars from Disney for an educational project my class did and I wanted a copy of the check before I deposited it at the credit union across the street." Sheryl tugged at my arm and we politely smiled as we left the shop.

When we got behind a wall of the credit union, we looked at each other and asked, "Where were we?!" We stood laughing, hoping none of our students or their parents happened to see us walking in or out of wherever we had been. I deposited my check and drove Sheryl home, playing over the morning's events in my mind. Who would have thought I would be five thousand dollars richer when I came home that day? And who would have thought on that same day I would have been in a shop full of leather paraphernalia and another full of pictures of NM? Hopefully, nobody!

Tip for New Teachers: If you need to make copies of anything, school-related or not, I would stick to places like Kinkos, Office Depot, Staples...it might save you some time — and your reputation.

Twenty-Nine

The Truth Is...If I'd Known What I Was Getting Myself into, I Probably Wouldn't Have Done It

My principal, Karen Wallace, was very good to me and so when she asked me for a special favor I felt I couldn't refuse.

One evening my friend Sheryl was visiting and the phone rang. It was Karen. "Becky," she began with her northern Florida accent, "I have an idea and I wondered if you would be willing to be part of it."

"What is it?" I asked before committing myself. Karen went on to explain that her nephew was going to propose to his girlfriend and he wanted it to be a surprise. Karen wondered if I would dress up like a vagabond and pretend I was selling rings to get money to buy a train ticket to New Jersey. Placed amongst the costume jewelry rings I'd be "selling" would be the engagement ring Alex was going to give to his girlfriend. It sounded kind of fun, but before agreeing to play the part, I wanted to know where this would be taking place.

"It'll be in a small park in Winter Park," Karen said.

Winter Park is an upscale town peppered with beautiful million dollar homes. I knew some people living in Winter Park and not far from their home was a small park called Kraft Gardens. It was off the beaten path and if anyone saw me, it would only be a handful of people. Sheryl told me that if I dressed as a vagabond, she'd dress up as a bum and lie on a bench with a newspaper over her face. Sheryl's support gave me the courage to tell Karen I'd do it.

The day of the big event came and Karen was going to pick Sheryl and me up at my house and then drop us off at the park. Karen would park her van behind some trees so she could watch the proposal without being seen. I called Sheryl to tell her when to be at my house.

"I've decided not to do it," Sheryl said.

"What?! You have to come! I don't want to do this alone."

"Nah, I changed my mind." She didn't even gave me a reason. My brain was in a frenzy, but it was too late to back out on Karen so I got ready. I dressed myself in a mismatched outfit, put Preparation H in my hair to make it greasy and then ratted it, covered my lips with pale pink, frosted lipstick, smeared my eye make-up with Vaseline so that I looked extremely tired, and left my face its natural color — pale.

When Karen arrived, she couldn't have been happier.

"You're perfect!" She was grinning and laughing at the same time. Karen was carrying a large case made specifically for rings. In the middle of seventy or so inexpensive rings was the elegant engagement ring for her nephew's proposal.

We got into the van and as she drove, Karen explained the plan. "When we get to the park, I'll hide my van and you can walk to the fountain area."

I didn't remember there being a fountain at Kraft Gardens.

"Alex and Stacy are eating dinner at one of the restaurants across the street," Karen continued. "Alex will bring Stacy to the fountain and that's when you'll approach them to sell the ring." I *knew* there were no restaurants across the street from Kraft Gardens.

"Where is this park?" I asked.

"Downtown Winter Park," Karen answered, acting as though what I was doing was a perfectly normal thing to do in downtown Winter Park where, on a Saturday night, couples dressed to the hilt would be taking romantic strolls after dining in high-end restaurants.

"Downtown? I thought we were going to Kraft Gardens!" I couldn't do this.

"You'll be all right," Karen assured me. Easy for her to say; she'd be hiding.

She dropped me off at the park and then found a concealed parking place where she could spy. There is a train depot in downtown Winter Park and that was my supposed departure spot to New Jersey. I sat on a bench, watching people go in and out of the restaurants across the street, and noticing that the people who walked by me kept their distance. I was feeling anxious and then I saw a young couple walk out of a restaurant and cross the street to the park. I had never met Alex's girlfriend, but this man was thin, with long hair and a beard. It was Alex and they were coming in my direction. I gripped the handle of the ring case with my left hand and used my right hand to beckon them to me. They both gave me a strange look and went the other way. It wasn't Alex and Stacy. I left the park to find Karen so she could update me on Alex's looks.

"Oh, no, Alex doesn't have a beard anymore. He's clean-shaven, got a haircut, and put on some weight."

Now she tells me.

I went back to the park and it wasn't long before the real Alex and his girlfriend, Stacy, were walking by the fountain. I walked up to them and asked, "'Scuse me, would you be interested in buyin' a ring?"

Alex's girlfriend was beautiful. She had gorgeous, shiny blonde hair and flawless skin. She looked like a Cover Girl model and I could imagine what she was thinking I looked like. Softly she said to Alex, "Come on," and tugged at his hand, trying to pull him in a different direction.

"Please," I drawled, "I need a train ticket to New Jersey and I'd really appreciate it if you'd help me by buyin' a ring." I opened the ring case.

"Honey, let's see what she has." Alex turned to me and his girlfriend grabbed his arm, while at the same time looking at Alex like he'd lost his mind.

"Let's go." She sounded desperate as she pulled his arm, turning him towards her and away from me. I grabbed his other arm and pulled him back to me. I, too, was desperate.

"Please! Just one ring. It would really help." Stacy was obviously panicked that a crazy woman was about to do something her friends would hear about on the news. And I wanted this to be over, possibly even more than Stacy did. Alex scanned the contents of the case, trying to find the engagement ring. I babbled on while he looked and his girlfriend trembled.

"Hurry Alex," I thought.

He found the ring, pulled it out, and turning to Stacy said, "How about this one?" Stacy was too shaken to realize that the ring Alex was holding was the engagement ring she had *oooed* and *ahhhed* over at the jewelry store. He dropped down on one knee and asked, "Stacy, will you marry me?" She was confused, ecstatic, and shocked.

She began to cry, and I began to cry, and she said yes and then she grabbed Alex by the arm, looked in my direction and in a loud, bewildered voice said, "Do you know her?!"

My pink frosted lips smiled and said, "Hi. I'm Becky Thomas. I teach at Karen's school." I guessed she wouldn't be sending any of their future children to Karen's school.

All went well and everyone was happy — especially me. I didn't get arrested and Karen said she owed me big time. She really didn't because I had already gone to the beach on report card workday, but it was nice to know I had bargaining power!

Tip for New Teachers: You may think that as a teacher you will have one role and that is to teach. That is your primary role, but if you have a principal like Karen, you might want to start shopping for pink frosted lipstick, Vaseline, and Preparation H.

Thirty

The Truth Is...I Was Glad When the Dirt Marks Reappeared

I decided it was time to buy my first house. I wanted an old house with a little property and a house like that in Orlando was way over my budget. I was told about a town outside of the Orlando area that had hills, lakes, and affordable homes. I took a drive, found the town, and wanted to live there. I began my search for a house while I continued to live and teach in the Orlando area. I knew this would be my last year teaching with Karen. I blossomed as a teacher under her leadership, but life changes and it was time to move on.

I was offered a third grade teaching position fifteen minutes from my newly purchased house. The area was rural and lice was a problem. Every student, and in my case, teacher, had a weekly lice check. The school nurse, or a teacher's aide, would come to each classroom and call the students out one-by-one to check their hair. The school needed to be fumigated but it was against the law to do this with the children in it, and that's who was bringing lice to the school.

One of the girls in my class had beautiful long, silky blond hair. She was always nicely dressed and everything about her was shiny and clean. That's why I was surprised when a student came to me and said that there were lots of little bugs crawling around in Darlene's hair. I couldn't imagine. But when I checked her out, I saw, for the first time, uncountable live lice running around someone's scalp. Her hair was so light and her scalp so pink, they were easy and sickening to see. Immediately I felt itchy and told her to go to the nurse. The nurse was soon back in my class, checking everyone's head for lice. She also found lice in the scalp of one other girl, Monica, who sat next to Darlene. They were both sent home with directions telling them how to delouse their heads.

Solving the problem of a lice-ridden head takes a lot of work and money. Lice are stubborn creatures and it often takes more than one expensive lice treatment to kill them off. There were a few times that I saw students sent home with lice and return to school with no hair. It was humiliating for the child, but it quickly and cheaply took care of the infestation.

Monica came back to school the next day after being given the lice shampoo treatment. Darlene waited an extra day. It wasn't long after Darlene came back that Monica once again had lice. Her mother called and asked that I move her desk away from Darlene. I did, and despite another lice treatment, lice once again appeared in Monica's hair. Her mother called and asked that I move her desk away from everyone. I did. A few days later, after another lice treatment, lice reappeared in Monica's hair.

Monica's mom drove her daughter's school bus. One morning as I stood at the bus rider drop-off area, Monica's mother spotted me. She stopped the bus, causing a traffic jam, and in an irritated tone called out to me, "I can't afford to keep givin' Monica those shampoo treatments. I need you to do somethin' about this."

"I've done everything you've asked," I told her. "I don't know what else to do."

"Miss Thomas, you're holding up traffic. Quit talking to the bus driver." The assistant principal scowled at me.

"I want you to move her backpack away from everyone else's. Someone in that room has lice and you need to find out who it is!" Monica's mom drove away and the AP glared at me like I was to blame for the bus driver's decision to have a conference during morning rush hour.

All of the students had their weekly head checks and once in a while a nit might be found, but none of the kids with nits sat by or played with Monica. I moved her backpack to a spot all by itself and that didn't do a thing to keep Monica from getting lice. The mother continued to be upset with me about the situation, but other than having everyone in the classroom shave their heads, there was nothing more we could do. It wasn't long before the mystery of the reappearing lice was solved.

One day, as I was shopping in a local store, around the corner of the aisle where I was standing came Monica and her mother. When they saw me, they stopped and Monica's mother said, "Miss Thomas, I need to apologize to you. I didn't know that chickens carry lice."

When I was a child, I was told not to touch dead birds because they have lice (dead birds, like lying on the road, not cooking in the oven for dinner). Like Monica's mom, I didn't know that *live* chickens carried lice.

"We have chickens and Monica plays with them. That's where the lice were comin' from."

Despite the assistant principal blaming me for causing trouble at the bus area, and Monica's mom making me rearrange my classroom each day, it felt really good to be cleared as a negligent teacher in the lice mystery. It was also good to know there were still people around who would admit when they were wrong.

I recently looked on the internet for the chicken-lice-human being relationship and according to many different sites and posts, humans can't get lice from chickens. So I guess Monica and the head lice still remain a mystery. The good news for me is that the internet wasn't being used by the everyday person when Monica had lice. Otherwise, Monica's mom might have written some pretty bad reviews of her daughter's third grade teacher.

There were other adventures connected with teaching in the country. There was a retention pond close to the school and the neighborhood alligator would at times make an appearance on the school grounds. Then there was the playground equipment room where the children got basketballs and kick balls. Hiding amongst the playground equipment were black widow spiders. It didn't seem to bother anyone that the children might have to flick a black widow or two away before playing with the balls. There was also a day at the school when one of the primary children commented to his teacher that there were cows walking around the playground area. The teacher smiled at her student with the creative imagination and then glanced out the window to find that his imagination wasn't so creative after all. The neighbor's cows had walked through a hole in the fence that was supposed to be keeping them in their pasture, and they were now having a great time on the swings and slides.

The title "Principal" was irrelevant at this school because the custodian at the school was in charge and whatever she said, you did. Although I used the traditional methods of teaching, I also had my own ideas about how I could best educate my students. I liked to do hands-on activities and experiments so that the children could experience the practical application of the things they were learning. Judith, the custodian, got upset with me on more than one occasion because she didn't like the way I taught. She thought my teaching was causing a "dirty carpet problem" in my classroom.

When I started the year, the classroom carpet looked great. As time went on, it became dark with huge patches of what looked like dirt. In a teachers meeting, Judith, in an angry tone, announced to the whole staff that "Miss Thomas is making a mess of the carpet with whatever she's doing in the classroom, and it sure isn't teaching!"

"Oh, so that's what she thinks," I thought. Judith was never in my room to see what kind of teaching I did, but because she saw pots with sunflowers growing and projects on the counter, she supposed the transformation of the new carpet into yucky flooring was my fault. I had no idea why the carpet was changing and when I tried to plead my case before Judith, it just made her madder.

During the school year, on a Friday we had off, the carpets were cleaned. When Monday came, the children and I were happy to see what looked like a brand new carpet in our room. The entryway to the classroom was tile and from that day on, anytime we ate snacks or anything else in the classroom, we all sat on the tile. I allowed nothing around the carpet that might in any way stain it. Within a week, small dark spots once again began to appear on the carpet in the same places they had previously been. These spots soon grew into large, dirty areas and before long it looked as though the carpet had never been cleaned. When Judith saw it, she wanted to blame me, but it didn't make sense. Even Miss Thomas couldn't make that much of a mess in one week. Come to find out, it was the carpet glue leaking through the carpet that caused the stains. Unlike the mother with the chickens, Judith never apologized for the unkind words she had spoken in front of the school staff about my teaching and the dirty carpet.

One day as I worked outside at my house, I noticed a caterpillar hanging on one of the leaves of a red-flowering bush. Its body was covered with sticks so that it blended in with its surroundings. I had never seen anything like it. We were studying camouflage in science and this caterpillar would be a perfect example of the concept. I got a jar for the caterpillar and gently tried to pull the insect from the bush. It put up a fight to let go, and because I didn't want to smash it, I left it on its leaf and snapped off the small branch the leaf was attached to.

We had a great science lesson the next day as the students were able to see camouflage in action. After studying the caterpillar, we took it to a bush right outside of our classroom that happened to be the same type of bush it had been taken from. As a class, we would keep an eye on the caterpillar to see if it would grow bigger, or maybe change into a butterfly.

As the days went by, we forgot about the caterpillar and didn't pay attention to the bush. It was weeks later as I worked outside at my house that I noticed my red-flowering bushes were turning into dying, leafless plants. They were an extremely hardy bush and I couldn't imagine what was causing their demise. I closely examined what was left of the bushes and found, hanging throughout them, "stick" caterpillars like the one I had taken to school. My bushes were the caterpillars' sustenance and the only thing I could do to possibly save my bushes was to cut them down to the base. Before doing so, I pulled off as many of the parasites as I could and destroyed them.

The next day, as my students sat quietly working on their writing, I heard a *Snip! Snip! Snip!* sound coming from outside our classroom. I looked out the window and saw Judith with a pair of pruning shears, cutting off the dead branches of the large bush our science experiment had been living on. When she finished, there were no branches left.

I felt a tinge of guilt as I watched the beautiful shrub disappear. Should I tell Judith what I had done? "Nah," I thought, "she never believes anything I tell her." My shrubs at home grew back and I hoped that the shrub at school had also grown back. I never knew because I was soon moved to a different area to teach and I forgot about the bush.

I found out that the caterpillar I once thought was so cool is called a "bag worm" and is extremely destructive. I guess that's a lesson to us all. Watch out for things that appear "cool"; they might end up being the most uncool thing you'll ever come across.

Tip for New Teachers: Things found in nature are wonderful to share with elementary students. They will bring your lessons to life and create within the students an appreciation of, and love for, the beautiful things in this world. Just be sure that what you share is not poisonous, vicious, or bush-eating because if it is, Judith might get you.

Thirty-One

The Truth Is...I Never Wanted Computers in My Classroom

C all me a dinosaur — you won't be the first. Do I like computers? Yes. They're an amazing invention and it still boggles my mind how quickly information can be transmitted, looked up, received, and misconstrued through computer technology. How spoiled we've become not having to use sheets of papyrus like the Egyptians, or quill pens dipped in ink like our forefathers, or typewriters and white-out like yours truly to communicate the written word. The problem I have with computers in the elementary classroom isn't just *a* problem, it's *many* problems.

I was teaching in the rural school with the worm-eaten bush when we were first required to make computers a part of our curriculum. It was one more thing we had to squeeze in, and by doing so it meant something else was going to get squeezed out. In the schools where I taught, handwriting was eventually eliminated. Students from kindergarten on up were no longer officially taught handwriting. There was no time.

At the time I was teaching at the rural school, each classroom had only one computer. I witnessed then, and in all of the following years I taught, that if one student was on the computer, the majority of the students watched that student on the computer rather than pay attention to what I was teaching. Another problem was the constant malfunction of computers in the classroom, especially on the primary level. Often this was due to students pressing every button they saw, hoping to get to a game site they weren't supposed to be on while their teacher was working with other students. The student who messed up the computer would then interrupt me and the student who I was working with, asking that I fix the computer.

Another problem was that, although there were many good academic sites and software programs available for schools, many students were experts at figuring out how to get to the highest level of whatever they were working on without actually doing the work required to get to that highest level. In other words, they learned how to beat the system and in the process weren't learning the academic skill.

These things probably don't bother the teachers who have grown up with computers. And even I think that computers in the media center and in the computer lab are great for elementary students. I just didn't want student computers in my classroom.

Maybe I was jealous of the computer. Maybe I was jealous that the students seemed to like the computer better than they liked me. When I told them to take out their math, spelling, or reading books, they often seemed to have hearing problems. When I announced that it was time to go to computer lab, they immediately sat up straight and smiled, each student hoping that he would be the first in line.

One day, a speaker had been invited to talk to the third graders about his service in World War II. He spoke about never giving up when you want something. He proceeded to tell the children that he got into the army during World War II by tricking the doctors so he could pass the eye examine. He then went on to tell about Eisenhower and Patton and the great war heroes they were. He concluded his presentation by sharing some of his personal war stories.

After attending the program, I announced to my students that they would be writing thank-you notes to our speaker, Mr. Belfonte. I then told them that they'd be typing the notes on the computer. I had decided that this would be the easiest way to cover the technology benchmark requirement.

The class was still and quiet, but I could hear their thoughts.

"Does she know how to turn the computer on?"

"I hope she dusts the keyboard so that I can see the letters."

"Is it April Fools' Day?"

At that time, we didn't have the internet at school and the computer consisted basically of word processing. I felt like we were putting the cart before the horse in teaching students how to use the word processing program before they knew how to properly use the keyboard. I took typing class in high school and it proved to be one of the most valuable classes I ever attended. To have students use the computer and take five minutes to type their names was an excruciating experience for me. If they knew how to use the keyboard without looking, they could type their names in ten seconds. It didn't matter how much I complained about this to other educators, we went forward with the hunt and peck method and every time I glanced at a student sitting at the keyboard looking for a letter, it made me grimace.

Nevertheless, despite my personal objections, we were going to use the dust-covered computer and type our thank yous to Mr. Belfonte. I explained that one child at a time, when he was finished with his seatwork, could go to the computer and type a few words of thanks to our speaker. Everything was in order and I actually felt proud of myself for finally dipping my toes into the world of technology. I wrote the class assignments on the board and let the students go to work.

Mary Ann was the brightest child in my class that year. Despite the speed at which she always worked, she was meticulous and accurate and as I suspected would happen, was the first to be done with her work that day. She quietly put her pencil down and went to the computer. As the rest of the class worked feverishly to complete their assignments so they could get to the computer, I sat down for a few moments to grade papers. I had graded one multiple-choice question on the first paper when I looked up to see Mary Ann standing at my desk.

"Miss Thomas," she quietly whispered, "how do you put spaces between the words?" I calmly got up and went with her to the computer. I showed her the space bar and how it worked and then walked back to my desk.

I was on the second multiple-choice question on the first paper when Mary Ann's hand went up. "Yes, Mary Ann?" I said in a loud whisper, trying not to disturb the rest of the class.

"Could you come here, Miss Thomas? I left a word out. How do I put it in?" I again got up and walked to the computer, trying not to feel annoyed. Mary Ann was a good child and a good student. I didn't want to transfer my annoyance with classroom computers onto her. I showed her how to insert a word and quickly went back to my seat to get at least one paper graded. I don't know how, but Mary Ann was at my desk and on her next question for me before I even picked up my grading pen.

"Miss Thomas, I made a spelling mistake. How do I erase the word and start over?"

"There's a backspace key. Hit it and you can erase any error you make."

"Thanks, Miss Thomas." She smiled and went back to the computer. Mary Ann was my brightest student. She had been on the computer less than four minutes, had asked three questions and I had only graded two questions on my first paper. It was going to be a long day.

"Miss Thomas, I'm finished with my work. May I get on the computer?" asked James.

"As soon as Mary Ann is done," I said.

"Miss Thomas, I'm done too," said Melany.

"You can go after James, Melany."

"Miss Thomas, how do you spell didn't?" Mary Ann asked from across the room.

"Just sound it out, Mary Ann. Remember, it's a contraction formed from the words did and not."

This wasn't (was not) going well. Three hands were up to go to the computer. Four...five...I had never seen my students work so fast. "Class, it seems everyone is getting done with their assignments very quickly, so read a book until it's your turn for the computer."

"A book? I don't have a book," James said.

"Why not?" I asked. "You just went to the library." Wasn't anything simple anymore?

"I didn't bring back the one I checked out last week so Mrs. Gray wouldn't let me get another one."

"Me neither," added Juan.

"I finished my book. May I go to the library and get another one?" asked Hannah.

Five students spoke out, "May I go, too?"

"Cindy, you may go with Hannah," I said and wished I could send the whole class so I could finish the paper I was grading.

"Miss Thomas, what's this word?" asked Grace pointing at the word *ridiculous* in the book she was reading.

"Ridiculous," I said.

"What does that mean?" she asked.

"Look it up," I answered.

"Where?" she asked.

"In the dictionary," I answered.

"Where's the dictionary?" she asked.

"On the shelf where it's been all year." This was ridiculous.

"Class, forget the part about reading a book. Let's do some math."

"Ohhh," wailed a student, "I want to go to the computer."

"You can't until Mary Ann is done. You'll get your turn." And so we did math and Mary Ann worked on the computer. We went to lunch and when we got back, Mary Ann was back on the computer. It was three o'clock, time to go home, and Mary Ann wasn't quite finished so I told her she could finish her note the next day.

The next day came and James finally got his turn. When he had a question, I let Mary Ann help him. When the next student had a question, I let James help and so it went. I was proud that I had worked out a system and couldn't help but think the students were also proud of themselves for being able to teach each other. Yes, I was beginning to understand why people were so crazy about computers. They really did have a place in the schools. There was a spell check so I didn't have to deal with spelling on these thank-you notes. There was a grammar check and a key for just about anything the students wanted to do. I began to see that I was wrong about computers in the classroom and the students needing to know how to use the keyboard without looking. My mind was enlightened and I had finally accepted the age of technology.

Although only one third of the class had written their thank-you notes, after a week of allowing the children to work on their notes without interference, I was ready to read them. I'd like to share them with you. I hope you enjoy them as much as I did.

I started the letter:

September 5, 2000

Dear Mr. Belfonte,

Thank you for coming to our school today and sharing your military experiences with us. The following are comments from my students. I hope you enjoy reading them.

Sincerely,
Rebecca Thomas

When you said you did't past the eye test I was sad so I put my head down. Then I heard you say that you took it again that time you past it I was surprised. I'm glad you past the test. Love Always Mary Ann About how many days did it take you to around the wornd.
    From James
    Thank you for coming to our school. I lick your story about the boats. It's a good storyd.
    Melany
    From Kyle I just want to know how it was in the army? Hope I see you again.

Dear Mr. Belfonte

I just want to know if you were ok all around those states and I'm glad you past the eye test and how the army I bet you were rich when you did not travel any were From, C

I'am glad to see the frist man that was on the shap. Why was you in WWTWO but not in WWONE when you shud been in WWONE and TWO? From Stacy

From Jackson

I realy was amased when I herd your stories.I was hoping that thar whould be more.It was So god

From Ashley

Dear Mr. Belfonte

I hope you are doing ok? I realy did like it. It was WONDERFULL. I can't Belive you traveled that far. I wish I could read that book again. One day I am going to like you.

Well I'll see you..

Definition of Ridiculous: Using a classroom computer for written assignments before you can spell, write a sensible sentence, or have taken a typing class!

Tip for New Teachers: This is a category that you will do much better in than I did. You've most likely grown up with computers and you may have been one of the students I taught when computers first came to the schools. If so, I'm sorry. There is one tip I'd like to give you, or maybe it's more of a reminder. No matter how great the invention, NOTHING will ever take the place of your love for your students — even if they'd rather look at the computer than listen to your lessons. A computer can't hug.

Thirty-Two

The Truth Is...I'm Ashamed that I Put the Success of the Show over the Wellbeing of the Children

We were learning about the skeletal system in health, and Halloween was a week away. "Hey," I thought, "I could teach the students the song 'Dem Bones' to help them remember which bone is connected to what and they could sing it for other classes as a Halloween treat."

Before telling the class my idea, I taught them the song. They loved it! After learning the words, I showed them some simple movements to go along with the song. They started out by lying on the floor and as the song progressed they slowly sat up and then eventually stood up and walked around the room, shaking their bones to the music. At the end, they all slowly lay back down, kept still and then popped up and shook their arms in the air. For the rest of the week, this little activity became their favorite part of the day. As I watched them, more ideas came to me.

I said to my assistant, Kelly, "How about us making a child-size skeleton out of paper for each student, taping the skeletons on them, and then I'll bring in my black light so that they will glow?" I was sure this would be a hit with the performers and audience.

Kelly agreed. She and I drew twenty-four detailed paper skeletons, and then wonderful Kelly began the tedious job of cutting out each one. I invited a few classes to our Halloween Day performance, and when the day came, we were practiced and anxious to have an audience.

In keeping with the Halloween tradition of this school, the students and teachers came dressed in costumes. I had a few odds and ends at home that I put together to make a Cleopatra outfit. With the help of a wig, my hair went from blonde to black and from wavy-frizzy to straight. Everyone thought I was Elvira.

As any person who has worked in theater knows, dress rehearsal is one of the most crucial elements to a successful performance. That's why I should have had a dress rehearsal before the day of the performance. The morning of the "Dem Bones" routine I brought in the black light and had the students hold their cutout skeletons in front of their bodies.

"Okay, Kelly," I called to the assistant, "turn out the lights!" With anticipation, we waited for the skeletons to come to life as the black light hit them. The only problem was, they didn't. Not only did they not come to life, you couldn't see them at all.

"What's wrong?" I called out, "I can't see them!" Science has never been my strength and at that moment I knew there was a scientific explanation as to why the skeletons weren't glowing. The only things glowing were the teeth of the students and one third grader's white "Bo Peep" dress. She got in front of the black light and began to waltz around, dazzling the onlookers.

"Look, Miss Thomas, she glows!" called my students.

"I know. Sit down Tammy, I need to figure out why the skeletons aren't glowing." Tammy danced around for a few more moments and then reluctantly sat down. It was time for lunch, so we turned the lights on and lined up. I was completely discouraged. All of the time and energy we had put into "Dem Bones" and no one would truly appreciate it without the skeletons glowing.

"Oh well, that's show biz," I thought. After dropping the students off at the cafeteria, I sadly walked into the teachers' lounge and sat down.

"What's wrong?" asked Nicole, a fellow third grade teacher. I explained to the three teachers sitting at the table how my "Dem Bones" show was ruined because of the non-glowing skeletons.

Jokingly Nicole said, "Well, if you had some Tide detergent you could use it to make the skeletons glow."

I came to life. "What do you mean?" Was there actually hope of saving the show?

"Tide and other detergents have fluorescents in them," Nicole explained.

"You know what?" I was talking more to myself than to Nicole, "I do have a box of Tide in my car! Thanks!"

I excitedly exited the lounge and ran to my car to get the Tide I had left there after washing my clothes at the laundromat. The box was almost full. My mind was working out the details as I carried the Tide to my room. I would need to cover the carpet with newspaper so no detergent would get on the floor. Judith would kill me. I had a stack of newspapers on the counter. I grabbed the stack and began to lay the papers on the floor, overlapping the edges to keep the detergent from escaping to the carpet. I finished just in time to pick up my class from lunch.

It was our normal routine to go to recess after lunch, but today there was a change in plans. "Boys and Girls," I announced, "we need to go back to the classroom instead of going to recess."

"No!" cried the class. "We want to go to recess. Why can't we go to recess?"

"You'll still get recess. In fact, I'll give you more time for recess today. But right now we have to get to the classroom to put detergent on our skeletons before our guests come."

"Why are we putting laundry soap on our skeletons?" asked James.

"Because Tide detergent glows under a black light and if we put it on our skeletons, they'll glow!" I was too happy about the new plan to notice if the students were excited about it. "So we're going to get things ready for the show now, and then after the show we'll go outside."

The students quit complaining and when we got to our classroom, they each picked a spot on the floor and Kelly brought them their skeletons. I placed a styrofoam bowl of detergent next to each student and then filled other bowls with white glue and placed them between students to share.

"How are we supposed to do this?" Margaret asked. I hadn't thought through those details so I looked around and saw a box of toothpicks.

"Here, dunk your toothpick in the glue and wipe it off on the skeleton." I gave each student a toothpick and that idea worked for zero seconds.

The clock was ticking and our guests would be coming in thirty minutes. Only one other idea came to mind. "Okay everyone, just use your hands. Get as much glue as you can on your hands and wipe it all over the skeletons."

The next twenty minutes were filled with mayhem. As students drenched their hands with white glue and tried to wipe it off on the skeletons, their hands stuck to the skeletons and it was then hard to get the skeletons off of their hands. Kelly and I went from student to student, freeing them from skeletons and then telling them to keep smearing the glue on their skeletons. Students had glue everywhere. I prayed that at that moment Judith was unclogging a sink somewhere.

"All right, I think you have enough glue on your skeletons. Now we're going to put the Tide on the glue." I showed them how to sprinkle it on and told them to try hard to keep the soap on the skeletons; we didn't want any on the carpet! After washing the glue off their hands, the students worked hard to cover their papers with detergent.

"Kelly, would you mind taping the skeletons onto the students when they finish? I'm going to pick up the newspapers." I was drenched under my Cleovira outfit. Between nerves, humidity, the heat of the wig, and the heavy makeup, perspiration was dripping everywhere. I looked up and saw through the window in the door a few parents waiting in the hall.

"Parents are here!" I thought. More tension! I never minded parents coming to class, but when I was desperately trying to pull something together that wasn't coming together, I didn't want parents around. I only wanted them to see me in complete control of my stewardship — their children. Maybe they would think I was an Egyptian custodian and that Miss Thomas was at the office.

I began to carefully pick up the newspapers so that the detergent wouldn't spill off. Why did I bother to be careful? Under the newspapers and on the carpet there seemed to be more Tide than was in the box to begin with.

"Kelly, I need to get the vacuum cleaner!" I ran towards the door and could see the invited classes standing outside in the hall waiting for the performance. When I opened the door, I quickly explained that it would be a few minutes, but that we were almost ready for them. I then darted off to the utility closet where one of the vacuum cleaners was kept. I got it, pushed it back to the room and maniacally swept the carpet before Judith saw the vacuum cleaner was missing. Meanwhile, Kelly and some of the parents who had been standing outside the door were taping the skeletons on the students. The tape was not holding and some of the bones of the skeletons were tearing.

I turned off the vacuum cleaner. *"Boys and Girls,* as soon as your skeleton is taped on, I want you to lie down at your assigned spot. Don't move or the skeletons will rip!" I turned the vacuum back on and madly finished the job. By now my make-up was smearing and my wig needed shampooing. I wrapped the cord around the holding pegs on the vacuum cleaner and rushed it back down the hall to the closet. I came back and as I passed the sixty or so students, teachers, and parents standing in the hall, I assured them it would be just another minute and the show would start.

I entered the room to see most of my students lying in a row looking like mummies. Tammy Bo Peep did not have her skeleton on. "I don't want to do it, Miss Thomas," she said.

I had gotten pretty good at reading students' minds and I told her, "Okay, but you are not to get up in front of the black light during the song. Do you understand?"

"Yes, Ma'am," she said with a disappointed look.

Everyone but Bo Peep was lying on the floor when a few of my students began to complain.

"Miss Thomas, I have soap in my eyes," complained Juan through his little cut out mouth hole. "It's coming through the eyeholes and it's burning my eyes."

"Oh, no! Our audience is waiting," I thought. I needed every one of my performers.

"You'll be all right for the song, don't you think?" I asked. Yes, that was a shameful moment in my life. How could I let fame and glory get in the way of my students' eyesight? Kelly took the students who were complaining into the restroom and I told the others to "break a leg."

I finally opened the door and welcomed the anxious audience. We had moved the desks and chairs so that the students could sit on the floor. Once everyone was in and seated, I introduced our song, turned off the lights, started the music, and turned on the black light. The skeletons glowed! The trouble was, no one in the audience noticed because they were looking at each other's teeth and glowing clothes.

"Wow! Look at Ricky's jacket!"

"You should see your teeth!"

"Yours too!"

I looked at my students singing and dancing, but they were hard to see because Bo Peep was in front of them all, waltzing in her glowing white dress and petticoats. Pieces of skeletons were falling on the floor as the paper and tape ripped from the dancing students. I have no idea if the audience listened to the song or watched the dance. I do know that they were happy and smiling because you could see their teeth glowing. If only they had been smiling at the performers and not at each other.

The entire performance was about three minutes and the audience who had waited in the hall for twenty minutes, left. We cleaned up the second mess of more detergent on the floor, threw away the costumes that took days to draw and cut out, and made sure the students who had soap in their eyes could see. I couldn't wait to be dressed like a teacher again.

What lesson did I learn from the "Dem Bones" experience? I learned that no matter how disastrous something might seem in the classroom, if the students have learned, then it wasn't a waste. To this day, I'll bet my Halloween performers can sing "Dem Bones" to you and know what bone is connected to what bone. And, if you're ever having skeletal surgery and you hear your surgeon singing "Dem Bones," you can be sure he knows what he's doing — just pray he can see.

Tip for New Teachers: Anytime you have a class performance, make sure your dress rehearsal is at least one day before the actual performance. And always carry Tide in your car.

Thirty-Three

The Truth Is...I Was Leading the Children to Believe in Magic

A favorite book that I read to my classes every year was *The Indian in the Cupboard*. It's about a magic key that unlocks a bathroom medicine cabinet. The key brings plastic cowboys, Indians, and other things made of plastic to life, and while the transformation takes place, the objects are also transferred from their time to the present. My students always loved the story, and while teaching my third graders I decided to add another dimension to my reading by bringing in an old bathroom medicine cabinet that I had taken out of my 1920's home. The cabinet had a beveled mirror, just like the one in the story, and for the most part resembled the cupboard in every other way.

The first day I brought the cabinet to class, the effect surprised even me. The children loved it and believed it was magical. Without saying a word, and when they thought I wasn't looking, they quietly opened the cabinet door and stuck plastic figures on the shelves inside. After closing the cabinet for a few seconds, they again opened the door hoping to find flesh and bone miniature men in place of the plastic ones. Although they didn't verbalize it, I could see disappointment on their faces when the figures were still plastic.

"We need a key," I said. "The cupboard in the story doesn't work without a key." The next day keys of different shapes and sizes were

brought to class. None of them fit. The children even had me searching my house for a key that might work. None of mine fit either.
Then Shawn moved in. He asked about the medicine cabinet and we
explained. The next day he produced a key that fit. But it wouldn't
turn the lock because the lock was old and painted over so that it
wouldn't move.

"Miss Thomas, you need to bring in a flathead screwdriver,"
Shawn told me. "If you do, I can get the lock to work." He was only a
third grader, but I believed him.

I brought in the flathead and as soon as Shawn saw it lying on his
desk, he went to work. Within seconds, two other boys were assisting
him. They decided they needed to take the beveled mirror out of the
cabinet door so that they could more easily work on the lock. They
amazed me. Within minutes they had scraped the old paint away and
loosened the screws. Twelve old screws were laid in a plastic cup and
the door was taken off the cabinet. The boys carefully placed the door
with the heavy mirror on the counter top. I lifted the mirror out of the
door and there between the mirror and the wood encasement was
part of a newspaper from Philadelphia. I was thrilled.

"Class!" I got their attention. "Look what was behind the mirror!"
The students looked and I held up the paper.

"It's from 1926! It's the society page. Look at the fashions and
travel ads. Listen to this. 'Come now to Miami. Get the thrill that
this amazing city gives every visitor. See this history-making city in
the building. Visit the City which the Seaboard Air Line Railroad is
spending more than six million dollars to reach. Gratify now your
desire to visit the American Tropics. Plan to spend your vacation
here. Forty-five of the largest and best hotels guarantee seven thousand nine hundred rooms at attractive rates. Single — three dollars to
five dollars per day. Many accommodations at even less.' " I turned
to the back of the newspaper and there was an ad for Bermuda with
a drawing of people lounging on the beach in bathing suits worn in
the 1920's. I held up the paper.

"If I pass this around, will you be especially careful as you look
at it?" Every child assured me that he would. The newspaper slowly

went from desk to desk and the magic of the cupboard started to work. Children who had never been interested in reading were pouring over the newspaper.

"Look what it says here, Miss Thomas. 'Children in Japan are looking for jobs.' "

"Yes," I answered, "that was in 1926 — 15 years before Japan bombed Pearl Harbor in Hawaii. When this paper written, the people of the United States didn't know that they'd soon be fighting the Japanese in World War Two."

"Wow!" the children exclaimed in unison.

The magic was real. This old newspaper that had been placed in the cupboard seventy-five years earlier came to life for a classroom of third graders. Or perhaps the magic of this cupboard was different. It was bringing my students to life. Suddenly the things I had been trying to teach them about history intrigued them. Touching that newspaper connected them to a time that, until that moment, they couldn't imagine. Yes, *The Indian in the Cupboard* is one of my favorite children's books. Why? Because it teaches lessons about human needs — the need to be loved, respected, and, to believe in magic.

Tip for New Teachers: We're now living in a society that is very hard to read. Mentioning things in the classroom like Santa Claus or the Easter Bunny or magic cupboards might be frowned upon. Knowing how to make-believe is an important part of childhood. It promotes creativity and gives children something to dream about. Besides, as a teacher you live in a world of make-believe. Somehow you are supposed to teach ten or more hours of curriculum a day in less than six hours AND you're held accountable for it. Now who believes in magic?

Thirty-Four

The Truth Is...I Hate Paper Mache Projects

I t was the day of the paper mache Viking helmets. Thursday was open house and I needed something to prove to the parents that their children were getting a rewarding education. I thought the students would enjoy doing a paper mache project and we were studying the Vikings, so I thought making a paper mache Viking helmet would be perfect. The only problem was, I hated working with paper mache. My disdain for paper mache came when I was in second grade, which is the only time I remember ever working with it.

When my older brother, Steve, was in second grade, his teacher had a life-sized paper mache donkey in her classroom. Every year, the students in her class got to add paper mache strips to the donkey and repaint it. When I got to second grade, I really wanted to be in her class so I could do the donkey project. Unfortunately I wasn't, so that year I decided to make my own paper mache donkey.

In one of Mom's pans I mixed handfuls of flour, glasses of water, and some salt. I didn't measure anything so I had no clue if the mix was going to work. I also didn't develop patience until I was in my forties so I ended up with lots of unmixed flour lumps floating around in the watery paste. I then ripped newspaper into many jagged strips of varying lengths which I dunked into my watery, lumpy mixture.

When I pulled a strip out of the paste to glue onto Mom's mixing bowl that I had borrowed to use as a mold for my donkey's head, water, salt, and flour dripped all over the kitchen floor and the strips slid around on the bowl as I tried to smooth them down. It wasn't long before my impatience turned into a tantrum and I balled up all of the slippery strips of paper and threw them on the kitchen floor, adding to the disaster I had already created. What I took from that experience was a feeling of frustration, stickiness, and hating paper mache so that all of my life I stayed away from it — that is, until the day of the paper mache Viking helmets.

I had the children tear newspapers into strips and put them at the corner of their desks the day before the actual project. I only had to throw away one child's set of strips for wearing them around his neck and on his head during math. Instead of using mixing bowls as molds for our helmets, I thought balloons would work well, so I had the students blow up balloons before leaving that day. I then had the children put their balloons into their cubbies so we could get an early start on the project the next day. Just as I opened the door for dismissal, one of the balloons popped, initiating a student pushing and screaming frenzy as they exited into the hallway.

The Viking helmet day had arrived and it was time to make paper mache. Unlike the days growing up when I winged everything, I looked up a paper mache recipe in a library book. It was simple: *Mix one cup of white glue and one cup of water and dunk the strips in. Wipe excess mixture off with fingers and put strips on balloon.*

The mixing process wasn't too bad. I asked Tommy to get a little water for the mixture because we didn't have quite enough. A teaspoon would do. He filled a cup and then when I wasn't looking, dumped it into the mixture. I heard it go in and he denied that it was more than a little bit.

"I only filled it to the top," he said pointing to the top of the cup.

I added lots more glue and told everyone to sit down — half of the class was out of their seats to see how much water Tommy had added to the mixture.

A balloon popped. I gave another balloon to the owner of the balloon that popped. Another balloon popped. I gave another balloon to the owner of that balloon.

I decided we'd work on the paper mache projects at the picnic tables that were right outside of our classroom. The picnic tables were also right outside of the cafeteria, and the cafeteria had really big windows. Four students sat at each table with their newspaper strips. (Seven children were in special pull-out classes at the time so they didn't start the project with us.) I proceeded to tell the class how to lay the strips on the balloons and wipe off the excess glue and not to go below a certain point on the balloon because these were going to be helmets to put on their heads and without a hole it wouldn't fit on their heads and not to put the strips on the pointy end but on the round end otherwise they would be Conehead Vikings.

POP! The same child's balloon popped whose balloon had popped in the classroom. Blew up another balloon and gave it to that child.

"Miss Thomas, there are love bugs in the glue." Pulled them out.

POP! The other child's balloon, whose balloon had popped in the classroom, popped. I blew up another balloon and gave it to that child.

"Miss Thomas, we're out of paste."

"How can you be out of paste when I just gave you a bowl of it? David! Those strips are supposed to be one inch wide. Take those half-foot-wide strips off your balloon!"

POP! The same child's balloon popped.

"Sorry, there aren't any more balloons." I stood above the other child who had lost two of her balloons.

POP! Her third balloon burst, flew into the air, and landed in my hair where it stuck to my bangs and hung down over my paste-splattered forehead and face.

My children laughed. "Ha! Ha! Ha! Look at Miss Thomas! A balloon is stuck in her hair!" The children in the cafeteria who were eating lunch and looking through the really big windows laughed. The principal on duty in the cafeteria laughed, and as the balloon hanging over my forehead flapped in the breeze, I also laughed because the other choice was to cry.

"All right boys, sit down on the grass!" scolded a teacher passing by. With paste on my face and a balloon stuck in my hair, I turned to see what was going on.

The scolding teacher looked at me. "These boys were walking on top of the picnic tables and pulling leaves off the branches of the trees." They were doing this while I had a balloon stuck in my hair.

I heard an unintelligible voice coming from the PA system. "The office is calling you Miss Thomas," the upset teacher informed me. "They said that Delrae has a doctor's appointment and she has to leave now. Her mom wants her homework."

"Please tell them I can't give her mom the homework because I have paste all over my hands and face and a balloon stuck in my hair."

"We're here Miss Thomas!" exclaimed the seven children running towards me who were no longer in their pull-out classes. "May we make our helmets now?"

"No! You can help clean up this mess!" Poor children. Victims of undeserved teacher anger.

"Miss Thomas, Scott and Juan are fighting in the bathroom! They're sticking their gluey hands on each other!"

"Tell them they're going to miss recess!" I exploded.

"They're already missing recess because they didn't do their homework."

"Miss Thomas, I'm done. How does it look?" asked Clover.

"Like a Conehead. I told you to cover the round end of the balloon. Don't blame me when people laugh at you. Okay, everyone who has a balloon left, please put them on the empty picnic table so they can dry."

The end of the day came and it was time to go back outside and bring in our dried paper mache balloons. "Miss Thomas, look at my balloon!" Michael cried.

"What balloon?" There was nothing there but a smashed-in paper mache mess.

"I know, what happened to it?" Michael asked.

"Miss Thomas, my balloon shrunk. Look at my helmet. It looks awful!" Candace was close to tears.

"Hmmm...it looks like a shrunken head," I said trying to cheer her up. "That might add an interesting twist to our display."

There were seven balloons left that we hoped would become Viking helmets. We had two more coats of paper mache to put on them and then they had to be painted. My biggest dilemma was, what was I going to do with the other eighteen children while the seven worked on their helmets?

They could build a Viking ship!

Tip for New Teachers: Don't make anything with paper mache. (You won't have time anyway, you have data to record.)

Thirty-Five

The Truth Is...If It Hadn't Been for My New Position, I Would Have Quit

how-stopping performances like "Dem Bones" and "fun" projects like the Viking helmets were becoming harder to fit into the school day. Before leaving my last school, a state writing test had become part of the requirements for passing fourth grade. I believe in standards, whether in the classroom, in one's personal life, or in a great country like America. If we aren't aspiring to become better as individuals and as a people, mediocrity will be our norm and the United States will no longer be known as the land of free enterprise and ingenuity. So having standardized tests as part of a public school's assessment program always seemed logical and necessary to me. What wasn't logical to me was how the state tests were affecting the way teachers were being told to teach and the way students were being made to learn.

We now had to relate all of our lesson plans and daily activities to the skills required to pass the state test. We were told how long each lesson was to last and the materials we were to use to teach the lesson. Teaching moments such as the one I had that led to the *World of Wonders Museum*, for the most part, had to be ignored. There was no time to veer off the set curriculum and schedule.

Although I still tried to make learning fun and interesting, the underlying stress of knowing the students wouldn't pass to the next grade if they didn't pass the state test was hard on both the students and the teachers. Some students didn't test well and yet they were able to do grade-level work throughout the year. The teachers no longer had the final say as to whether a student would be promoted or not. The test decided that.

But the stakes weren't high just for the students and teachers. Government monetary rewards for public schools were connected to test scores, so the stress also became greater for the administrators. The state test was given in March, and to me, one of the greatest travesties of this new system was that once the test was over, the students felt as though school was out and it was hard to keep them on task for the rest of the year. Because the creativity I was once allowed to use in my teaching was slowly being eliminated, my desire to teach in the public schools was fading.

It was a month before school would be out and I had made up my mind to leave the public schools. We were at an after school teachers meeting and our principal, Mr. Green, told us that he'd be hiring a teacher for a new position he was creating for the next year. This teacher would use the arts to teach skills related to the state test. As he talked about the position, I thought, "I could do that." Mr. Green moved on to another topic while I mulled over the fine arts position.

"If I could be in a classroom setting that lent itself to creativity," I thought, "I would enjoy my job." My only negative thought about the position was that some students probably wouldn't like coming to music class, and I wondered what that would do to my love of music. I could remember my elementary music teacher hurling a hardbound music book at one of the boys in my class who wanted to talk to his friends rather than sing. How would I handle students who had no interest in one of the things I loved most — especially now that we weren't allowed to throw books? Mr. Green offered me the position and I decided I would walk into my fear. I took the job.

It turned out that I really enjoyed teaching the class. I was able to connect the music and art lessons to state test material in a much more relaxed and enjoyable atmosphere than what I had to deal with in the regular classroom. I formed two choruses. One was a large chorus that any student could be in, the other was a select group that sang for special events in the county. I was now doing what I had never imagined doing, and loving it. I was glad Mr. Green asked me to teach the special fine arts class. I was glad I had stayed in education.

Tip for New Teachers: As a teacher, you may be in a teaching job you don't like. Don't give up. Next year you may be teaching something different and loving it!

Thirty-Six

The Truth Is...I Wanted to Die

Summer had come and I agreed to teach a keyboard class at summer school. I needed the extra money and the classes I taught were only offered in the mornings so I still had my afternoons to work on the house. That summer a friend of mine, who owned six horses, was taking a cruise with her husband the last week I'd be teaching. She asked if I would horse-sit while she was gone. I loved horses and because I got along well with hers, she begged me to take care of them. She would pay me for the week, and after paying for the gas to make the hour and a half drive to her house every evening to feed and water her horses, and then the same drive back to the school every morning for summer school, I would profit thirty dollars for the week. That would pay for a tank of gas. I'd take it!

It was the last week of summer school and every day that week had been filled with gray skies and rain. I wanted to ride the horses but because of the rain, was unable to do so until Friday morning. When Friday came, the grass was damp and the skies were overcast, but it wasn't raining. I decided that the only opportunity I would have to ride would be to climb onto Deja, the largest horse, and ride bareback and without reins to the barn to put out the feed before leaving that morning. I had ridden Deja bareback before. She was a plodder and when I made the trek to the barn each morning, she kept the other horses at bay so that I could fill the buckets with grain before they got to the barn and knocked me over to get to their food.

I stood on the wood flooring of the front deck connected to the house and called to Deja. "Come on, Deja! Come here, Girl."

She came to me, but she was not happy about me climbing onto her back. I didn't know if it was due to the mood of the overcast day or if she was hungry and wanted me to get to the barn ahead of her to fill the grain buckets. Whatever the reason, I ignored her protests. "Deja," I said, "today's my last day and I really want a ride before I go home. We're just going to the barn to get your food."

She stood at the side of the deck as I grabbed her mane and swung my right leg over her back. She grumbled with a low snigger. "Thank you, Deja. I appreciate the lift." I clicked my tongue against my teeth and pushed my legs into her sides to signal that we were ready. She began her plodding walk to the barn, when suddenly her ears shot back and she took off in a gallop. She was mad and this was her way to get even with me for riding her against her objections.

I had never been afraid of horses until that moment. Deja's belly was too wide for me to get any kind of grip with my short legs. I tried to grab her mane, but as she galloped, her bobbing head made it impossible. I had no way to stay on her back and knew I was in serious trouble. My friend who owned the horses once told me that horses want the rider to be in control. When a horse feels fear from its rider, it can cause the horse to react in unpredictable ways. At that moment, I didn't just feel fear, it took control of my entire being. Every part of me was on high alert when Deja suddenly kicked her hind legs up into the air and I went flying. I was even with the high branches of a tree we had galloped past and when I came down, I landed under the tree on my backside, the right side of my rear taking the full impact of the fall.

I lay there motionless for a few minutes, trying to gather my scattered thoughts. Because I was conscious and felt no immediate pain in my body, I made an attempt to get up. I slowly pushed my hands against the hard ground. As I did so, terrifying and horrific pain coursed through my body as I tried to move my right leg to stand up. Instead of pulling up towards my body, my leg flopped over because my femur, the largest bone in the body, was broken and unable to support me or keep my leg straight.

Never had I screamed with such volume, fear, and desperation. I was alone on my friend's ten acres and all of the surrounding houses were also on ten or more acres. No one could hear me. I tried to breathe deeply to gain some sort of control over the pain and fear that engulfed me. I prayed in agony, "Oh, God, please send an angel to me; I don't want to be alone."

In response to my prayer, strong, definite words came into my mind. "There is a miracle in this."

Those words gave me hope, but I saw no way to get help except to drag myself back to the house, two hundred feet away, and call 9-1-1. How could I do this? I thought of the man who, while mountain climbing, got trapped by a boulder and cut off his own arm to save his life. I thought of pioneers who crossed the prairies in the winter and lost limbs due to frost bite, and even worse, had to bury their dead children in shallow graves as they made their trek west. The mental images of these courageous people gave me hope.

Like so many others in the U.S., I was raised a Christian. I found that sometimes holy words spoken by Christians came across as commonplace and powerless, even when they were spoken with great emotion. As I lay on my back, fighting the terror that overwhelmed me, a picture of Christ in Gethsemane came to mind. I had been taught that in Gethsemane, Christ had felt every mental, emotional, and physical illness and pain that the entire human race had suffered. For the first time, in my own suffering, I began to realize that what he had done was so far beyond what anyone on this earth could comprehend, the power of his strength gave me the courage to try.

I grabbed my bad leg with both hands and placed it on top of my good leg. I then dug my nails into the wet grass and sand and pulled my body towards the house. I got about ten feet when my broken leg flopped off onto the ground and excruciating pain paralyzed me. Again I screamed and called for help, but no one came. I couldn't do this. I knew that if I closed my eyes I would die, and at that moment I couldn't think of anything I wanted more. As I lay there contemplating the idea of leaving this earth, two of the horses came walking from a field that was a few acres away and when they got to me, both placed a heavy hoof right on top of the break in my leg. I wailed loudly in pain and shouted at them to go away. They stood stoic, as though obeying a voice of command that I couldn't hear.

"Get away!" I screamed as I tried to push their hooves off of my leg. They didn't move until I grabbed my broken leg, placed it on my other leg, screamed in agony, and again dragged myself towards the house. The horses left me and went back to the field.

I got about halfway to the house when my broken leg slipped off my good leg and once again hit the ground, sending unbearable pain through my body. A second time I made the decision to close my eyes and drift into the life beyond, and again the same two horses walked from the pasture to where I lay, and placed their hooves on the break in my leg. I yelled at them to leave, but they wouldn't. I knew then that these horses were not to let me die. As much as I didn't want to go through the agony of dragging myself to the house, somehow the pain of that seemed more bearable than the pain of the horses' hooves resting on my leg. At least I at times could steady my bad leg on my good leg and get a few moments of respite. I moved towards the house and the horses walked away.

After what seemed an eternity, I reached the steps to the deck of the house. I would have to pull my body up the steps and then across the deck to get to another step that led into the house and to the phone.

I told myself that I was about to go through the most painful experience of my life. I thought through how I was going to do this. When I pulled my body up the steps and then onto the deck, I would stop, scream until the pain subsided, rest, and then psyche myself up so that I could drag myself across the deck and do it all again. I assured myself that I would make it, and that the pain, which I knew would be more severe than I allowed myself to think about, would not last forever.

The experience was just as I had imagined. The days of teaching my class to visualize were now helping me in the direst circumstance of my life. "You can be what your mind can see." I saw myself making it to the phone after going through what I could only describe as torture.

I did get inside the house, grabbed the broom next to where I was lying and used it to knock the phone off of the wall. Within minutes after dialing 9-1-1, an ambulance arrived and I grabbed the hand of the first paramedic I saw, mentally vowing I would not let go. I had never in my life been so thankful to see another human. After being asked for my insurance card and telling the paramedics it was in my purse, they checked it and then sent for a medical helicopter. I was airlifted to the nearest hospital with a trauma unit. When I arrived at the hospital, I was wheeled into the trauma center on the gurney and was again asked for my insurance card. They checked it and I was soon admitted to surgery. Within a few hours I had been operated on and put back together. Now with a titanium rod, a bracket, and multiple screws in my leg I would eventually be able to walk.

As anyone who has broken a femur knows, the recovery process is long and often painful. I would not be going back to school until right before Christmas. For me, this recovery was particularly painful because the nationally known high-profile insurance company provider for our county schools was in dispute with the hospital I had been taken to. They would not cover my stay in the hospital and I owed twenty-five thousand dollars. Now that was painful!

Tip for New Teachers: It's important to know your health insurance policy and what's covered. And if you are involved in a situation like mine where your insurance does not cover your medical needs, don't stay in the hospital after your surgery. Stay at a nice hotel and order room service. The food will be good, no one will wake you up to take your vitals every time you fall asleep, and your bill will be about twenty thousand dollars less than mine was!

Thirty-Seven

The Truth Is...I Thought This Was Just the Beginning of a Successful Experience

Although I couldn't go to work, I called the students in the select singing group I had formed the year before and asked if they'd like to sing at a recording studio. A private donor had given me one thousand dollars for the choral group to record a CD of children's songs I'd written. Any money made from CD sales could be used to transport the group to singing events. The girls were excited about recording and were even more excited when I asked them to come for a sleepover at my house the night before their recording gig.

I had been working on my house for four years now and had made progress, but there was still a spooky quality to it. First of all, you rarely find a basement in a Florida house, but there was a small, unfinished basement in mine. After buying the house, an AC man came to inspect my air conditioning ducts in the basement. We stood in the basement as he explained what needed to be done to the ducts. As he talked, I noticed a large wolf spider hanging over his head. I reacted the way any person who is scared of large spiders would react — I screamed and hit the AC man. He had no clue why I was attacking him, and to be honest, I had no idea why I was attacking him either, but I smacked him a few times as I screamed and then ran up the stairs. He ran after me yelling, "What's wrong?" When we were safely upstairs I told him.

"There was a huge, brown spider hanging over your head!"

"Oh," he said in relief, "I thought it was a snake."

"Nah, snakes don't bother me," I answered, relieved that someone in the house wasn't afraid of big spiders.

After I had the bug man fumigate my house, I didn't see any more of those hand-sized, thick-bodied spiders hanging from the basement ceiling. Nevertheless, when I made a trip down to get a can of food or a jug of water that I kept stored in the basement, the moist, earthy smell and feel of the subterranean vault always had me looking over my head or eyeing dark corners for hairy bodies with long legs.

The rest of the house was on its way to losing its creepy feeling. There were still water stains on the dining and living room ceilings, and the kitchen cupboards were crooked and in need of replacement, but other than that, I thought things were shaping up pretty well.

When the girls arrived, I took them on a two minute tour of the house. They were terrified of the basement, especially when I told them about the spider. As we walked away from the basement door, I noticed a few girls looking back to make sure the door was closed. The chorus stayed close to one another as we traveled through the house, so that just in case a spider jumped out at them, they could all scream together.

I took them upstairs to show them the two bedrooms and the bathroom. The bedroom across from my mine had what I considered a beautiful oil print of a dark-haired girl dressed in turn-of-the-century clothing standing amongst large white and pink flowers — hydrangeas. It hung over the couch and when the doors were open, could be seen from my bedroom. The girls didn't say anything about the picture. They didn't say much of anything about anything in the house — except the basement and the spiders.

When it was time to go to bed, I put two girls in the bedroom with the picture, two girls downstairs on the couch in the living room, two girls in sleeping bags on the living room floor, and two girls in the T.V. room which was next to the basement door. After getting the girls situated, I fell asleep in my queen-sized bed. Not long after I drifted off, I was awakened by whispers.

"She's on that side. There's room over here."

"Get in the middle so I can sleep on this side."

I didn't say a word, pretending I was asleep, but I recognized the voices of Beth and Paula, the two girls I had put in the T.V. room. I guess they thought the spiders could climb up the basement steps to the T.V. room, but not up the steps leading to my bedroom.

I was still recuperating from my surgery and was a little nervous that the girls might push me out of the bed or kick my healing leg while they were sleeping. I stayed close to the edge of the bed hoping the girls wouldn't be able to reach my bad leg.

I was again on my way to dreamland when Stacy and Francis, who had been sleeping in the sleeping bags on the living room floor, joined us. I wasn't sure why, but I guessed it probably had something to do with being afraid of spiders — or maybe they saw the snakes under the living room couch that I hadn't told them about.

I heard footsteps in the hall and then the voice of another chorus member.

"We can't sleep in that room with the picture. That girl is creepy!" Gloria said.

Two more bodies crawled into my bed. There were now seven bodies in the bed and it was all I could do to hang onto the side of the mattress to keep from falling off. The herd of girls fell asleep and I lay awake fearful of another broken femur. I finally got up, got my crutches, and made my way to the room with the creepy girl picture. I had the couch all to myself and I was finally able to sleep.

The next morning I was awakened by the sound of crying. "Someone took her! She's not here!"

"Who's missing?" I wondered.

Before I had the chance to get up and find out, Stacy opened my door and whispered, "She's in here!" There was an audible sigh of relief and the girls quietly closed my door and went downstairs. Twenty minutes later they came into my room with a plate of eggs, burnt toast, and a glass of orange juice.

"We made you breakfast in bed, Miss Thomas!" The girls were beaming and I was honestly surprised. "Go ahead and eat it."

The girls sat around me, excited to have surprised me and anxious to get my review of their cooking. I already knew how the toast would taste. I took a bite of the eggs and cringed, grabbed my orange juice and washed the eggs down my throat to keep from spitting them out.

"How are they?" asked Gloria.

"They're a little salty and I think there were some egg shells in them." I didn't want to hurt the girls' feelings so I answered them as politely as I could. The eggs were awful! There must have been at least a tablespoon of salt on them. The salt mixed with the egg shells made them inedible.

"We told you, Gloria!" more than one girl blurted out.

Stacy turned to me and said, "We told her not to dump the salt on the eggs but she did anyway."

"Sorry, Miss Thomas. I've never made eggs before." Gloria was smiling.

"Well this was really thoughtful, Girls. Thanks so much." None of the girls had eaten so I pulled myself together and hobbled down to the kitchen. It was a disaster! On the stove top were egg shells stuck to slimy uncooked egg whites. The loaf of bread was spilling out of its wrapper and salt was scattered over the counter top. The orange juice carton sat on the counter, its lid missing. Splashes of escaped juice dotted the floor and counter top and somehow the girls managed to fill the sink with pots, pans, and dishes they had used in preparing my breakfast. After our recording session we'd start our home management class.

We ate breakfast and then left for the studio. Jim, our audio engineer, was great to work with. His upbeat disposition worked well with these children and before long they were situated in the sound booths, ready for their recording debuts.

The group sang to the accompaniments I had arranged and recorded on my one hundred dollar keyboard. The arrangements weren't Broadway quality, but I was able to put a few synthesized instruments in to at least give some sort of variety to the sound. The children started out with enthusiasm, but by the time I asked them to sing the Thanksgiving song for the tenth time, they asked if they could please not have to sing it again and one by one, lay down on the studio floor, their lack of sleep and the monotony of singing the song so many times making them groggy.

I remembered those days as a kid, going to a sleepover when no one slept, being revved up by adrenaline from the excitement of a new adventure. I also remembered what followed: feeling drugged, foggy, and desperate for sleep. Who cared if the voices on "Thanksgiving Day" were together? This CD was for the parents, and parents love any performance their children are in. I let the singers sleep.

I went back to school after my six months of recuperation and was happy to once again be with the students and teachers. I felt love and support, answered questions, and told the story of my accident, and the miracle that I was alive, many times. When students came to my class, they wanted to hear the details of my ordeal. Depending on the age of the students, I told them what I thought was appropriate. When my fourth grade class came that day, they insisted on knowing all about my surgery. They wanted to know how the doctors got the rod inside my leg. I firmly told them that they didn't want to know, but they were relentless and so I explained that the surgeon had to cut my leg open and then "split" the muscles to get to the bone where he screwed a titanium rod and placed a bracket. The moment I finished my story, I heard a thud and noticed one of the students lying on the floor.

"Gus! Gus!" I called the student's name, but there was no response. The class laughed.

"Good one, Gus!" a student called out. Gus didn't look good enough to pull a "good one." He was pasty white and extremely still.

"Gus!" I called. He was out cold. "Tamera, buzz the office."

"Yes?" came the voice from the office.

"Please send help. One of my students has fainted." Within a few minutes, an administrator was in our portable. Gus soon came to, disoriented and still deathly white. His mother was called and Gus went home.

I felt bad that the description of my surgery made Gus faint. His teacher, and others who knew and had taught Gus, told me not to give it a second thought. "He's always been squeamish and the slightest thing will make him sick."

I had the feeling that if I had listened to the description of my surgery that I, too, would have been sick. Neither Gus nor I would ever be doctors.

The songs the students recorded were now available to the parents on a CD and considering none of the children were professional singers, I thought they did a great job. They sang their recorded songs at a few programs and we sold some CDs. "This is just the beginning," I thought. I learned from the experience and was planning for our next year's recording session. Then a different principal was assigned to our school and she got rid of art and music. I would be leaving.

Tip for New Teachers: If you teach at a school where there are no art or music programs, find a way to incorporate these important subjects into your teaching. It's a sure bet that every person reading this can spell a word or define a part of speech or a math term because of an art project taught or a song learned.

 E-N-C-Y-C-L-O-P-E-D-I-A Thanks, Disney!

Thirty-Eight

The Truth Is...I Didn't Know What I Was Going to Say to Destine

"Hi, Susan, this is Becky Thomas."

"Becky! Hi!" Susan was always kind and cheerful. She and I had worked together in a school with Karen Wallace. Karen had retired from education and now Susan was a principal in a different school. If I had to move again, I couldn't think of anyone I'd rather work for.

"I was wondering if you have any openings at your school," I said.

"I do and I would love for you to come." Susan knew my style of teaching. In fact, she was the one who encouraged me to apply for the Disney Teacherrific award for my *Solving the World Puzzle* project.

"I would like to incorporate into my teaching a system I've been using for the last two years. I teach math through music, movement, and related activities."

"You could probably work it in," Susan replied, but I noticed that she didn't promise me. Because the freedom to educate in a way unique to a teacher's personal style was disappearing, I wasn't so sure I could work it in, but at least Susan was willing to let me try.

"I have a third grade position if you'd like it," she offered.

Susan was African American and all of the children at her school were African American. I am very white. I get excited when my face is sunburned because it gives me some color. I didn't know how the students would react to a white teacher with frosted blonde hair.

"How do your students feel about white people?" I was the minority going into someone else's territory and I wasn't sure how I'd be welcomed.

"About half the teachers here are white. The students will be fine with you."

"I'll take the position," I answered and began one of the hardest teaching experiences of my life.

It was great to see Susan again. She truly was one of the nicest people I had ever met. How did she survive in the school she was supervising? In the school where I had previously worked with Susan, she took care of discipline problems when Mrs. Wallace was unavailable. Susan's idea of disciplining a child was to give him a cookie and ask him to promise not to be "bad" again. I remember one student in particular that I sent to Susan for discipline. When I sent the student, I also sent a note saying, "Do not give him a cookie. He needs discipline! Thank you." When I saw her later in the day, we both laughed at the note. It didn't work. She gave him a cookie. Now she was in a school located in a neighborhood riddled with drug abuse, drug dealing, prostitution, and sometimes murder. How could she handle it? How could I handle it?

To get to the school, I had to take toll roads. There was a man who worked in one of the toll booths who always made me feel uncomfortable when I gave him my toll money.

"Hello, Beautiful," he'd say as he took the money, holding my hand for a moment as the money exchanged hands.

"How're you doing today, Sugar?" he'd ask, winking while I quickly gave him my money.

"You have a wonderful weekend, Honey," he'd say, sugarcoating each word as I cringed inside. When possible, I purposely avoided his toll booth.

It was the first day of school and I sat at my desk organizing last minute odds and ends. My classroom was on the second floor of the building and the hallways were quiet as other teachers were also in their classrooms preparing for the first day of school. I had encountered the toll booth man that morning and as I put a paperclip on a set of forms to go home, I decided I'd start taking the back roads to get to work.

"Hey." A large, tough-looking middle schooler walked through the classroom door.

"Hello," I said. "May I help you?"

"Are you a mean teacher?" she snarled. No "hello," no "my name is," just, "are you a mean teacher?"

I was rattled by her boldness and didn't think to ask why she was in my room. "If my students are nice, so am I. If my students aren't nice, well, I guess you can figure out what kind of a teacher I would be. Are you a nice person?"

Now she looked at me like I was the stupidest person in the room. "No."

"What's your name?"

She curled up her lip and snapped, "Destine Rousseau."

"Rousseau. That's French, isn't it?" She didn't answer, but instead turned around and walked out the door. Whoa! I was glad I was teaching third grade! I looked over my student list and towards the bottom, in the R section, was the name *Rousseau, Destine*. I needed the toll booth man to hold my hand.

The bell rang and the students silently walked into the classroom. I said good morning to each child as he or she walked by and not one of them answered or smiled at me. Destine walked by and glared. I told the students to find a seat. I usually let my students sit where they wanted on the first day. It never failed that within a few days I'd have to change the seating arrangement, but I liked to at least give them the chance to prove to me that they couldn't sit by a friend and be quiet. They got settled and I introduced myself.

Destine ignored everything I told her and the class. She got up when she wanted and when I asked her to sit down, she wouldn't. At one point, Destine walked to the back of the room where the backpacks were hanging. I quietly went to her and asked, "Destine, what are you doing?"

She wouldn't look at me. "I want my Mama."

"I want my Mama, too. But I can't have her right now and you can't have your Mama either, because you're in school, and so you need to sit down." I had been nice to Destine all morning and she wouldn't respond. Although I wasn't mean, I was getting firmer with her. She did sit down, but she wasn't through testing me.

As far as the order of events, it was a typical first day. I went over the class rules and the schedule, assigned books to the students, and took the students to lunch. The cafeteria was mass chaos. I dropped my students off and escaped to the teachers' lounge. I sat and listened to the other teachers as I ate, wondering how their day was going. Lunch went by too fast, and with knotted stomach, I applied some fresh lipstick and gathered my courage to face the class and Destine. When I got back to the cafeteria my class stood in line waiting for me, and when Destine saw me she screamed, "What wrong with your lips?!" I immediately put my hand to my mouth, feeling my lips, when Destine exclaimed, "They all bloody!"

Bloody? How could they be bloody? My heart was racing and I didn't know what to think when the girl behind her, Tamika said, "That not blood, Destine, that lipstick." Destine gave me a white, toothy, smark-alecky smile and I wanted to smack her for taking a few years off of my life.

Because of the frequent fights that broke out on the playground, there was no recess in this school, so we immediately went back to class and I read to my students. I had a repertoire of books that I read every year (except to the Vietnamese children). I always started out with *The Lion, the Witch and the Wardrobe*. I read it with a British accent, but this day as I began, I suddenly felt very strange reading with my accent to this particular group of children. When I began the book each year, most students giggled a little as they listened to my attempt at speaking with an English accent. However, they soon settled into the story and cheered each day when I announced I was going to read.

The feeling was very different this time. Could children who came from neighborhoods of drugs, prostitution, and other crimes relate to a world of proper etiquette and perfect English? Looking at Destine, the answer would be no. She was obviously making fun of me, and she knew how to do it without me being able to accuse her of anything. In fact, as time went on I found that the majority of the children in the classroom were able to do the same thing, and on top of that they were masters at manipulation, telling stories that weren't true, and talking really loudly. Although Destine was the one making faces as I read, other students were making comments under their breath. I finally stopped reading. "Boys and Girls, I need you all to look at me, and please stop talking."

It took a minute before the talking stopped and all eyes were on me. Many of those eyes looked away when my eyes met theirs. "Some of you probably think it's weird to hear your teacher speaking the way I am as I read this story. Reading can take us anywhere in the world. This story takes us to England during World War II, so I read it with an English accent. Do any of you know what happened during World War II?" If any of the children knew, they didn't answer. "It was pretty complicated, but one terrible thing that happened was that a powerful man by the name of Adolf Hitler was trying to take over the world."

"Yeah, I heard of Hitler," Shadrack called out.

Other students chimed in, "Yeah, me too!"

"Then you probably know of the awful things he did. The children in this story," I said as I held up the book, "Lucy, Edmund, Susan, and Peter, were living in London, England during World War II. Night after night Hitler sent bombers over London, destroying buildings and killing many people." The class became quiet and interested. "Can you imagine what it must have been like for the people living there, hearing the air raid sirens, never knowing if their houses would be a target of the bombing? Because of these conditions, the children in the story had to leave their parents and live in the country in a huge old house with an elderly professor. In this house they found a magic land and met all kinds of creatures that could talk."

The class was now quiet and wanting to hear the adventures of Lucy, Edmund, Susan, and Peter. I again began to read, and this time, everyone was listening and we all got lost in the land of Narnia. Everyone, that is, but Destine — she was still making faces at me.

I left that day feeling pretty beat up and wondering if I was going to be able to test my music program. Somehow these children didn't seem like they'd be into singing skill songs.

The next day in the middle of math, Destine again walked to the backpack area. She put on her backpack and deliberately pulled her straps up in a way that I could see she was getting ready to leave. There were two doors in the room — one where she was standing and one where I was teaching. Now, if she had really wanted to leave she would have snuck out the back door. But instead, she sauntered up to the door where I was teaching. After finishing my multiplication lesson, I quietly walked to Destine and asked, "Are you going somewhere?"

"Yes, I'm going home."

I answered quietly, "Okay, but I'll need to call the office so someone can walk with you. You can't go alone."

She screamed, "No! Don't call the office!" She put her backpack on a hook and sat down. I didn't even ask her to, she just did. Later that day she loudly said that I was old, really old, and told me I looked like the dinosaur in the *Dinosaur 3* movie. I was beginning to feel like a dinosaur — with long claws and sharp teeth.

Thursday came and I was very worn down. I was tired of being ignored, criticized, and looked at strangely, not just by Destine, but by most of the class. Destine was the ringleader and was the worst, but the majority of the others followed to varying degrees.

School started and I was at the board teaching. Destine got up from her chair and walked to the back of the room. I had had it. There was no more nice left in me. "Destine, what are you doing out of your seat?" As I mentioned before, Destine was large. She had failed third grade twice because she couldn't pass the state test and she now looked at me like she was going to beat me up.

"You wouldn't let me sharpen my pencil!" she growled.

"You never even asked to sharpen your pencil!" I gave it back to her.

"She's mad!" Clarence called out, telling me something he thought I didn't know.

There comes a moment in most people's lives when they are pushed to their breaking point. When that happens, there is no predicting what will transpire. I was now at that breaking point. I turned to the class and spoke in a stern voice that they had not yet heard from me.

"Destine's always mad!" I said with anger. All eyes were on me, wide open and full of surprise. The whites of the students' eyes stood out against their dark skin. The entire class sat up and leaned forward, many of them grabbing the fronts of their desks. For the first time since the school year began I had everyone's attention, including Destine's.

"And do you know why Destine is always mad?" I continued, "Because Destine wants her way and when she doesn't get it, she gets mad." I looked directly at Destine, my eyes locking with hers. "Well, let me tell you something, Destine." I didn't know what I was going to tell her so I hoped that whatever it was, it was going to be good. "You might as well get used to not getting your way in this life because most people don't get their way. If I got my way, I'd be married to a rich man and live in a house that was all fixed up and there wouldn't be leaks in my roof. But I'm single, and my roof leaks, and I have to come to work every day so I can take care of myself. But do you know what? I'm thankful my health is good so that I can come to work." My voice became firmer and louder as I admonished Destine. "And you should be thankful that your health is good so that you can come to school and learn instead of being bedridden in a hospital somewhere BARELY HANGING ONTO LIFE!" Wow! That *was* good. Not a child moved, except for Destine. She quietly sat down in her chair, and raised her hand.

"Yes, Destine?" I talked to her as if we were exchanging pleasantries over tea and crumpets.

"May I sharpen my pencil?" This was the first time she spoke to me without being sarcastic, rude, or intimidating.

"Sure," I politely answered.

First thing the next morning Destine came to my desk. "Miss Thomas, I been thinking and I decided I'm gonna change my attitude."

"I'm really glad to hear that, Destine." I really was glad because I didn't think there was anything else I could say that would top the bit about the hospital.

Destine really did change. She often made me laugh and actually asked if she could come live with me. In fact, one of the best moments in my entire teaching career happened one day with Destine. I was bringing my students back from their special area class and Destine stepped out of line and took my hand. She walked proudly with her head held high in front of all of her peers. I didn't tell her to get back in line. I held onto her hand and felt the love pass from her to me and then back again. I loved it. And the truth was, I loved Destine with all of my very old heart.

Tip for New Teachers: Don't be afraid to be stern with a student if that's what is needed. Sometimes that's all a student wants and she doesn't even know it. I would, however, be careful about the words you use. There must be a dictionary of "politically correct" terms somewhere. Find it and study it. (And let me know if I'm in trouble.)

Thirty-Nine

The Truth Is...I Was Pleasantly Surprised by My Students

Unlike the Vietnamese students, the students in this school struggled with academics because education was not a priority in most of their homes. Almost every student in the school came from a family who was on welfare and many of those families on welfare abused the system. This misuse of funds instilled in the children of the abusers a feeling of entitlement, rather than the desire to work hard to achieve success. When I questioned one student about his future dreams and plans he responded, "I don't need to do nothin' when I get older 'cause I'll get a check like my mama do." How could I compete with that? In every school I had taught, there were children who did poorly in academics and it was often for the same reason the students I was now teaching did poorly — their parents were not educated and didn't value the opportunity they had to encourage their children to achieve in ways they never did.

For many parents of the students I now taught, the public schools were largely viewed as a baby-sitting service and anything the children learned was the responsibility of the teacher. When most of the students in the classroom didn't care about learning and this attitude was modeled by the parents, what was the answer to getting these students to learn?

It also didn't help that the school advocated methods that didn't inspire students to actively learn. The school had purchased a new reading program and when I saw how we were to teach from it, I could feel my blood pressure rising. The whole book was scripted. Instead of me teaching the students with my own words, creativity, and the techniques I had learned over the years, I was to read, word for word, what was written in the teacher's manual. I no longer had a voice in how the students would learn, it was all spelled out for me. I could see that if this type of curriculum replaced the standard curriculum, sometime in the near future real teachers would no longer be needed. How could I motivate a group of students about reading when *I* wasn't motivated by the reading program?

The math program was solid, but the majority of my students were unable to sit still and many also struggled with memorizing. The more I thought about the situation, the more I felt that using my math songs would benefit the students, even if the songs weren't part of the prescribed curriculum. I brought in my keyboard and began teaching a song about a fat ant who needed to lose weight. The students learned about ounces, pounds, and tons and I learned about the incredible music ability of these students. The moment the song started, the students pounded out counter rhythms on their desks. Some pulled out pencils to use as drumsticks, others used their hands. I was taken completely by surprise, but I don't think one student noticed. They were instantaneously transformed by the music to another world and all else around them disappeared. They took my straight, 4/4 music and made it into a song of syncopation and exotic counter beats. Not only did they liven up the rhythm of the song, they sang the song with feeling. I was taking these kids on the road!

I taught my students all of the academic songs I had written and was pleased with the results. I began to get comments and notes from special education teachers and counselors working with some of my students, who said that the songs were not only helping them to remember math terms and formulas, but they were also helping to change the attitude of some of the more difficult students. It wasn't that all of my students suddenly became cooperative and easy to work with, but the songs were noticeably helping them to remember things they would have to know for the state test, which in turn gave them more confidence in their abilities and a better attitude towards school.

As we practiced our songs, Cecilia, who had a particularly negative attitude, transformed into a different person. She asked if she could sing a solo in a song I had written about time. The melody of the song spoke to her soul, so much so that one day she came to me and said, "Miss Thomas, I know what I want to do when I get older." It was rare for any of these children to talk about what they wanted to do when they got older. It was as though they couldn't dream.

"What do you want to do?" I asked her.

"I want to teach children to learn through music like you do."

Knowing that Cecilia felt direction in her life and that it involved serving others, I wanted to shout, "Hurrah!" Instead I smiled at her and told her I was glad.

Because the children in this school struggled so much, many professionals from the community volunteered their time to read with the students or to help them with math. One of these volunteers happened to belong to the Orlando University Club, a prestigious club whose members are involved in helping the community. I got to know this member and told him about the academic songs the students were learning. He was interested in hearing them, and after paying a visit to the classroom and getting a short concert, invited us to sing at a University Club meeting and join the members for breakfast. I didn't know who was more excited about this — the students or me. None of us had ever been to the club.

When imagining our visit to the club, I wasn't worried about the students and the songs, I was worried about the students and their etiquette. With the exception of a student or two, they had none. We spent time in the classroom talking about manners when out in public, and then we practiced those manners. We talked about keeping our voices down when in public, and saying thank you and please. We practiced everything I could think of and then I said some prayers. Whatever was going to happen was going to happen.

Because we had to be at the University Club at 8:00 a.m., the students arrived at school early the day of their performance. I was thrilled that all but one of the students were there on time. They were all dressed in their best and made me proud to be their teacher. Even though we were missing one student, we had to leave for the club if we were to arrive on time.

Susan, Mrs. Sharp the reading coach, and I transported the children in our cars. As the last students were getting out of the cars to go into the club, the parent of the student who was missing drove up, parked, and out jumped her son looking dapper in his dark suit and white shirt. It was a miracle; all of the students made it!

The children walked quietly into the club, but couldn't contain their hushed "ooo" and "ahhh" whispers as they stepped into a world that most of them had never before experienced. There were glass chandeliers hanging from the ceilings and beautiful china was set out on linen cloth-covered tables. I heard a student whisper that he wanted to live in a house like this someday and other students softly said, "Me too."

I wanted them to have this, and much more in their lives. But until they could see that these things existed, they wouldn't know how to dream about them.

The students sang wonderfully. They were charming and the club members enjoyed the performance. After singing, the students sat down, six to a table, and were served breakfast. I held my breath, thinking that would keep them from spilling their juice or help them to remember not to wipe their fingers on their clothes. I didn't have to hold my breath; they were fine. Because I didn't know what would be served for breakfast, I didn't think of everything to tell them. I walked around to the children and told them how proud I was of them and their performance. As I talked to a group of boys at a table, Jerome picked up a large link sausage from his plate and with his fingers, stuffed the whole thing into his mouth.

"Jerome," I said, "don't put the whole sausage in your mouth. You need to cut it up." He immediately opened his mouth and pulled the whole sausage back out with his fingers. I should've known better.

"Miss Thomas," Alexander asked, "may I use the restroom?"

"Yes," I answered, "and make sure you wash your hands before coming back to the table." When Alexander came back, he smelled like he had been dunked in a vat of cologne.

"Wow, Alexander, why you smell like that? You smell good!" Shadrack exclaimed.

"There's a bottle of spray stuff in the bathroom," Alexander said.

"Miss Thomas, can I go to the bathroom?" asked Shadrack. "I really gotta go." We weren't in the middle of a lesson and the students hadn't used the restroom for at least two hours. I didn't know if Shadrack really had to use the restroom, but I did know what he was going to smell like when he returned from it.

"Go ahead," I said and knew exactly what that answer meant. It meant that every student in the class would now ask to go to the restroom. One by one the students made a trip to the bathroom, and one by one they came back smelling like they had fallen into a tub of cologne — the boys and girls alike. At first I thought the club members might be upset with the students' excessive use of their spray, but the members were happy to see that something so simple could make these children so happy. It was a good morning in every way.

Quite a few members commented on how well-dressed the students were. They knew of the circumstances these children came from and were surprised that they had such nice clothes to wear. I agreed that they did look great and commented that they always dressed nicely at school, too. I didn't bring up Ruby Payne's book *Understanding Poverty*. Payne explains in her book that people who live in poverty, when receiving a government check, will spend the money on things that show the public they are able to take care of their own. I didn't feel it was an appropriate setting to explain why these students dressed nicely, but didn't have money for food or school supplies. It was my hope that as the students had positive experiences with communities outside of their own, they would come to see that they could go beyond the achievement boundaries that seemed to have been set for them and become as successful as they were determined to be. Our wonderful day at the University Club was a step in that direction.

Tip for New Teachers: If you ever go out to eat with your students, order ahead so you know what to expect. And only order sausage if it's on a pizza.

Forty

The Truth Is...I Was Happy to Hear His Aunt's Screaming Voice

Many of the students at this school had been held back, some of them more than once. Destine had been held back twice because she couldn't pass the state test, so she acted and looked like a fifth grader (or maybe a senior). For most students, I could see the problems that had played a part in their learning difficulties. But then there was Juleanne. She was repeating third grade and I couldn't understand why. She knew the material and the only thing repeating third grade seemed to be doing for her was making her angry. It was very hard to work with Juleanne because she didn't want to be there — and for good reason. When I questioned the principal about why Juleanne was held back, I was told that she couldn't pass the state test.

"She freezes up on tests and she failed it," Susan told me. "She even went to summer school classes and then took another test, but again she failed." If I were Juleanne, I'd be angry too.

Because Juleanne didn't want to be in third grade again, she made it hard for me, on a daily basis, to teach the rest of the class. If she couldn't pass the test, apparently she didn't want anyone else to pass it either. Trying to keep a balance between being a kind and loving teacher and an ogre was very tricky. Juleanne, and another student she had cemented with, brought out the worst in me. Destine kept me laughing and there were other students who were respectful and really did want to do well with their school work. I tried to stay sane.

Then there was my student, Jerome — the one who put the whole sausage in his mouth. Jerome was not a trouble maker, per se, but he could be a little sarcastic and didn't care much for school. He never did his homework and despite the notes I sent home to his mother, he still never did his homework. I was suspicious that his mother never got my notes and since Jerome's family had no working phone, I decided I needed to pay Jerome's mom a visit. This was before GPS's and so I figured the best way to get to Jerome's house was to follow him. There were two problems with this idea: first, I dressed up for work and that meant I wore heels, and second, Jerome could run about ten times faster than I could, even if I was wearing running shoes. The few times I tried to follow Jerome, he walked so that I could keep up with him until we reached the woodsy area of the path, and then he took off. By the time I got through the thicket of trees, he was nowhere to be found and I didn't know which house was his. Many of the houses and apartments didn't have numbers, so I had no idea where to look for him.

Jerome acted pretty high and mighty in class, knowing I couldn't follow him home. Somehow I would get the best of him. Growing up with scheming brothers, sisters, and cousins served me well in my teaching profession. I learned to think like my opponent and then outwit him. One day before school, I asked a teacher's assistant if she would watch my class the last five minutes before dismissal that day. She agreed to do this for me and when she arrived, I made my getaway.

I knew that Jerome lived somewhere on the other side of the thicket of trees. I walked as fast as I could in my heels and dress, across the school property, down the path and through the trees towards Jerome's house. At the end of the trees were some apartments and then some homes — and a dumpster.

The dismissal bell rang and I knew that the students would soon be coming down the path. I hid behind the dumpster and as I waited, I looked around and noticed behind me two elderly people sitting in rocking chairs on their front porches, looking at me with high suspicion. I smiled and assured them I was harmless. "Hi. I'm a teacher over at the school there," I said as I pointed towards the thicket. "I'm just waiting for a student." They didn't say a word but continued to rock as they stared at me.

Before long, I heard the happy voices of children being released from school and then saw bodies moving down the path towards me. My heart beat faster and I felt like a kid playing hide-and-go-seek. Students passed by and a few of them saw me. "Hi, Miss Thomas!" they called out in surprise. I put my finger to my mouth to signal I needed to remain unnoticed. I moved further back behind the dumpster, and frequently peeked around the corner. Then I saw him.

Jerome was walking with his younger sister and they were lost in conversation, unaware that I was about to join them. I gave them enough time to pass by me and then tiptoed out to the path and fell in step behind them. We made it twenty or so feet before Jerome glanced behind him, and then did a double take, shocked to see his teacher. He looked confused, and then I sensed within him the impulse to run.

"Keep walking," I said, "we're almost home." He and his sister didn't say another word as we walked the rest of the way to their house. When we arrived, the children went inside and closed the door, leaving me standing on the outside. I politely knocked on the door. A pleasant-looking lady greeted me.

"May I help you?" she asked.

"Yes. Hi, I'm Miss Thomas, Jerome's teacher. Are you Jerome's mother?"

"No, I'm his aunt." One thing I learned about these students and their lives was that a person might say she was a relative, but she really might not be related at all. I wasn't sure if this lady was truly his aunt, but when she told me that his mother wasn't home, I figured she would do.

"Jerome hasn't been doing any homework for weeks now. I've sent notes home to his mother and I've never received any correspondence back. I'd appreciate it if you'd tell her I came by and could you please ask her to be sure Jerome does his homework?"

She answered back in a most pleasant voice. "I'll do that. Thank you for comin' by. Have a nice afternoon." I smiled and nodded as she softly closed the door.

I hadn't gotten more than three steps down the sidewalk when I heard, "JEROME! WHAT SHE MEAN YOU HAVEN'T BEEN DOIN' YOUR HOMEWORK! YOUR TEACHER HAVE TO COME HERE TO TELL US THIS?! YOU BEST GET THAT HOMEWORK DONE..." I smiled and waved as I walked by the folks in the rocking chairs.

Tip for New Teachers: You never know what might be required of you to ensure that your students get a good education. Just be ready to think outside the box and to hide outside the dumpster.

Forty-One

The Truth Is...I Never Thought an African American Would Compliment My Dancing

I had been at Susan's school for a few months, and one day when I stopped by the teachers' mailroom to pick up my attendance roster, a fifth grade teacher walked in. Before getting his mail he turned to me and said, "Miss Thomas, I don't know what you've done to Destine, but whatever it is, it's a miracle."

"Really?" It sounded like this was a compliment, but on the other hand, how much did he know?

"Yes. Last year no one in this school could control her. She roamed the halls all day and since she's been with you, I haven't seen her in the hall once. How did you do it?" This teacher was truly impressed. He was also extremely mild and it wouldn't have surprised me if on a walk through the woods, birds sat on his shoulders and deer nuzzled up to him.

I quietly said, "You might not want to know."

He gave me a contemplative look. "Okay then," he said, "don't tell me. It is a miracle, though."

I guess in some ways it was a miracle. I just hoped that I wouldn't be pushed into another one of those miracles anytime soon.

When Halloween rolled around, I took Destine and Cecilia trick-or-treating at the mall. Before going in, we practiced saying please and thank you until I felt sure they wouldn't just grab the candy from the store keepers and run. After the mall, we went to a Halloween party at the place where I had house sat. It was a magical house and I wanted these girls to feel of its magic.

As they soaked in the invisible energy of ghosts and goblins and all things that make Halloween fun and mysterious, I took them on a tour of the house. We walked through the rooms amidst princesses and skeletons, witches and superheroes. Tables glowed with the light of candles that revealed bowls and platters holding sumptuous appetizers and side dishes, hotdogs and chili, chips and dips, and enticing festive treats. Smiling faces of carved pumpkins greeted us at every turn.

After the tour, the girls and I joined in with others to play "Unwrap the Mummy." Not too far into the game, I noticed that Destine was missing. I couldn't imagine why she had wandered away. Cecilia was having a good time unwrapping the mummy, so she stayed in the game while I looked for Destine.

I searched outside where many of the guests were conversing, but couldn't find Destine. I went through the house, trying to think like Destine. Where would she have gone, and why? I quietly walked into an empty room, not expecting to find her, but there she was sitting by herself with her eyes closed, silently moving her lips. I tried to leave before she could see me, but I wasn't fast enough. She opened her eyes and said, "I knew it. I knew it. Someday this house is gonna be mine." I didn't know if that particular house was going to be hers, but I wished for her to have a house she could love as much as my friends' house. I wished for all of my students an education that would bring them the things they could now only dream of.

After Halloween, and before Thanksgiving, we had parent/ teacher conferences. In most schools, specific days and evenings are set aside for the conferences and parents sign up for a fifteen to thirty minute time slot on one of the given dates to discuss their child's academic and social progress. I sent notes home to my parents asking them to fill out "the attached form" and to send it back if they wanted a conference. One form was returned.

Conference night came and two parents showed up. The first parent had sent back the form. The other parent showed up unannounced with her child, and after we talked for a few minutes she said, "Miss Thomas, I got some things to do at home so I'm gonna leave Jackson here with you so I can get my work done."

I was taken so off-guard by her presumption that I would babysit, that she walked out of the classroom, leaving Jackson behind, before I could think of anything to say. Her son didn't say a word to me, but went to the computer and immediately became engrossed in pressing keys and clicking the mouse. I sat at my desk grading papers until conference night was over, wondering if anyone in the state knew that some of their taxpayer money was being used to pay a college-educated babysitter thirty-two dollars an hour. That's something *I* never would have thought of.

As I was closing up, Jackson's mom came back and got her son. It never dawned on her that leaving her son in the classroom to be babysat by his teacher during parent/teacher conferences was really not acceptable. On the other hand, maybe she knew that no parents were going to show up and she wanted to give me purpose. I wasn't sure if I'd ever figure out my clientele.

As the school year went by, my students learned some things about white people they didn't know and I learned some things about African Americans that I didn't know. The room was quiet as I read to the class a story about Harriet Tubman. I always loved to read this story with its message of what the human spirit will do to gain its God-given right to freedom. As I read about Harriet and her group of runaways hiding in the swamps, Clarence asked, "What is that?"

The tone of his question told me that it had nothing to do with what I was reading. "What is what?" I asked.

"That?" Clarence pointed to my leg. More specifically, he pointed to a spider vein on my leg.

"That's a spider vein." I hated to admit it.

"What's a spider vein?" It suddenly occurred to me that because of their dark skin, these children didn't have to be concerned with spider veins showing on their legs. Lucky them.

The girls were constantly putting lotion on their legs because they didn't want them to look ashy. I'd never heard of that term before and when I realized that it meant that their legs were dry and whitish-looking, I knew this was something I didn't have to be concerned about. Unfortunately, nothing could make my legs look any whiter than they already were.

I also learned the difference between an African American perm and a Caucasian perm. One day, as I walked the students to lunch, one of the girls asked, "Miss Thomas, do you got a perm?"

I couldn't imagine what she was talking about. My hair is naturally wavy, but it definitely didn't look like it had been permed. It was actually pretty straight that day. "What did you ask, Gabriella?"

"Do you got a perm? You know, when your hair is straight and it looks fried?"

And then there was the way I danced. The students quickly let me know that my style of dancing was funny.

"Miss Thomas, you move your legs too much. Don't move your legs, just the top part of your body. Watch."

And then I was given a dance lesson. It was hard for me not to move my legs, but I soon got the gist of what they were doing and learned how to do the "Snap" with my neck, only moving my upper body while keeping my legs still. I felt very proud when the kids told me I was getting it! I "snapped my neck" all through recess and the next day I could hardly move my head.

"Miss Thomas, you know a girl broke her neck doin' that dance and she died," Destine said.

"Ummhmm...she shore did Miss Thomas. I seen it on the news," Jackson agreed.

"Me too. It showed her neck getting snapped while she was dancing." Juleanne made a face showing disgust.

I wondered if I would need x-rays. "When did this happen?" I asked.

"Yesterday. I saw it on the news yesterday."

"Yeah, it was bad. Her neck got broke in two."

It seemed every student in my class had seen the evening news and the girl with the broken neck. I could honestly imagine this happening to the poor girl. I moved very carefully until my neck stopped hurting and my head had some range of motion. Two assistant teachers had apparently seen me "snapping my neck" on the playground and as I walked by them they said, "Hey, Miss Thomas, who taught you to dance like that? You good!"

Now these women really were good dancers and I wasn't sure if they were pulling my leg and secretly laughing behind my back. "When did you see me dancing?" I asked with skepticism.

"The other day on the playground. How you know how to dance like that? You really good, Miss Thomas." I took them at their word and thought maybe it was time to start "snapping my neck" again.

It wasn't long after my neck began to feel normal that we had an outdoor celebration at school and a DJ was hired to oversee the dance part of the festivities. As the music blared, the third graders danced away on the cement floor of the pavilion. It was fun watching them, but I didn't know if my neck was strong enough to join in with them. The music stopped and the DJ made the announcement: "We have a special request for a teacher to come join the students. Miss Thomas, please come out to the dance floor."

Were they serious? The students cheered and pulled me out to where they were dancing. The music started and I joined in, my frosted blond hair sticking out amongst the sea of dark brown hair, and my pale white skin contrasting their dark brown skin. We might have looked a little different, but we were all "snapping our necks" and I prayed none of us would die.

Tip for New Teachers: No matter what your ethnicity, you will learn from students who are different from you. Buy a neck brace.

Forty-Two

The Truth Is...I Wouldn't Have Believed Destine if I Hadn't Seen It for Myself

I survived the dance and found out that the students had made up the story about the girl breaking her neck. I learned that storytelling amongst these students was a common occurrence. Someone in the class would start a story and the rest of the group would join in, seamlessly adding their parts, having no idea where the story would end up. They were so good at telling these stories with conviction, it was hard for me to detect the stories were made up until at some point something would be said that I knew wasn't true and that's when I would realize that I had been duped. Along with the completely false stories were the exaggerated stories. When a student told me something that seemed a little off, it's because it was. That's why I didn't pay attention to Destine's story about the Ferris wheel.

Destine was a big girl and she loved to eat. Lunch and snack time were her two favorite times of the day. Her snack could have passed for a lunch and on top of that, she would often try to get me to share my snack with her. That's why when she offered me her snack one day, I should have paid more attention.

"Miss Thomas," she said with half-closed eyes, "do you want my snack?" I laughed until I saw she wasn't kidding. "I'm so tired. They was putting up the Ferris wheel last night and I couldn't sleep. I watched them all night. They was right outside my window. I coulda touched that Ferris wheel."

A small carnival had come to town and they were setting up in the same area where Destine lived. I could imagine that it would be hard to sleep, hearing the sound of the clanging metal as the rides were banged together. It was easy to transport myself back to childhood days and feel the excitement Destine must be feeling to know the carnival was in town, and to be able to see it come to life through a bedroom window. I didn't take her snack, but I let her put her head down to rest.

Destine was tired all that week. "I can't sleep. That Ferris wheel's keepin' me up all night. I could jump outta my window and go for a ride if I wanted."

"Only a couple more days and it will be gone." I smiled at her and figured she would be a little sad when it wasn't there for her to watch through her window. I was sure she'd miss the lights and the sounds of the rides in the distance. Sunday the carnival would be on its way to another town and Destine's neighborhood would turn back into itself.

Destine lived with her grandmother, and I had some clothes that Destine thought her grandmother's friend would like. The clothes were in my truck and since I was taking the clothes to her house, I offered Destine a ride home.

As we got closer to her house, I could see the carnival. It was on a lot at the corner of a street in an area where I'd never been. As we came to that street, Destine yelled, "Turn here!" and then looked at me like I was some kind of ignoramus because I didn't know that's where I was supposed to turn. As we came to the first house on the street, Destine again yelled, "Turn here!" and gave me that same look. I pulled into a driveway and there was the house where Destine lived. It was an older wooden house and I liked it — except for one thing — there was a Ferris wheel about three feet from Destine's bedroom window. She really could've jumped out of her window and taken a ride.

"I don't believe it!" I could not fathom that a carnival could be set up right next to a house that was inhabited. And with all of the restrictions elementary teachers had to live by, I couldn't believe there were "no Ferris Wheels by bedroom windows" restrictions in this country.

"I told you it was right outside my window." Destine gave me a look that put me in my place. I guess it didn't occur to her that with all of the story-telling and exaggerations she and the other students pulled on me, I might have a little trouble believing her when she said she could touch the Ferris wheel through her bedroom window. I met her grandmother and we conversed for a few minutes, but the whole time my mind kept going back to the Ferris wheel.

"Would it be okay if I went into Destine's room to take a look at the Ferris wheel through the window in there?" Destine's grandmother gave me permission and Destine smiled with satisfaction, knowing that her bigger than life story was true and now I knew it too.

The window was open and a breeze blew through the screen, pushing the curtains out, away from the window frame. And there, literally a yard from her window, was a carnival-sized red Ferris wheel. My mouth hung open and I chuckled, knowing that no one would believe me if I told them the truth about Destine and the Ferris wheel. "Wow! No wonder you couldn't sleep."

"I told you, Miss Thomas. When they was putting it up..." and as she went on to describe how the construction had kept her up all night I thought of the day she offered me her snack because she was too tired to eat it. I guess I should have taken her at her word, but I had been taken too many times because I believed the words my students told me. Destine offering up her snack should have been a dead give-away.

When Monday came, Destine cheerfully ate her snack and I knew the carnival had gone. I wondered if somewhere, in another elementary school, a child was having a hard time keeping his eyes open because the carnival had come to his town. And I wondered if he had a teacher who would believe his story. Hopefully he had a camera.

Tip for New Teachers: You can't always know if a student is telling the truth. If it's important to a child's safety to find out the truth of what he says, then investigate. Otherwise, enjoy his story and don't worry about it. And then, if you find out it really is true, enjoy it for a second time!

Forty-Three

The Truth Is...I Didn't Like Going to the Symphony when I Was a Child

I t was symphony orchestra day. Personally, classical music does more for my soul than any music I listen to, but that wasn't always the case. My grandfather was a percussionist for the Cleveland Orchestra, and so growing up, I was very familiar with symphonic music. Every year in elementary school we went on a field trip to hear the Cleveland Orchestra perform and I would see Grandpa standing at the back of the stage playing the kettle drums, or xylophone, or cymbals, and it was all I could do to stay awake.

At school, we were taught proper concert etiquette and we dressed in our best church clothes on the day of the concert. We were quieter than mice during the performance and I can honestly say that at the time, I didn't have a proper appreciation for symphonic music. I thought it was pretty, but it made me drowsy and I liked music that I could dance to. Now I was the teacher and the class I was taking to the symphony loved to make up counter beats and dance to any music they heard. I was very apprehensive about going to the symphony with these children.

The day of the symphony field trip, for the millionth time, I rehearsed concert manners with the class. I asked them questions about how they should behave at the concert and reminded them about not clapping until the director's arms were at his side with the baton down. I told them that they were not to whistle, or call out, or clap while the orchestra was playing and when the orchestra finished playing, the students were still not to whistle or call out. They were not to help the percussion section by beating their hands on the backs of the seats in front of them, or by hitting anything else with their hands. In other words, they were not to move.

Destine showed me a ten dollar bill she had brought to buy a souvenir. "Destine," I asked, "what are you planning to buy at a symphony concert?"

She looked at me like I knew nothing about classical music and said in a condescendingly serious tone, "A violin."

The students looked great; much the same as they looked on the day of their performance at the Orlando University Club. We filed onto the bus, found a seat, and were off to the performing arts center. When we arrived and got off of the bus, Destine immediately told me that she had a run in her pantyhose and she couldn't wear them into the concert hall. It was hard to tell she was even wearing pantyhose and it was nearly impossible to tell she had a run in them. "Destine, you can't even see it. I promise, no one is going to know."

"No, Miss Thomas, I can't wear them." I wasn't sure how she planned to get them off since we were standing with crowds of students from other schools. If she took her pantyhose off there, no one would notice the run because they'd be noticing a crazy child undressing in public.

"Please follow your guide," came directions from a woman whose hair and makeup were in perfect order. Our line began to move and Destine moved with it, run pantyhose and all.

Anyone who has ever been to the symphony with classes of elementary school children knows that it can be a nerve-wracking experience. If a teacher is like me, she will never relax during the program because she is hyper-aware of every move her students make. She wants to be sure all of the classes seated anywhere near her class are in no way distracted during the concert because of one of her students misbehaving. And then there are the teachers who have probably never been taught concert etiquette or who know it, but don't want to be bothered with it because it takes a lot of effort to keep a class quiet during a concert. So the students of those teachers clap to any rhythm they can catch, move their arms as they pretend to be the director, and talk and laugh during the performance. This makes the nervous teachers like me even more nervous because we feel it is our personal responsibility to make sure every child in the concert hall is quiet so that the performers can concentrate. I really didn't want to be on this field trip.

I got my class seated and made sure I gave them threatening looks until the lights went out and they could no longer see my eyes. We were welcomed to the concert and the director was introduced. The audience applauded, so I gave my class the applaud nod. The music started and I gave my students the signal to stop clapping. Every ten seconds or so I'd glance down the row to make sure no one was talking or dancing. They were being exceptionally good. I finally relaxed a little and that's when the student next to me handed me something I couldn't immediately identify.

"Destine said to give you these." I felt a silky, stretchy material and it suddenly dawned on me that I was holding Destine's pantyhose. I looked down the row and could see her white teeth smiling at me in the dark. I wondered if there was anything in the concert etiquette book about swinging pantyhose around instead of clapping at the end of a number.

The concert went on and I was amazed at how well my students were behaving. They didn't move, they didn't make a sound, in fact, they didn't even have their eyes open because they were all asleep. I decided not to wake them because first, they were quiet and second, I remembered how the symphony affected me when I was a child. Some things never change.

Tip for New Teachers: You may not like taking your class to the symphony for a field trip. If this is true, you're not alone. It is good for the students to go, however. For some children, this will be the

only opportunity they get to hear a symphony orchestra perform live. Unless they're like the children I took, and then they still won't hear a symphony orchestra perform live because they'll be sleeping. If so, you enjoy the concert!

Forty-Four

The Truth Is...I Hoped Our Guest Would

Have a Hard Time

I have taught in small towns where the schools were run by the townspeople, and I have taught in large districts where there were so many people involved in running the schools that it got pretty complicated. One area of complication was construction on buildings that were in use. As we all know, everything manmade on this planet will eventually weather, rot, and fall apart if we don't maintain it. Schools fall into the manmade category and so part of our taxpayer money has to go to maintaining schools. A problem I experienced in schools in the large districts was that there were so many schools to be maintained, there was never enough non-school time to get the big jobs done, so, much of the construction work took place while school was in session. This made for some interesting teaching situations.

I once taught in a school where the roofs were tarred during the school year. Most of the students and teachers got ill from breathing in the tar fumes. I ended up extremely sick and when I visited the doctor, I told him that the tar fumes had caused my condition. He said that my theory couldn't be proven and I suspected he had stock in the tar industry.

Another school where I taught was over-crowded, so portables had to be set up while the students tried to learn. The bulldozers and cement mixers were so loud the teachers couldn't teach and the students couldn't hear or concentrate because their classrooms were rumbling.

The school where I taught Destine's class was old and many rooms were in need of repair. The decision was made to start repairs upstairs on the empty room right next to my room, and when those repairs were complete, my class would move into the refurbished room and the repair work would then start on my classroom. It sounded good in theory, but the application of that theory wasn't so good. I guess if the classroom walls had been ten feet thick, with state-of-the-art insulation, the plan might have worked. Unfortunately, everything going on in the room next door could be heard in my room and it was impossible for me to teach. The construction workers used hammers, drills, electric saws, and any other tool they could buy that was noisy. The workers did take breaks, but it just so happened that their breaks were at the same time my class had its breaks for lunch and special area classes. We had no downtime from the noise. Once in a while there would be a short lull in the construction work and I would take advantage of the moment, giving the students any important information I could. Most of the time I had to shout over the noise and hope something was getting through to the kids. I went to the principal and explained the situation, telling her that my students couldn't hear me teach. She told me that the county made construction decisions and there was really nothing she could do about it.

During the renovation project, I got a call from a county reading specialist asking if I'd like her to give a presentation for my class. "A *county* reading specialist," I thought, "now, that might be beneficial in ways the county's not considering." I told her that I'd love to have her come and secretly hoped the day she came would be especially noisy.

Our visitor was an amiable person and I liked her at once. I introduced her to the class and when she began her presentation, to my delight, the symphony of tools began. The students immediately put their fingers in their ears, which I knew would only last for a moment. After adjusting to the noise, they unplugged their ears and tried to focus on our guest who was still smiling as she yelled to the class her encouraging words about reading.

Although I truly liked this person, I sat at an empty desk at the side of the room feeling a tinge of pleasure in knowing that she was experiencing what the students and I had been experiencing every day for two weeks. She pushed forward, trying to connect with the students, until she finally cupped her hands around her mouth and shouted to me, "This is ridiculous! How can you teach with this going on?!"

I smiled and yelled, "I can't!" She finally gave up and left for the county office. I was sure the story she would share with fellow county workers would cause some sort of stir. As a teacher, I might not have had a lot of clout, but if I was smart, I could figure out ways to take advantage of those who did. A day later, my class was moved to an empty portable.

Tip for New Teachers: It's okay to be sly if it's helping the children.

Forty-Five

The Truth Is...I Didn't Know What the Outcome of My Controversial Lessons Would Be

As the days went by I had many opportunities to teach, and also learn, material not in the curriculum. For instance, I learned that the students at this school used the term "passed" when someone they knew died. Destine talked with me about a relative of hers who had passed. Then one day, she came to school visibly upset and told me that her grandmother, with whom she stayed, was sick. Her grandmother had gone to the hospital and they were afraid she was going to pass. I knew Destine's grandmother meant everything to Destine so I did my best to console her. Every day that week Destine gave me a report on her grandmother's health, and every day Destine said that she was afraid her grandmother was going to pass. Then on Friday, Destine came in with a light step and a smile on her face.

"Miss Thomas, she passed! She passed! My grandmother passed!" I was surprised that Destine was so happy about this. I do know that many, including myself, view death as a positive thing because of what awaits us after this life. Even so, there is the natural sadness associated with losing someone you love.

"I'm sorry to hear that, Destine. When did she die?" I asked.

"Die?! You think I'd be smilin' like this if she died? She passed the physical at the hospital and she's comin' home!" How was I supposed to know that this time using the word "passed" meant something totally different from the way Destine had been using it all week? And how was it that Destine was able to make me feel like I didn't know anything?

One day as my students and I were returning to class from the science lab, we walked by some flowering bushes and saw a beautiful, large, yellow butterfly flitting from one bush to another. The class screamed, "Ahhh, Miss Thomas, get it away! It gonna bite us!" The students then darted away from the bushes and were on the verge of tears thinking that the butterfly might get them.

After I calmed the students down, I taught them about butterflies and what wonderful insects they were. In fact, butterflies were probably my favorite insect on the whole earth and if one landed on me, I would consider it good luck. It was hard for the students to let go of their fear of those beautiful creatures. I couldn't imagine what made them so afraid. I guess their unsubstantiated fear of butterflies could be applied to many things in life. What we don't understand we often misjudge and are afraid of, or make fun of — no matter how beautiful it might be.

I felt this truth manifesting itself to me as I taught the children at this school. I found that within this group of students, and the general population at this school, there was prejudice against one another. Lighter skinned students made fun of students who were the darkest — just like people teased me growing up because I was so white. Although the students where I now taught were all African American, students from the U.S. made fun of students who spoke with a Caribbean Island accent or who were not culturally the same as African Americans from the U.S. It reminded me of the students in my school who were Caucasian, but made fun of other Caucasian students who were in some way different from themselves. And many of the students where I now taught had mixed feelings about white people.

At times my students would tell me that "so and so" didn't like white people. When I talked to a student who felt this way, I could never get a straight answer as to why he felt the way he did. The most I could get out of these students was that their families just didn't like whites. That seemed to be a common thread amongst people I had met throughout life who were prejudiced. Prejudice had been passed down through families, and so I guessed it was going to take families to rid this world of prejudice.

We were in the second half of the school year when a new boy moved in. He was brought to my class, unannounced, and after being introduced as Ben, was left with his new classmates and me. As I welcomed him to our class, my entire group of students burst out laughing and pointed their fingers at him.

"He white! Ha! Ha! He white! Miss Thomas, he white!"

The child was small and frail-looking. He stood in front of the class with his head down and I could feel my underdog protection instinct getting ready to strike.

"Class," I said in a loud, angry voice, "in case you hadn't noticed, your teacher is also white!"

"No, Miss Thomas, you kinda red," Juleanne informed me.

"That's because I'm always yelling at you!"

I was completely shocked at their disdain for this child because of his color. Growing up, I thought that prejudice came from white people towards African Americans and when I could, I stood up to white people who expressed this prejudice. These children were confirming what I had sadly come to understand as I grew older — prejudice seemed to exist among all groups of people.

One day as I was teaching a social studies lesson, I asked the students what they thought of slavery.

"We so glad there's no slavery!" Jimmal answered.

"That's right," piped in Clarence. "It's good slavery's over."

I contradicted my students. "But slavery's not over." When I spoke these words, a quiet came over the room as the students stared at me. Like a person taking the same route as he commuted to work each day, conversations about slavery seemed to be routine in the public schools, and when I changed the routine, students slammed on the brakes and without saying a word, their questioning looks told me that they were curious to hear about the new direction I was taking them.

"What you mean, Miss Thomas? Abraham Lincoln freed the slaves," Cecelia challenged.

"Yes, Abraham Lincoln fought for a law that said one human could not own another, and eventually the slaves in our country were free to find their own way, but there are all kinds of slavery. The worst kind is when a person's thoughts and actions are controlled by another person's thoughts and actions."

"What's that mean?" Destine asked.

"That means that if a person isn't educated and doesn't understand the world around him, another person who does understand will be able to control the uneducated and unenlightened person. Anyone who is controlled by another has in some way become that person's slave. Or, what if a person is healthy and able to work, but decides she'd rather get money for doing nothing? She becomes a slave to the person or to the institution giving her that money. She will never reach the potential God intended for her. I never want that for any of you. I want you children to be so educated and so enlightened that you will always think for yourselves and will have the life you want because you were able to make that life. I don't want any of you to be stuck in a life that goes nowhere because someone or something else is controlling you."

It was quiet in the room. I was hoping the students were finding a new way to think. As I had learned earlier that year, the idea of welfare and government reliance was so ingrained in most of my students, that neither their parents, nor they, saw much need for education. I wished that I had the money to take these students on a trip to every state in these wonderful United States. Maybe then they could see the beauty, and richness, and opportunities for them if they could just rise above a way of thinking that had kept most of their families enslaved way beyond the passage of the Thirteenth Amendment.

Another day, the discussion led to slavery again — this time its roots. I explained to the students that slavery had existed in one form or another pretty much since the beginning of time. It had always been an evil practice, but the slaves hadn't always been the same. Sometimes the Greeks were slaves, sometimes the Israelis. In the United States, most slaves were of black African descent. Some of these black Africans were sold to white people from Europe by other black Africans who wanted the goods the white man had to offer. As I shared this information with the students, their mouths dropped open and they looked at me like I was the biggest liar that had ever lied.

Then one of the students spoke up. "It's true. My parents taught me about what she's saying."

I addressed the class. "So in that case, who was wrong — those who sold the slaves or those who bought them?"

"They were all wrong," answered more than one student.

They were finding new ways to think that I could only hope would lead them to new freedoms in their lives. "To be honest," I told them, "I don't know if anyone knows the complete truth behind slavery in our country because we don't know what was in the minds and hearts of all the different people involved. I do know, however, that if a nation wants to be strong, the people in that nation need to be united." My students were listening, really listening. "Don't just accept what I'm telling you. Search out the truth for yourselves. Ask your parents what they think. Ask your minister or pastor what he thinks. Read books and articles and then search your soul. You are going to hear many differing views on every topic there is in this world. The more you educate yourselves and seek after the truth, the better choices you can make and the happier lives you will live. Honesty and forgiveness will bring you peace. Being angry at, and blaming others will keep you from being the wonderful person you're meant to be."

I couldn't relate to what many African Americans had been through, but I could relate to how hatred towards another keeps a person from progressing towards true freedom and inner peace. I learned in my own life that forgiving is the only way to release ourselves from the unseen bondage of anger or hatred. I shared with my students my hope that we, as a country, would be able to forgive where forgiveness was needed and that we could work together to become a happier people and a stronger nation. I could only hope that the children would take to heart this lesson with which many adults still struggled.

Tip for New Teachers: Just because something is written in a textbook or found in an educational video doesn't mean that it's true. We are living in a miraculous time when more information is at our fingertips than ever before in the history of this world. Read and research. Talk with people from differing points of view, and then search your heart. It's surprising how much more your heart knows about the truth than your head.

Forty-Six

The Truth Is...I Was Afraid Juleanne Wouldn't Pass the State Test

The state test was just around the corner and tension was in the air. I presented as much information as I could in the short time we had left before test week. The class sang through all of the math songs and then reviewed the skills they contained. Juleanne was becoming more and more belligerent and I knew it was due to her fear of failing the test again. Destine seemed pretty unaffected and did little to make sure she understood the material. There is only so much a teacher can do to help her students and I felt that I had reached my limit. It was now time to find out how much effort the students had put into learning the material.

The morning of the first test, the children were unusually quiet. I knew it was because they were scared. All of the students in my class were God-fearing people and so I did something that was highly unusual in the public schools. I told the class that I would give them a few minutes of silence and if they wanted to pray, they were free to do so. I had barely gotten the words out of my mouth when half of the class got down on their knees beside their desks, some praying silently, some out loud. I was taken off-guard. Growing up in a church whose members were very reserved in their expression of worship, I didn't expect such an outward display of supplication for help. It made me smile and I said a silent prayer that the students would be calm and their minds would be clear so that they could do their best.

After prayer meeting, I read the test instructions to the class exactly as they were written in the teacher's test manual. There was a proctor in the room who would help with tasks such as passing out pencils, and who would also verify that I in no way aided the students with the test answers. I finished reading the instructions, told the class to begin, and wrote down their starting time. I also wrote down when they were to finish and then began walking around the room. Juleanne sat at her desk doing nothing.

"Juleanne, this is a timed test. You need to start." She gave me a dirty look. What was she thinking? I knew she didn't want to repeat third grade again.

"Juleanne, you don't have much time. You need to get busy." She wouldn't budge. And then it occurred to me that she was so afraid of not passing the test, that if she purposely failed it she would be able to save face. I knew of Juleanne's stubbornness and so I had to in some way outsmart her.

"Juleanne, I don't care if you pass the test, but I will not let you leave this room until you've marked something on the answer sheet." Of course I really couldn't keep her until she marked something, but she didn't know that.

"Mark anything you want, I don't care, but you have to mark something." I knew Juleanne well enough to know that she had too much pride to mark answers at random. If she had to mark answers, she would try to get them right. My hope was that because I told her she couldn't leave until something was marked, she would start filling in answers. I nonchalantly walked away and used every ounce of discipline I had to not look back to see if she was working. I thought I'd give her a few minutes and then casually walk by her desk to check on her.

Meanwhile, Destine called out — something that is forbidden during state tests. "I'm finished!" She turned around and smiled at the class.

My heart jumped. How could she be finished? These tests were difficult and for Destine to finish, with her inability to focus, she'd need the whole day. Students looked up from their tests, their concentration broken. Destine saw the surprised and puzzled look on my face.

"They can't fail me more than twice in elementary school so I just marked any answer and now I'm done." She was smart when she wanted to be. I told her to check over her answers and not to make a sound until the test time was officially over. It was going to be a long week.

Cecelia raised her hand for my help. I walked to her desk. "Yes, Cecelia?"

"Miss Thomas, how does the mode song go?" She wanted me to sing it to her.

"I can't tell you," I said. Oh, so badly I wanted to.

"I can't get past the part, 'Are you in the mood for the mode...' "

The next few words of the song told what the mode was. "It's the number you see most frequently."

She skipped over those words and sang to herself, "If you have five threes and three fives, the mode will be the three."

"Oh, it's three," she whispered and then marked the answer *three* that just happened to be one of the answers on the test, and just happened to be the wrong answer. I walked away to keep from singing the words that would give her the right answer, and then, with indifference, walked past Juleanne's desk. She didn't look up at me. She was deep in concentration, reading math problems and filling in answers. I was smiling inside.

Monday was over and then we tested on Tuesday, Wednesday, and Thursday of that week. Friday was makeup day and the students, and teachers, were tired. It's easier and much more enjoyable to teach all day than it is to test all day. The following week we had more tests and then the tests were over for the year.

For the first time all year, I felt relaxed as I taught. Unfortunately, once the state tests were over the students also felt that school was over for the year. Regardless, the students and I laughed more and I felt a different relationship building. The last two months of school were close to enjoyable.

Although it was a relief when the tests were over, the stress was never gone until the test scores were in. It was late May, a couple of weeks before school was out, when the state test scores arrived. Each teacher was given her class scores and when I got to my room, I eagerly scanned down the roster. Destine failed — what a surprise. I skimmed the roster looking for Juleanne's name. I was as fearful as I was anxious to see her results. If she failed, I did not want to be the one to tell her. My shaky finger stopped by the name *Williams, Juleanne*. I traced across the numbers and under each subject tested was a passing score. I couldn't wait for the students to arrive!

When the students came to class that day, I didn't let on that the test scores had come in. All of the class, but Destine, had passed. Destine would be leaving third grade anyway because she had already failed the tests twice and also because she would soon be old enough to teach third grade. I took care of the morning business and then got the students settled in with their writing assignment. As they busily worked, I called Juleanne's name and signaled for her to follow me out to the hall. I closed the door behind us and then looked at her. "Juleanne," I said in a serious tone, "the test scores came in today." She looked down, not wanting to show the dread that had instantly filled her eyes. "You passed."

It took a moment for Juleanne to register what I had said, but she suddenly looked up at me and with more happiness than I thought possible for her to express, she responded in a breathless shout, "I did?!" I smiled and shook my head in the affirmative. She threw her arms around me and began to cry. "Oh, Miss Thomas, I thought you was gonna tell me I failed again."

"I knew you wouldn't fail, Juleanne. You're a smart girl, but it's a good thing I knew how to outsmart you so that you actually filled in the test answers." She gave out a relieved laugh and wiped the tears from her cheeks. "I'm so happy for you," I said.

Another school year was over and it had been hard. It turned out that it was nothing, though, compared to the year ahead.

Tip for New Teachers: Not all stories about tests will have the happy ending this one did. Sometimes, no matter how hard you try to help a child, she won't do as well as you had hoped and may even fail. You haven't failed, though, if you did the best you could in teaching her. And there's no doubt that you did. After all, you're an elementary school teacher.

Forty-Seven

The Truth Is...Though I Might Have Been Crazy, I Wasn't Scared

After college, I worked in Washington, D.C. While living there I met many interesting people from around the world. One of those people was a member of the Black Panthers.

My small town impression of the Black Panthers was that they were a scary group of people that I would have a really hard time relating to. Steve, one of my brothers, had a best friend who was African American and I could never picture him in a group like the Black Panthers — he was too happy. So when the Black Panther I met in D.C. asked me to lunch, I was curious and a little nervous. What would we talk about? Whether I was right or not, I thought of the Black Panthers as being sort of like the Hell's Angels, and growing up in a home where we watched *Leave It To Beaver* and *Father Knows Best*, I wasn't too familiar with the jargon I might have to know to carry on a conversation with my lunch date.

My worrying was for naught because my date never gave me a chance to speak. He was full of anger towards white people and he spent the entire lunch telling me why white people were evil, and how they should be made to pay for their treatment of black people. I had never seen anyone so angry for so long. The fury in his eyes told volumes about what filled his soul. At the end of lunch, he asked me for another date. Why? According to his words, he hated me because I was white.

"I don't want to go out to lunch with you again," I told him with a slight edge to my voice.

"Because you're prejudiced," he instantly shot back.

"If I were prejudiced I never would have gone out with you in the first place. I don't want to go out with you again because the entire time I've been with you, you've told me how awful white people are. Why would I want to be with someone who hates who I am?" He didn't respond so I guess what I said made some kind of sense to him.

It was a new school year and I was now teaching fifth grade. One of the boys in this class reminded me a great deal of the Black Panther I had lunched with. This child was handsome, but had a look in his eyes that also made him scary. He didn't respect authority and when I mentioned to the counselors from the independent school counseling service we used that Samuel Johnson was in my class, they simultaneously said, "You have Samuel Johnson?!" And then Dr. Palmer said, "Well don't send him to us because we won't see him." That's how bad he was.

I have a theory, and since I have no way to prove it, it's just that. I think that principals watch their teachers to see which ones can handle the tough kids and when they find out which teachers can, they load that teacher with as many problem students as they can get away with. This year I felt like I was one of those teachers. I guess after keeping Destine out of the halls and out of trouble, I passed the tough teacher test. I had Samuel, and on top of that I had so many other students who loved to fight, I couldn't teach.

The first day of school is always tiring. This first day was not only tiring, but frustrating, exasperating, maddening, and just about impossible. Talking with the students, I might have gotten three words out before someone shouted something rude to either a student or to the whole class. This would cause a verbal war amongst the students, words being fired at machine gun speed so that I had no idea what was being said. I tried to intercede, but the students were so loud, they couldn't hear me. When I did manage to get them quiet, inevitably Samuel would make some snide remark about me or school. Reprimanding him was next to impossible because he didn't care anything about what I was saying, giving me a mocking smile the whole time I lectured him. The entire day went this way until I finally threatened Samuel.

"If you make one more disrespectful comment to me, I'm going to your home after school to talk with your parents." He laughed.

There was no doubt in my mind that Samuel would make another rude comment to me, so before making the threat to him I had to be sure I was willing to carry through on going to his apartment. In the movie *The Blind Side,* Sandra Bullock makes a visit to the apartment of the young man she eventually adopts. The apartment is in a neighborhood full of violence and drugs. That was the kind of neighborhood Samuel lived in. Nonetheless, Samuel made the determining remark and I told him I'd see him at his apartment. He gave out a laugh that said, "Yeah, right, like you would ever come to *my* neighborhood."

I dismissed the students for the day and went to the office. I asked for Samuel's address and with my purse strapped over my shoulder, walked down the sidewalk by the school and crossed the street to Samuel's neighborhood. I supposed it was crazy that I was walking through this area alone, but I was so mad at Samuel I think the energy I was giving off protected me from anyone thinking of harassing me. I found the apartment with the same number I had written on the paper I was carrying and out walked Samuel. He smirked at me, but I noticed some nervous twitches in that smirk, telling me that he thought his teacher was either really tough or really insane to be there, and either way she might be dangerous.

"Hello Samuel," I said with a terse smile. "Is your mother home?"

"She ain't here." He was beginning to get his confidence back. Just then a man walked out of the apartment, his pants down below his boxer shorts and barely hanging onto his upper thighs.

"What goin' on?" he asked. His eyes were bloodshot and I wasn't sure if he had been drinking or smoking pot.

"Are you Samuel's father?"

He gave an offhanded laugh followed by a sarcastic smile. "I'm Samuel's uncle. What chu want?"

I figured he was a live-in boyfriend and like Samuel, this man had absolutely no respect for authority and no respect for me. That's all it took for me to not care if he had a gun hidden in his boxers. "Well, I'm Samuel's teacher and he has been rude to me the whole day!"

Samuel's "uncle" let out a hoot and said, "Samuel, it chur first day and you already in trouble? Ha!"

So this guy thought it was funny that his "nephew" was disrespectful? I began to speak, enunciating each word so that he could clearly hear what I was saying. I started out speaking slowly, but my delivery sped up as I became angrier.

"Yes, it was his first day and he was extremely rude to me and disruptive to the class. I am not at school to babysit Samuel. I'm there to teach him and if he doesn't want to learn, I really don't care, but I do care about the other students and if he continues to interfere with their learning, either you or Samuel's mother will be sitting in my class babysitting Samuel while I teach!" As my words got louder and firmer, Samuel's "uncle's" pants got closer to his waist. He grabbed the belt that was attached to the pants and pulled it up so that I could no longer see his plaid boxers. He then grabbed the end of the belt and tightened it around his waist so that his pants were snuggly sitting where they were made to sit.

He turned to Samuel and said, "I better not hear nothin' more from school 'bout bad behavior, Samuel." Now that this man had his pants on, he seemed to better understand his responsibility in guiding Samuel.

"Thank you," I said. "I'll see you at school tomorrow, Samuel." I turned and walked back to the school. When I got there, the two assistants who had talked to me about my dancing were sitting together on a bench by the school fence. They verbally attacked me.

"Miss Thomas, what chu doin' in that neighborhood?!" one of them asked.

"A white woman goin' over there alone? And carrying yo purse? What chu thinkin'?!" the other demanded.

"We black and we won't go over there alone! You never go there by yourself again, you hear?" I promised them that I wouldn't, but there were a few times that year I needed to go back. Happily, it was for good things.

Tip for New Teachers: Only go into a rough neighborhood if you have no fear of death — or of plaid boxers. Although, either might be easier to handle than a student like Samuel. I still haven't reached a verdict on that one.

Forty-Eight

The Truth Is...I Knew Keeping Janet in the Room Might Be Against Policy

School started on the ninth of August that year, and because of Hurricane Charley, it was cancelled on the thirteenth, the sixteenth through the twentieth, and then on the twenty-third of August. When we came back on the twenty-fourth, it was like starting the first week all over again, except this time there were a million stories to tell about the hurricane and it was hard to get the students settled to do anything. Then Hurricane Francis came and school was cancelled September third through the seventh. When we came back to school, it was worse than starting the first week all over again and now there were a billion stories to tell. Then Hurricane Jean came through and school was cancelled on the twenty-seventh and twenty-eighth of September and when the students came back, it was almost as bad as living through the hurricanes.

I had some tough classes throughout my years of teaching, but none compared to this class. The students spent the entire day verbally fighting and I spent the entire day verbally threatening them about what would happen if they didn't quit fighting. My threats didn't faze them. There might have been three students in the class who wanted to learn, but the others took the learning time away with their nonstop disruptions. Sometimes a teacher can't help but wonder if a class might be the way it is because of her teaching style or because of her lack of class management. I talked to the administration and shared my fears about my students and the education they weren't getting.

"I can't teach. I spend the whole day trying to keep order. They're not going to pass the state test." I couldn't have been more serious.

My principal was not at all worried. "You always say your students won't do well, and then they always do well."

It was true, I was a worry wart and was constantly fearful of my students not making gains. "This is different. I've never taught a class like this and they aren't learning anything."

My principal gave me a smile and then she chuckled. "They'll be fine." As I said, I loved my principal, but at that moment I wanted her to see the seriousness of the situation. She had so much confidence in me that she wouldn't even consider that I might have a need to be concerned.

At this school, most of the students' parents hadn't been taught acceptable social behavior. A counselor paying a home visit might conference with a parent while a video of hard core porn played in the living room where the parent, the counselor, and the children all sat. A child might be walked to school by his mother who was still dressed in a low cut silky nightgown and bedroom slippers. Other students were delivered to the school by mothers dressed in outfits that were made to fit a Barbie Doll. How was I supposed to teach students whose parents needed to be taught?

One day as I sat alone in my portable, a mother walked in and said she needed to talk with me. I welcomed her to sit down and asked what I could do for her. "Could you give me money for my 'lectric bill?" she asked. "They gonna turn my 'lectric off if I don' pay it."

"Mrs. Grayson, I wish I could give you the money, but I don't think that's the best thing," I said. "I want you to go to the front office and talk with the school counselor. She can tell you where to get help. She'll probably even make some calls for you. Please let me know what happens, and if you still need help, I'll see what I can do." She thanked me and made her way to the office.

It was now January and although the weather never stays cold for long in Central Florida, there are days that force Floridians to turn on the heat. It was one of those days and Janet Grayson came to school coughing like she'd been smoking Camels since birth.

"Janet, what's wrong?" I asked.

Her eyes were cloudy and half closed. "I don' feel well." She began hacking again.

"Have you been to the doctor?" If her mother had no money for electricity, I was sure Janet hadn't seen a doctor.

She shook her head no and then went to her desk and put her head down. After writing a note to the school nurse, I asked a student to walk Janet to the clinic. Not long after the students left for the clinic, they came back.

"What did Mrs. Styles say?" I asked Janet.

"She gonna get in touch with my mother." The Graysons had no phone, so getting in touch with her mother would be tricky. Until I received word, I would make Janet as comfortable as possible. I made a "bed" in the back of the room with a blanket that I kept in the classroom cabinet. Janet lay on the blanket and quickly fell asleep. The day went on and we were still unable to contact Janet's mother. Janet spent the entire day sleeping. She didn't come to school the following day, but the day after she was back and was no better than when she had last been with us. Again, I made a bed for her and she slept.

I called the clinic and told the nurse the situation. "Is there any way we can get her to a doctor?" I asked. "She is really sick and probably shouldn't be here with the other students."

"Yes, we'll arrange for Janet to see a doctor," the nurse replied. Because so many families at this school were living in poverty, there were special benefits for the students, and being able to get a doctor for them was one of those benefits.

Janet saw the doctor and was diagnosed with pneumonia. He gave her antibiotics and said that she needed to stay at home for at least a week. She was home three days and then came back, still sick — although she was no longer contagious.

"Janet, why are you at school?" I asked, knowing that she should have stayed home for at least five days.

She looked down and began hacking. When she stopped long enough to answer she said, "Ain't no 'lectricity at home. It cold." I would look into that, but meanwhile I made a bed in the back of the class where she could sleep during school hours until there was heat in her house.

There are times teachers have to make tough calls. Should I have kept Janet there? Should I have forced her mother to keep her home in a house with no heat and probably nothing nutritious to eat?

Ten years before, I had a student in my class who became extremely sick at school. She was pale and weak and was shivering with a fever. I took her to the clinic where she could lie down until her mother came. We had no regular nurse at the school, so I was her "nurse" at that moment. I could find no blanket to cover her, so I walked across the hall to the office and asked if they knew where there might be a blanket.

"The blankets are here in the office, but we're not allowed to let the students use them anymore because they might pass their germs on and then the school will be sued."

I wasn't mad at the secretary — she was just following orders — I was mad at what the fear of lawsuits had done to our benevolent American society.

"Give me a blanket, please!" My mothering instinct took over. "Grace is shivering with a fever. If someone wants to sue, let them sue me!" The secretary immediately handed me the blanket. After the student used it, I took it home and washed it.

I don't know if what I did in these two cases was in compliance with school policy, but my decisions concerning these students were in compliance with my conscience — and that's what should guide an elementary school teacher.

Tip for New Teachers: There are times you will have to make some tough calls. Sometimes your heart will rule against the policies set up in your school. I would never tell anyone to go against authority,

but I will say that all humans make mistakes and that includes those in authority. Remember that you are responsible for the safety and well-being of the children in your stewardship. If that is always foremost in your thoughts, your decisions concerning your students will always be correct. And what else matters?

Forty-Nine

The Truth Is...I Felt Relieved That There Might Be a Way Out

It was true that most of the students I taught the year of the hurricanes did not do well in their academics, but that didn't mean they weren't smart. They were extremely smart when it came to anything they wanted to learn. The problem was that what they wanted to learn had nothing to do with what I was teaching them. I felt that if I could work with these students long enough to teach them what was important in life, they would eventually do well in their schoolwork. Unfortunately I'd probably only live to be ninety.

One day I had a rare moment when every child in the class was focused on the math lesson I was teaching. It was quiet, no one was giving the evil eye to anyone else, and I could actually feel all brain waves traveling in my direction. While I wrote some problems on the board, Janet took a large comb from her desk and placed it in her thick, curly hair. Then, out of nowhere, I heard a high-pitched voice scream, "Whachu doin' wid dat comb in yo hair? Get dat comb out, NOW!" My head flew around in the direction of the screaming voice and there I saw Janet's mother. She had walked into the portable, unannounced, and completely disrupted the one actual teaching moment I was blessed with that entire year.

"Miss Thomas," she went on in her fast, high-pitched voice, "I got dis pile of papers you needs to fill out right away."

I wasn't too happy with Mrs. Grayson's disruption of the class and I really wasn't happy that she was telling me what to do, especially without the mention of a "please." I found that many parents in this school demanded and expected things without thinking much about what their part in the process might be and without thinking that a please or thank you might motivate the teacher to want to help them.

Without smiling I said, "Put them on my desk. I'll get to them when I finish the other papers you see piled on my desk." Every year the piles of paperwork became higher and higher and at this school, with so many families getting government assistance, the piles were taking over. She did thank me when she left, but now the class had lost their focus and the one magic teaching moment had vanished.

I asked the administration to please come to my room and observe my class. I sensed that I had the most difficult class in the school and really needed support. I was told that all of the classes in the school were difficult and that I was probably having a hard time because of all of the hurricanes we had battled, and the craziness that had come from their disruptions. I suppose a small part of what I was experiencing came from the hurricanes, but even before the first storm hit, my class was out of control. No one came to my room.

It seemed that someone would figure out that my class was pretty tough when the music teacher sent, not just one of my students to the detention center, but at times took the entire class to the detention center instead of teaching them music. It seemed that someone would wonder how Samuel was behaving in my class, knowing that he was so out of control the school counselors wouldn't even see him. It seemed someone would suspect my bunch was pretty rough when I shared with my colleagues how during a school lockdown, while the police ran past our portable windows chasing the criminal, the majority of my class jumped out of their seats and ran to the windows, whooping and hollering for the criminal as they watched him get away. And then there was the conference I had with the mother of one of my students. When the conference ended and the parent walked away from the school, a school counselor said to me, "I wouldn't meet with that parent alone."

"Why not," I asked.

"Because she just got out of jail for murder." Why wouldn't anyone believe me when I said I had an extremely tough class?

I decided to meet with the assistant principal to discuss the concerns I had about my class. After listening to my sad story she said, "Maybe you don't belong in an inner-city school."

When she said this, I felt a weight lift off of my shoulders. Maybe I didn't belong there and it wasn't my fault that I didn't have what it took to get these kids in line. When I picked up my class from science lab, I told the lab teacher about my meeting.

"Mrs. Fischer thinks that maybe I don't belong here."

Mr. Clark's response surprised me. "Please, please, please don't leave. You really care about these children. Please don't leave."

I was happy that he knew I cared about the students, and a little surprised that it showed. I really did care about them, but I felt like a drill sergeant always barking orders at them hoping to keep them in line. I never wanted to be that dictator my first supervisor was afraid I would be, but I felt like that's what I was turning into.

"But I feel like they're not learning anything," I confided, "and I'm always so stern with them."

"You have to be stern," Mr. Clark assured me. "Do you realize what a miracle you've worked with their behavior? You have the hardest class in the school and you've worked wonders with them."

Yay! Someone finally confirmed what I believed all along — I had the hardest students in the school. For a moment I felt lighter inside knowing that Mr. Clark thought I was doing a good job with them. Unfortunately, there was no test to measure the growth of a child's character or attitude. These students may have been changing for the better, but their test scores weren't going to show academic growth. I knew this, and was plagued by it all year.

Because there was a large population of unwed mothers in the neighborhoods of this school, my fifth grade girls were required to go to a pregnancy prevention class. Fortunately, I didn't have to teach the class. But when my girls went to their class, I needed to teach something to the boys who were left behind. I knew that half of the problem with these girls getting pregnant was the boys, so I decided I would talk with my boys about females and what makes them tick. I was surprised at how eager the boys were to learn the truth about women. They pulled their chairs away from their desks and formed a semi-circle around me as I sat in my chair. They rested their chins on their hands and listened intently as I began. "All girls want to be treated with respect. Sometimes they don't even know it because they've never been treated that way."

"How do you show respect to a girl?" Phillip asked.

"Well, there are lots of ways. I'll start with some simple things. Hold the door open for a girl. Pull a girl's chair out for her so that she can sit down. Let her go in front of you when you're going through doors." I had never seen these boys look so sweet. They really wanted to become gentlemen.

Our time alone passed quickly and before we knew it, the girls were coming up the ramp to our classroom portable. Immediately one of the boys opened the door for the girls. The first girl walked through the door and slapped him. The second girl walked through the door and hit him. I told him to get away from the door before I had to take him to the hospital. I wasn't sure what the girls had been taught in their pregnancy prevention class, but from what I could see they didn't have to worry about any boys getting too close to them. That was in the early nineties. I have no idea what's being taught in elementary health classes now and I don't think I want to know. I'm just glad my time has been served!

Tip for New Teachers: If you are required to teach sex education in your elementary class, don't forget to tell them it's time to wear deodorant. At their age, that's the most important piece of information they can be given.

Fifty

The Truth Is...It Never Occurred to Me that Superstition Could Keep a Person from Advancing in Life

Another state test was on the horizon and I saw little hope that more than a few of my students would pass. Other than the days I was observed for my evaluation, the administration never visited my class that year. This was a tough school and on top of that, the paperwork in all schools was becoming unmanageable. Like the teachers, the administrators were being loaded down with forms and emails and meetings, and their time for teachers and students was becoming scarce.

I was unable to use my songs in the classroom that year because the students couldn't handle anything that wasn't structured. My energy was low and my frustrations high. Would I ever get through to these children? One morning on my drive to work, I searched my brain for ideas that might help these students. I offered up a silent, heart-felt prayer asking, "How can I reach these children?"

Immediately an unexpected, yet distinct impression came into my heart. "You must help rid them of superstition."

"Rid them of superstition? What does that mean?" I received no more instruction, but pondered the inspired words as I drove into the school parking lot. It didn't take long before I began to understand what I had been told.

"Don't walk under a ladder or you'll have bad luck!" As kids, we always walked around a ladder leaning against a wall. And when Dad drove past a cemetery, my sister and I would hold our breath because we didn't want to wake the dead. Superstitions were part of growing up, but other than adding interest to life, they really didn't mean anything to us. With these students it was different.

That day, for the first time, I was aware of how superstitions were controlling my students' lives. As we walked from lunch, the first student in line stepped on a crack in the sidewalk. Terry lectured him, "You stepped on that crack! Your mama gonna break her back!" The rest of the class walked around the crack and none of them were smiling.

Alonzo turned to Terry and said, "My uncle's right palm was itchin' the other day and he won five dolla's in the lottery."

"I know. My mama had the same thing happen and she found ten dolla's when we was walking to the store."

For the next five minutes, students shared stories about superstitious sayings that had come true for them or for someone they knew. Had they been talking about superstitions all year and I just hadn't noticed; or was I now purposely being made aware of how superstitions were affecting many of these students and their progress?

The most surprising incident concerning superstition happened after school that day. There was a fourth grade student who sang with an after-school group I had organized. She was one of the most negative and angry children I had ever worked with. Many times I tried to help her get beyond her bad attitude, but she was stubborn and set in her dark ways. The day of my superstition inspiration, she was especially cantankerous with me and mean to the girls in the group. I pulled her into a classroom and asked her to sit down.

"Okay, Serena, tell me what's going on." She was sullen and wouldn't make eye contact with me. Again I asked, "What's going on?"

"I don' know what chu mean." She knew exactly what I meant.

"You always seem mad. I never see you smile. You're hurting the girls' feelings with your unkind remarks. What's going on?"

Her answer took me by surprise and opened a new world of understanding to the inspired counsel I had been given that morning. "It's voodoo. Black magic. Superstition. It bring you down, make you negative, keep you trapped so you can't be free to move on."

My heart was racing. It was as though her tongue had been unlocked by an invisible key and she was giving me all of the answers to my question of how superstition was holding these students back.

Serena came from Haiti, as did many of the children in this school, and had been taught the practice of voodoo. It never occurred to me that these young children were being held back by a practice that had been passed down from their ancestors.

There was so much more to being a teacher than most people ever considered. There was absolutely nothing in the teacher manuals about superstition.

Tip for New Teachers: There will be times that you'll be surprised by what you have to deal with. There are answers for every situation that comes up. After all, there's the internet, and if that doesn't work, try prayer.

Fifty-One

The Truth Is...I Was Glad the Truth about My Students Was Finally Recognized

State test week came and nothing out of the ordinary happened. When the test scores came back, nothing out of the ordinary happened there either. Only four of my students passed. Although it was exactly what I had predicted, I was sick at the news. In the past, no matter how difficult school was for some of my students, they always showed progress. This group had no clue how to answer and solve the problems on the test. They made it look like I had taught them nothing all year. That wasn't true. I *had* taught them. The problem was that there weren't any questions on the test about why fighting wasn't a good way to solve problems, or why wearing skirts that barely covered your underwear wasn't acceptable, or why opening a door for a girl in my class might be dangerous.

There is an underground communication system in the public schools and as soon as something gets out that could be considered a juicy bit of gossip, there's no chance of keeping the lid on it. I've never been one to hide what's going on in my life and when I saw my students' test scores, I immediately shared my dismay with a few other teachers. That's all it took to get the news around the school that Miss Thomas's class had failed the state test.

Four students did pass: Terry, who was a math whiz and technology genius, Alonzo, who was also strong in math and a friend of

Terry's, Patricia, one of my girls in the after-school singing program, and Samuel, the very intelligent future leader of the Black Panthers.

The day the test scores came out, Terry and Alonzo had stayed after school to work on a project in the classroom. I needed to pick up some forms from the office and the rule was that students couldn't be in the classrooms alone, so the boys waited outside the classroom door until I got back. After finishing my errand, I walked from the office to my portable and before I could get to the portable ramp, Terry and Alonzo came running towards me.

"Miss Thomas, we tried to keep her out!" Terry shouted.

"We told Ms. Filson she wasn't allowed in the room unless you was there!" Alonzo's words caught me by surprise. What was Ms. Filson doing in my room? Ms. Filson had taught these two boys the year before and whatever approach she used in her classroom worked to create a fierce loyalty towards her from her students.

Terry continued, "We blocked the door and she pushed us aside. She went to your computer and got into our test scores!"

Alonzo was as upset as Terry. "We told her to get out of the room, but she wouldn't listen."

I was extremely proud of my boys for trying to defend me. They knew what was right and they did their best to stand up to a teacher for whom they once had undying loyalty, but who was now displaying unethical behavior. Some of my students really had learned that year.

I told the administration what Ms. Filson had done and they said it would be taken care of. I never found out how it was taken care of because Ms. Filson and I never talked after that.

It was time for another fifth grade end-of-the-year banquet and awards ceremony. As was typical of these events, it was held in the multipurpose room cafeteria where food could be served and the stage utilized. Usually, when a student is out of control it's because parents have not set boundaries at home. When my students' parents arrived for the banquet, it was obvious that their parents hadn't set boundaries in their homes growing up either. With the exception of two or three parents, my students' parents were worse than their children in behavior. Throughout the entire banquet and awards ceremony, the parents whooped and hollered, laughed and talked loudly, showed no signs of having manners, and basically disregarded most of the school rules I had been trying to teach their children all year.

With dismay, I watched the parents' unacceptable behavior and was reminded of another time that year I had felt that same dismay. I had just walked into the cafeteria of bedlam when the announcement came that we were in lockdown. When that happens, every door in the school is locked and you have to stay where you are until the coast is clear. There I was with one other teacher, and a few teachers' aides, locked in the cafeteria with one hundred fifty wild children. The lockdown lasted an hour and afterwards I wanted to be locked in a quiet, padded room. Now these parents were making me feel the same way.

I politely asked them to quiet down and that didn't work. Even their children seemed embarrassed and asked their parents to calm down, but the parents were too busy running around taking pictures and making noise to pay attention to anyone but themselves. I was never so happy to see a school activity come to an end. It was the last day of school with the students and as we walked out of the cafeteria one of the fifth grade teachers said, "Wow, you really did have a rough class this year. I had no idea." I had tried to tell her and quite a few other people that year about my class, but because the majority of students in the school were difficult, everyone probably thought that *they* had the roughest class. I knew that wasn't true because not everyone had a future Black Panthers leader as a student. I guess I was just lucky.

Tip for New Teachers: If you have an especially difficult class, let me know. I'll listen, give you understanding, and I'll find Samuel Johnson for you. He will scare your students into being good.

Fifty-Two

The Truth Is...I Felt Like There Was No Difference between the Principal and My Student

Another year ended and I wasn't sure what to make of the year. I tried to teach my students correct English but they were so busy yelling at each other in incorrect English they couldn't hear me.

I tried to teach them to ignore ridiculous statements other students made, but when it came to their *mamas*, nothing I said made a difference.

"Don' talk 'bout my mama like that!" Kadrick screamed at Benji. Benji smiled at Kadrick.

"Miss Thomas," Kadrick whined, "he sayin' bad things 'bout my mama."

"Benji, what did you say about his mother?" I really didn't think he'd tell me.

Kadrick answered, "He say she ugly."

I looked at Benji, "That's not nice, Benji. How would you like it if he said that about your mother?"

"He don' know my mama," Kadrick said.

I asked Benji, "Do you know Kadrick's mom?"

"No," Benji answered

I couldn't believe it. "Kadrick, if Benji has never seen your mother, he has no idea how she looks. He's just saying she's ugly to make you mad."

"No one say nothin' 'bout my mama!" Kadrick was dead serious. Benji continued to smile. I soon learned that if ever these children wanted to get a rise out of someone, they only needed to say the words "your mama" and they would get the desired effect.

I also learned that when a group of students are extremely difficult, like mine were, ways would be found to pass them on to the next grade, even if they failed the state test. All of my students, but two, were passed on to middle school. And, although I had no proof, I suspected that when a teacher's students' test scores were low, the teacher would be placed in a grade level where she could do the least amount of damage. It was the last day of school for the teachers, and as I walked through the hall to the exit, my principal handed me my assignment for the following year — first grade.

First graders were cute, but I didn't think I had the patience to work with their short attention spans. I declined the offer and started looking for a new school.

I knew that I wanted to teach academic skills through song and dance, but I also knew that before I could promote the idea, I had to test it. So far that hadn't worked too well because of the ever-increasing controls that were being put on the classroom teachers. It was getting harder and harder to find a moment to teach in any way but the test-centered way.

That summer I talked with a friend, Gary, about wanting to teach academic skills through music and dance. He mentioned that a principal friend of his, Mrs. Patterson, was looking for a fifth grade teacher. Gary thought that perhaps this principal would allow me to use my music in teaching academic skills. I gave Mrs. Patterson a call.

"Hello, Mrs. Patterson, my name is Becky Thomas and I was talking with Gary White yesterday. He mentioned that you might need a fifth grade teacher."

Mrs. Patterson seemed a little surprised by my call, but she also sounded happy. "Yes, I do need a fifth grade teacher. Have you taught fifth grade?"

I told her that I had and when she asked about my evaluations, I told her that I never had a problem with any evaluation.

"Okay, you're hired."

"Wow," I thought, "that was easy!"

"Could I ask you a few questions before I accept?" She said yes, so I went on. "I write skill songs to help teach math and reading and I wondered if you would have any objections to me using these songs as part of my teaching curriculum."

Mrs. Patterson was extremely open to the idea, which put my mind at ease. I then asked her if I would receive administrative support when it came to discipline problems.

"Oh, you'll receive constant support. Our school has many difficult students and so we have support and then backup support."

Her words were reassuring, and I asked her one more question. "Don't you want to meet me before you hire me?"

"No, if Gary recommended you that's all I need." I had a job.

The first thing I did when I arrived at Mrs. Patterson's school was go to the office to meet my new boss. She was tall and very thin, had thick glasses, and her hair was frizzy-curly. There were other teachers in her office, saying hello, asking about schedules, and talking with each other. I stood quietly until she noticed me.

"Hello," I said, "I'm Becky Thomas, the teacher you hired over the phone."

I reached out to shake her hand, but before I could make contact, she stood up and came around to the front of the desk. She shook my hand and then embraced me.

"We're so glad to have you here!" she beamed. I sensed this was going to be a good year.

The school was in a crime-ridden area and so some of the students were difficult. Compared to my last school, however, I felt like I was in heaven. My students actually looked at me when I taught. They were talkative, but they listened when I asked them not to talk and their parents responded when there was a problem. Although this was a Title I school and received government assistance, most of the parents had jobs. Because they had jobs, they felt more of a responsibility for their children's education and took more of an interest in it than the parents of the school I had just left.

The school year was moving along pretty well, until Shane moved in. I had never met a child like Shane. He was nice-looking and proved to be intelligent and creative. He also proved to keep the class in a continual uproar. I had heard the term Borderline Personality Disorder before meeting Shane, but I had no idea what it meant. Shane taught me. When presenting a lesson to the class, no matter how slowly I went, it was never slow enough for Shane. He demanded that I repeat the information over and over until he was satisfied. Even my academically challenged students didn't want the information repeated as often as Shane did. Shane would get fixated on a particular word and until his mind would let go of that word, he couldn't move on. It was important that I kept the lessons going so that I could teach what was scheduled for the day. Shane didn't see it that way. "No, Miss Thomas," he would yell, "you can't move on. I don't understand this!"

"Shane, I'll help you after I finish the lesson. I promise you'll understand, but we need to move on."

"No! No, you can't. I don't get it!" Shane was willful and until he felt he understood what I was teaching, he caused disruptions so that he controlled when I could move forward with a lesson.

I never knew where I stood with Shane. One minute he told me I was unfair and he was going to report me, the next minute he told me he loved me. I asked the principal to observe Shane.

In the short time I had been at this school, my principal had changed. I noticed that she was putting on weight and working out. Her thin frame was becoming shapely, she no longer wore glasses, and she had her hair straightened and highlighted. She went from dowdy to chic in her appearance, and with this change in appearance came a change in personality. The warmth I first felt from her was replaced by a feeling of detachment and even arrogance. I didn't know what had caused this change, but she had changed and she didn't come to observe Shane.

I was told by Shane's social workers that Shane was living in a foster home. He would be getting counseling from an outside service and his counselor would pull him out of class for his sessions. The diagnosis hadn't been confirmed, but the professionals working with Shane were confident that he had Borderline Personality Disorder. There was no such thing as a "normal" elementary class anymore.

One day, Shane's disruptions forced me to take him to the principal's office. I rarely asked for principal intervention with my students, but since the principal hadn't come to me, I would take the student to her. As my class lined up for special area, I told Shane he was to follow me to the principal's office.

"I'm not following you to the principal's office!" Shane yelled.

I ignored him. "Rachel, please go through the door on the right side," I calmly instructed the student at the front of the line.

Shane was on my heels. "You can't make me go to the office!" The class quietly walked through the door and then turned down the sidewalk to music class. I watched them go into the music room and then I turned the opposite direction and began my walk with Shane to see the principal. I hadn't said one word to Shane since I first told him he was going with me, but he hadn't stopped talking since I told him. It took three minutes for us to get to the office, and the entire time Shane stood right behind my left ear and made comments.

"This isn't fair. You can't do this. I'm not going with you. You can't make me follow you. I'm not going to follow you..." I wondered if Gollum had taken over Shane's body. Although he insisted he would not go to the office, when I opened the door to go in, Shane followed right behind me and continued with his rude remarks.

"I don't have to do what you say. I'm not going to listen to you."

Mrs. Patterson was standing at the front desk, and when she heard the way Shane talked to me she reprimanded him. "Don't you talk to your teacher like that!"

Shane looked at Mrs. Patterson and said, "I can talk to her anyway I want. It's none of your business."

"You're suspended!" Mrs. Patterson shot back.

I had been dealing with Shane's disrespectful behavior for three months now and had gotten no support when it came to disciplining him. Mrs. Patterson had dealt with Shane's behavior for three seconds and suspended him. Why did I feel powerless as an elementary school teacher?

Mrs. Patterson then called my name and held out a picture for me to look at. It was a picture of Mrs. Patterson.

"Miss Thomas, look at this picture," she said. "I was so skinny. Look at me now. Quite a difference." Her self-centeredness left me speechless.

Mrs. Patterson suspended Shane for three days but offered me no suggestions in the way of handling Shane's behavior when he returned. So much for the guarantee of support.

Tip for New Teachers: One of the most beneficial lessons I learned over the years when it came to discipline was to not get drawn in by a child's anger. If the child has no one to argue with, it takes the wind out of his sails. Of course, you might want him to keep a little of that wind so he can sail behind you to the office.

Fifty-Three

The Truth Is...I Was Smiling on the Inside While the Assistant Principal Talked and the Boys Argued

The students I was now teaching struggled in math and reading. In this school, the students with the highest scores were put in accelerated classes and the rest of the students were put in the teachers like me's classes. From the start, trying to get my students to understand fifth grade math was a challenge. I had written quite a few math songs that I had used in my previous classes and so I brought them to this class and surprisingly, they liked them. As they learned the songs, they requested that I write more songs for math terms they couldn't remember.

"Could you write a song for maximum and minimum? I always get those two mixed up." I wrote a song.

"I can't remember which coordinate goes across and which one goes up or down." I wrote a song.

"I get confused with the mode and the mean and the median." I wrote three songs. I found a studio where I could cheaply get these songs recorded on a CD, and then for a Christmas present, I gave each of my students a copy of the CD. I'm not sure if they appreciated receiving an academic CD for a Christmas present, but they acted like they were happy. When we came back from Christmas break, we did a math review. I put a list of numbers on the board.

"Class, look at these numbers and tell me what the mode is."

Within a few seconds, more than one answer came. "Six!"

"That's right. Okay, tell me the median."

Again, a number of students answered, "Eight!"

"Very good! Now the range."

As the review went on, I was amazed at how well the class was doing. I finally stopped and asked, "Did you take genius pills over break? How do you know these answers?"

A chorus of voices called out, "Because we listened to your CD." Could math concepts put to music really make that much difference in a student's ability to learn? Excitement ran through me as I thought that maybe, just maybe, my math songs really were helping these children. There was only one way to find out — I'd write more songs.

With each song I wrote and taught, I made up a movement or a dance. It seemed to me that music combined with motion would do even more to help the students remember the concepts in the songs. The students were having fun and learning at the same time, and I was teaching the way I thought would be most beneficial to the students.

Shane had a difficult time interacting with the other students. When we sang our songs and danced, he was always causing some sort of fiasco so that even the most enjoyable things we did were never without an element of frustration. Then Dante moved in. He was a likeable boy, but he had serious anger management problems and with Shane's impulsive anti-social behavior being directed at him, and Dante's anger being directed at Shane, they made a lovely pair.

The combination of Shane and Dante's behavior often inter-rupted my teaching. Shane inevitably started the conflict with Dante, knowing he could provoke him to anger. And he did — every time. Neither of them was willing to let the other get the last word, so their arguments went on until I became the banshee woman. They would not listen to me until I screamed at them, and once again I told the administration about this situation, and once again I received no visits or answers.

One day the assistant principal, Mrs. Kowalski, who was a very nice person, came to my class to deliver awards to the students who had perfect attendance, and also to those who were on the honor roll for the nine weeks grading period. She stood in front of the class and began. "I'm here to present certificates and pencils to those of you who made it to school every day this past nine weeks."

"You didn't," Shane said to Dante.

"Neither did you," Dante shot back.

"Did to."

"Did not." Shane *had* been at school every day. Teachers know those kinds of things — especially when it's a student that you hoped would stay home once in a while.

"Excuse me, Mrs. Kowalski," I interrupted. "Boys. Stop. Now."

Mrs. Kowalski continued, "I will also be giving awards to those who have all A's and B's on their report cards."

"I know you didn't," Shane said to Dante.

"Well, you're too stupid to get all A's and B's, so neither did you," Dante retorted.

"No, you're the one who's stupid." This time Mrs. Kowalski tried to stop them.

"Boys, please don't talk. You need to listen." They didn't listen.

"You've probably never gotten anything above a D in your life," Shane said to Dante.

"Have so."

"Have not."

My confession is that I took delight in this exchange of words. Once again, I had talked with my principal about this constant problem in my classroom but she must have forgotten her hearing aids that day. As much as I liked the assistant principal, I was glad that she was experiencing what I experienced on a daily basis.

"Boys," she was stern this time, "you need to stop. If I have to talk to you again about this, you're coming with me to the office." Well, that was a guaranteed break for the class and me. Mrs. Kowalski continued and so did the boys. While she announced the names of the certificate recipients, the boys bickered loudly.

"Sarah Newell," said Mrs. Kowalski.

"She's your *girlfriend*," said Shane.

"Is not!" said Dante. "She's *your* girlfriend."

"Is not!" said Shane.

"Boys," said Mrs. Kowalski, "when I leave, you're coming with me to the office."

"Am not," said Shane.

"Oh yes you are," said Mrs. Kowalski. I should have warned her not to respond. She would never win a verbal battle with Shane. She just needed to tell him once and let it go at that. He would follow her, telling her the whole way that he wasn't going to follow her. Dante on the other hand might punch Shane out on the way to the office. I learned with Dante that when he became angry, all living things needed to move away from him if they wanted to keep living. He would pace in the classroom, like a wild cat, until his anger dissipated. Mrs. Kowalski continued on with the names of the students receiving recognition, and Shane and Dante continued on with their disruptive remarks to each other.

Mrs. Kowalski finished and then told the boys to come with her. They both got up and Shane said, "I'm not going with you to the office."

Mrs. Kowalski tried to remain professional, "Just follow me, please," she said in an obviously controlled tone.

"I don't have to," said Shane.

"Yes, you do," said Dante.

"Don't tell me what to do," said Shane. This rhetoric continued as the three of them walked down the hall and out the door. I would have to find Mrs. Kowalski after school and give her banshee screaming lessons.

Tip for New Teachers: Don't feel bad if your typically disruptive students misbehave in front of your administrators. Sometimes that's the only way you'll get the help you need.

Fifty-Four

The Truth Is...Body Language Got Me into More Trouble than I Could Have Imagined

When teaching my fifth graders about communication skills, I taught them a lesson on body language. In many cases, body language is as important to understand as spoken language. In fact, it's often more important because it tends to be more honest and sometimes its message is clearer. However, it really is necessary for humans to communicate by the spoken or written word, and not being able to do so can lead to trouble.

One of the custodians at my school, Mr. Costa, spoke very limited English. Very limited as in maybe one hundred words. He never seemed happy and so I made an extra effort each day to let him know I appreciated the cleaning he did in my classroom. I tried to learn a little of his language, but that didn't go too well. Nevertheless, he appreciated my attempts and he seemed a little happier as he cleaned.

Being an unrealistic teacher, I thought that if I stayed late enough I could catch up on all of my work. I sometimes stayed at school until the custodians locked up. One night I stayed too long and got trapped on the school campus. Apparently no one noticed my car in the parking lot and the gates to the entrance and exit were padlocked. It was pitch black outside and as I wandered around the school yard looking for an escape, I actually felt a little frightened. Just as I decided that I could lock myself in the classroom and sleep on the floor, I heard a familiar voice. It was Mr. Costa! He was trying to tell me something in his language, and although I couldn't understand, I figured I was getting a mini-lecture. I probably deserved it.

While he walked to the gate, I walked to my car. Within a few minutes, I was at the gate and couldn't thank him enough for helping me. I wanted to say more than thank you. I pointed at him and said, "If you hadn't opened the gate," pointed at myself and said, "then I would have had to sleep here." I then put my hands together like I was praying, put my hands under my head and cocked my head like I was sleeping. He gave me a big smile and I waved goodnight as I drove through the gate.

The next day after school we had a teachers meeting. I was running a little late and so when I walked out of my room into the hallway to go to the meeting, I was the only person in the hallway, along with Mr. Costa. When he saw me, he immediately left his cleaning cart and quickly came to me. He put his arms around me and tried to kiss me.

"What is going on?" I wondered as I laughed nervously and pulled away. Mr. Costa was smiling and saying something in his native language and with laughter on his lips, again pulled me to him and kissed me. That's when I pushed him away with force.

"What are you doing? I have to get to the teachers meeting!" Did that sound like I was insinuating we could do a little more kissing after the meeting? How does one handle a situation when one doesn't want to be rude, but one also doesn't want to be kissed by a certain custodian? I quickly walked away, feeling wobbly and confused.

By the time I got to the meeting, Mrs. Patterson had already started. I sat down and tried to stay calm while my brain replayed over and over what had just happened. I had no idea what Mrs. Patterson was saying because my mind was on Mr. Costa. He had never shown any hint of this kind of behavior towards me. He was usually sullen and grumpy when he came into my room and I figured he couldn't wait to leave. Had I done something to bring this on? Then it hit me. The night before when I thanked him for letting me out of the school, I spoke, but he most likely didn't understand my words. So he read my hand and body language. I pointed to him, then pointed to me and then made the sign for sleep. I was in trouble.

I mentally debated the dilemma and came to the conclusion that somehow Mr. Costa had to know what I had really said. I knew it would be embarrassing for him, but I'd rather have him be embarrassed than have him chasing me around the room. I didn't want to get Mr. Costa in trouble, but I could see no other way to handle the situation than to go to Mrs. Patterson.

Mrs. Patterson listened to my plight and said that she would get one of the cafeteria workers who spoke English, as well as Mr. Costa's language, to translate in a meeting with Mr. Costa. We met the next day and I explained, through the interpreter, what I had said at the gate. I didn't know what Mr. Costa was saying in response to my explanation, but he was upset. I tried to be sensitive to what he must be feeling. I was sure this was humiliating for him, but he wasn't accepting my overtures of friendship and forgiveness very well. It was just a simple miscommunication. Why couldn't he leave it at that and forget it ever happened?

The next day when I arrived at school, the principal called me to her office. "I've been thinking about this situation," she said, "and no matter how I try to fight it, the thought is clear that you have to meet with county officials and fill out a report about Mr. Costa kissing you."

I didn't want to get this man in trouble with the county. I told Mrs. Patterson my feelings, but she was insistent. "If this gets out and it hasn't been reported, I'll be in trouble." Was there anything left in this country that we couldn't get in trouble for? I had no complaints against this man. We had settled things. Why couldn't we let it go? Mrs. Patterson got a teacher's assistant to cover my class and I went to the county office.

On my way out Mrs. Patterson said, "I sure hope we don't lose Mr. Costa. That would be a real hardship for me in trying to get this school cleaned." Then why couldn't we drop this?

As I told the story to the lady in human resources, I began to cry. "I don't want to get Mr. Costa in trouble. It was a miscommunication and we straightened it out." She was sensitive to my feelings and said that she understood, but that these things had to be reported. I asked if Mr. Costa was going to lose his job over the incident. She couldn't tell me, which made me feel worse.

I left the county office feeling sick to my stomach and emotionally drained. When I got back to the school, I stopped at the office to report to Mrs. Patterson. My face was blotchy from crying and my eyes were bloodshot. "How did it go?" asked Mrs. Patterson.

"It was hard," I answered.

"Did they say anything about me?" Why would they say anything about her? What was she so worried about?

"No, they didn't say anything about you. Just about Mr. Costa and me." I walked back to my room and felt like I had no support. Being an elementary teacher was becoming a lonely job.

Tip for New Teachers: These are the only words you should use when speaking to a custodian who doesn't speak English: hello, yes, please, no, thank you, and goodbye. And, DO NOT use your hands when you speak! (The words toilet paper, paper towels, soap, and tissue might also come in handy.) By the way, Mr. Costa was still working at that school when I left. However, he never talked to me again. I guess it was becoming a lonely job for him, too.

Fifty-Five

The Truth Is...Singing and Dancing Can be Educational

Another year, another state test. The classes were split according to student needs. This school kept their "English for Speakers of other Languages" students in the regular classroom instead of pulling them out for special instruction. For the state test, however, they were tested with a class made up only of ESOL students. I had quite a few ESOL students and when the test day came, they were escorted to the room next door.

The first day after the tests were over, my ESOL students came back to the room and Raquel confided, "We got in trouble with Mrs. Dover during the test."

The state test was the most serious thing in Florida education. Nobody fooled around during this test. "What did you do?" I asked.

"We were singing some of the math songs and she said we weren't allowed to do that. We had to sing them in our head." Hooray! They were using the math songs!

When the test results came back, I was thrilled. My students showed enough growth in math that I received a five thousand dollar stipend. I could pay more of my hospital bill. The songs had helped them and the test scores were evidence of that. Now I wanted to test my program on a larger scale.

I visited with Mrs. Patterson in her office and explained my idea. "My students had a tough time in math, but when they learned the math songs I wrote, their scores improved. I was wondering if you would consider letting me teach my program to the entire school."

"I think that would be a good idea." She answered so quickly I felt that she must have been thinking about it before I asked her. "Do you have enough material to teach all of the students, kindergarten on up?" She really had been thinking about it.

I didn't have the material at that moment, but I would write as many songs as possible over the summer so that I would be ready when the next school year started. I assured her that I would have a program for all of the children. "Then I'll put you in portable nine. I think your program will really help the students at this school." I was elated!

That summer I worked feverishly to not only write songs, but to put lesson plans together for each grade level, make cards for the activities I thought up to go with the skills, make up dances and movements for each song, and put together lyric booklets for the students. I was stressed, but I didn't mind because I believed in what I was doing. That summer I could have used an additional two months to get ready for the new school year.

I didn't need a gym membership that year. All day, every day was nonstop movement. There were some tough kids in this school and I had to teach those kids along with the well-behaved children. Some of the fourth and fifth graders fought the idea of dancing and singing in front of their peers, but once they broke through their feelings of self-consciousness, they looked forward to their *Academics through Music* class.

Although I was worn out by the end of each day, I was glad to be doing what I was doing. I had a million ideas bouncing around in my head. I could bring in dance instructors to teach these students dances that they would otherwise never learn. I could introduce the program into other schools and then the schools could compete against each other. The students at this school struggled in academics, but excelled in dancing and singing. Having a dancing/singing competition would give them a chance to shine. Of course, they would have to pass the skills taught in each song before they could be in the competition, but having the competition for motivation would help them learn the skills.

One day, about a month into teaching the program, I felt a band of pain around my lower back. Each day the pain grew worse, until one night such excruciating pain ran across my lower back, and then shot down my right leg, that I called 9-1-1.

Within minutes, an ambulance arrived and I was taken to the hospital in town where I was given an MRI. The image revealed that I had herniated discs that had sent splinters into my sciatic nerve. It was inconceivable to me that splinters could cause the agonizing and relentless pain in my back and leg. But once the discectomy surgery was performed and the splinters were removed, I was on the road to recovery, and after six weeks was able to go back to school.

While recovering, I often thought about ways I could better help students to understand math. I found that students made the same mistakes in math every year, and among those mistakes was plotting coordinates incorrectly. I had written a song to help them with this, but I felt that if the students could "walk out" the coordinates, they could better internalize the concept. I visualized making a large, masking tape coordinate grid for the students to walk on. There was carpet on the portable floor, but it already had some holes in it so I figured I wouldn't get in too much trouble if I put tape on the carpet.

The week I returned to work, I made the masking tape coordinate grid and the students loved it! I found that it significantly helped them better understand, and gave them practice on, a variety of math concepts and skills. I made up math mat games, and at times teachers asked if they could send students to my portable to "walk out" math problems they couldn't understand. I began to receive copies of emails the teachers were sending to Mrs. Patterson, telling her how the *Academics through Music* program was helping their students. One fifth grade teacher told me how happy she was to see her students acting like children in my classroom. They sang, danced, laughed, and learned while for forty-five minutes the program lifted the weight of the world from their shoulders.

Some of the students in this school came from split homes where drug abuse and other societal ills plagued their lives. They were often required to take over the role of the parent at a young age, making it hard for these students to come to school and relinquish their "parental" authority to the teachers. Many classroom discipline problems stemmed from such dynamics. These same students scoffed and made fun of the songs, dances, and activities I taught them. But once they allowed themselves to let go of their tough facades, they became the ten-year-olds that they were and joined in with the others as they sang and danced.

The work was exhausting. From the moment school started until the last child left, I was on my feet singing, dancing, moving, and instructing. When the students left, and I finished grading papers and recording grades, I went home to write new songs and come up with new activities for each song. Despite the demands of the program, I felt satisfaction knowing that the students were learning and were having fun in the process.

Tip for New Teachers: Don't make a masking tape coordinate grid on your floor. If you do, when you take up the tape, there will be a masking tape residue coordinate grid on your floor and you may end up with a few students who will be stuck to the carpet.

Fifty-Six

The Truth Is...I Was Beginning

to Feel Afraid

I could sugarcoat my experience with *Academics through Music* and say that the program was the answer to every student's struggle with math. But anyone who ever tells you that her educational product will solve all academic problems is not being honest. Every person has his own learning style, strengths and weaknesses in learning, his own attention span and ability to focus, and his unique likes and dislikes when it comes to any subject matter. While in school, I enjoyed doing algebra but could barely tolerate geometry. I enjoyed dissecting the English language, but I never liked dissecting frogs or any other specimen in science. Because I was teaching the whole school *Academics through Music*, I worked with every child in the school. There were some students who came to my class with an attention span of zero or who had other things going on in their lives that kept them from participating in an acceptable way. There was a whole kindergarten class at this school that seemed to exist within the Twilight Zone and when they arrived for my class, this fifth dimension engulfed my entire portable.

As I mentioned earlier, I believe that certain teachers are saddled with the most difficult students because they are willing to work with them. I had no doubt that the teacher of the Twilight Zone class had been targeted. After spending only forty-five minutes with her class,

I needed a week off. I didn't know how she was dealing with her students all day every school day.

In this class were three students diagnosed with autism and four others that I knew would be. Although an aide came with the class to my room, it was impossible to keep the students at an acceptable noise level. The "regular" students in the class inevitably put their heads down because they became invisible as the autistic students fed off of each other. Instead of teaching, most of my time was spent trying to get the autistic students under control. Among these students were twins — a brother and sister, Clarissa and Jacob — who were both autistic. I couldn't imagine how hard this must have been for their parents. They were intelligent children, but had absolutely no sense of boundaries or acceptable social behavior.

One day some specialists came to my portable to observe the autistic students. Counting the aide, there were four adults sitting at the back of the room. When the class entered the portable, I knew there had to be angels around the students because every one of them sat down quietly and waited for instruction. I had their attention for two whole minutes when Clarissa, the autistic twin, stood in front of me with her arms outstretched, blocking me from the students, and loudly proclaimed, "I'm sick and tired of this! Either get a job, get a hobby, or a get a few good friends!" I stood with my mouth open as the adults in the back laughed uncontrollably.

On the last day of school that year, when this class left my room, one by one they hugged me and said things like, "Goodbye, Miss Thomas. I'll miss you." "Goodbye, Miss Thomas. I love you." "Goodbye, Miss Thomas. Have a great summer."

Jacob, the autistic twin, stood two feet from me and said, "Goodbye, Stinky." For an elementary teacher, humility was never hard to come by.

I taught a first grade class in this school that had more than its share of problem students. One of the students in this class thought he was Superman as he jumped off of desks and threw chairs. Because of student behavior problems, this class also had a full-time aide. One day, a student in this class wouldn't follow directions and was causing problems with the other students. I told him to sit at a table until

I called for him to rejoin the group. There was a restroom in my portable and he decided he needed to use it, which I didn't know about until I heard, "Ahhhhh! Close the door!"

There stood Quintin at the bathroom door, holding it wide open. "I didn't know you were in there," he casually responded to the aide who was using the restroom.

The poor aide desperately yelled, "Close the door!"

Quintin didn't move. He conversed with her as though she were sitting at a desk and he was asking her questions about reading.

"How was I supposed to know you were in there? The door wasn't even locked."

"Quintin!" I called across the room, "close the door!"

"I didn't know she was in there," he said, still not closing the door. Quintin just couldn't understand that not knowing she was in there wasn't really the issue.

"Close it!" I yelled in exasperation. He did and I began to compose a song in my head about "Knock, knock, knockin' on the bathroom door" before opening it.

There was a fourth grade class with two boys who ended up in a lockdown class. A lockdown class consisted of students who were so out of control that the door to their classroom was always locked. The only time they were allowed to leave class was when they needed to use the restroom and when they did, the entire class, along with the aides and teachers, went with them. Their lunches were brought to them and the special area teachers taught in the lockdown class rather than the students going to the special area room. Police officers were often seen going to and coming from this class. It was good to know the police were there to keep us safe from the students on campus. The two fourth grade boys, who would eventually end up in the lockdown class, were at this point still in the regular class. I was teaching the students in that class about perimeter and the two soon-to-be lockdown boys tried to keep me from teaching by shouting out rude remarks.

"Boys, if I have to stop for you again I'm writing a note to your parents," I warned.

"Go to hell," Mark answered, obviously scared by my warning.

"What did you say?!" Why do we ask things like that when we know what was said and we really don't want to hear it again?

Before Mark could answer, Duane, his partner in crime said, "It's none of your business, you old lady!"

What?! Forget about writing Mark up for swearing at me; Duane had crossed the line. "Okay, that's it!" I said, "I'm writing you up, Duane!" No one was going to call me an old lady and get away with it — at least not as long as I could hear.

And then there was Ashley, the new third grade girl who came on Monday and tried to beat me up on Wednesday. From the start, I knew there was something not right about this new student. When I welcomed her, she gave me a twisted smile along with a look that projected suspicion and the desire to harm me. I made a mental note to keep an eye on her. When she was in the room, I felt that I had to measure every word I said and every move I made to keep her from flying into a rage.

It was Wednesday of her first week and we were playing a math game. When a student was out, he was to go to his seat and wait until only one person was left in the game and declared the winner. Ashley got out but didn't leave the game until I reminded her to go to her seat. She moved very slowly towards her table, eyeing me as she went. I could feel her icy stare, but went on with the game and pretended I didn't notice. As the class continued to play, I saw that Ashley was sitting on top of the table instead of in her chair and knew that she was testing me.

"Ashley, please sit in your seat." She continued to stare at me as she placed both of her feet on the chair.

"Ashley," reiterated the aide, "you heard Miss Thomas. Sit in your chair." Ashley didn't move but continued to stare at me.

Her defiance was evoking just the effect she wanted. I was feeling frustration inside because I wanted to take her by the arm and sit her in the chair myself. I knew I couldn't do that because one, she might try to sue me, and two, she might be carrying a switchblade. I walked to her and looked her in the eyes as I pulled the chair away so that she could no longer put her feet on it.

"Ashley," I said, "you need to sit in your chair or I'll have to send for someone to remove you from class."

With that, she got off the table, grabbed the chair from me, shoved it out of the way, and began to kick and hit me. I called out to the aide to buzz the office. We waited for a response, but there wasn't one. "Call them again!" I said. The aide once again buzzed the office. This time, someone answered.

"Front office."

"Please send someone to Miss Thomas's room. One of the students is hitting her."

"Okay." The voice coming through the speaker didn't sound too concerned. I guess when you have armed policemen on campus, hearing that a student is only hitting a teacher doesn't sound that serious.

I kept a calm façade as Ashley followed me around the room, keeping her eyes fixed on me. The rest of the students sat on the floor and continued to play the math game as I called out instructions to them. Not being able to lose Ashley, I turned to her and said, "Ashley, what is it that you want?"

She answered with a demonic voice, "I just want to be close to you." I was trying to recall any training I might have had in exorcism. At one point, I walked past the students and Ashley followed me, kicking a few of the students in the ribs as we walked by. It was right after that, and after what seemed an eternity, that the portable door opened and standing there was the dean of discipline. She looked at me as though I had interrupted the most important moment of her life.

With hands on her hips she asked, "What do you want?"

I explained what had just happened, including Ashley kicking students in the ribs, and the dean said, "Well, I was in the middle of a reading group and you made me come all the way to your portable."

Reluctantly, the dean took Ashley with her, angry with me because I hadn't handled the situation myself. What was expected of elementary school teachers these days? It seemed that a teacher had to be tied up and gagged before those in charge felt that help was warranted. Shaken as I was, I finished teaching the class, projecting as calm an energy as I could so that the students felt safe — although every day *I* was feeling less and less safe.

I wrote an email to the administration telling them what had happened and asking what I should do as a follow-up to the incident. Mrs. Kowalski called the police and then emailed me, profusely apologizing for the trauma I must have gone through and asked if there was anything she could do to help me. Just knowing I had her support gave me comfort. The next day a policeman and Mrs. Kowalski questioned me.

"Please tell me what happened," the policeman said. I explained the events of the day before, and I was then given some background on Ashley. She had come from an abusive situation and was now living with a foster family.

"Do you want to press charges?" Mrs. Kowalski asked me.

I knew from the start that Ashley was a deeply troubled eight-year-old and that her attack on me was not personal. "I want you to do what's best for Ashley," I said. "If you think counseling would help, then please get her counseling. If you think the juvenile detention center would help her, then I'll press charges. I truly only want what's best for her."

Ashley got counseling and I felt like I was going to need it — it was time to go to the lockdown class.

Duane and Mark, the boys who cursed at me and then said I was an old lady, were now in lockdown and compared to some of the other students in the class, they were a pleasure. The class was small, with not more than eight students, but teaching them was like teaching a thousand regular students. One day as I was teaching, a student named Gleason said, "Miss Thomas, you can go now."

"Actually, Gleason, I have ten more minutes," I said.

"No, you can go now. I'm bored," he insisted.

I hated to tell him the bad news. "We still have ten more minutes to sing and dance. Okay, repeat after me," I instructed. "Zero, two, four, six, eight, even numbers are so great..." A pair of sharp scissors went sailing past my head, just missing my left eye. I turned my head in the direction the scissors were traveling. Did I really see what I thought I saw? Yep, there were sharp, shiny scissors lying on the floor behind me.

"Uh, excuse me." I interrupted the aides who were sitting behind a partition, and showed them Gleason's weapon. "Gleason just threw these scissors at me."

The aides didn't say or ask anything. They quickly got up, grabbed Gleason by his arms, took him to the other side of the partition and pinned him to the floor. I was pleasantly surprised that anyone in the public schools was still allowed to touch a child in order to control dangerous behavior. Gleason began to yell and scream.

I guess Duane saw the questioning look in my eyes because he cupped his hands and shouted to me, "Keep teaching and just yell. This happens all of the time!" I did what he said, and when I left the room I wasn't sure if I'd ever be able to sing again; my vocal cords felt shot. As I walked across the campus to my portable, I could feel my body shaking from the near miss of the scissors and wondered what assault would be next. For the first time in my teaching career I began to wonder how long I could last as a teacher. I guessed it would be as long as I had to.

Teaching Tip: Keep a pair of safety glasses in your pocket and learn karate.

Fifty-Seven

The Truth Is...I Knew the Program Would Work

The year was quickly passing and the students were happy to come to *Academics through Music* class. I had finished paying off my hospital bill, so I saved any extra money I earned and invested it in the manufacture of a portable one hundred square foot math mat. Teachers shared stories with me about how the songs and math mat were helping different students and I knew this teaching method was what I wanted to do until my days of teaching were over. There was a special counseling service at the school for students who had extreme self-worth problems. The counselor told me that because of the songs and dances they were learning, the students he counseled were coming out of their shells and showing a confidence they had never before exhibited. Despite some of the difficult situations I was working with, the students were learning and growing.

For our state test rally, a radio station DJ was brought in and he got the students enthused about doing their best on the upcoming test. Then, students in third, fourth, and fifth grade performed the songs and dances they had learned in *Academics through Music* class. The show went well, and afterwards, teacher after teacher commented on how great the students had done.

Like many school districts in the United States, our district had a television station dedicated to all that was going on in the many schools across the county. Two of the audiovisual personnel came to my classroom, taped students as they sang and danced, and then interviewed four students. Three of the students' interviews were very complimentary. The other student's interview went something like this:

Interviewer: So, Jason, how do you like learning math through song and dance?

Jason: I don't.

Interviewer: So do you like math?

Jason: It's okay, but I like to read better.

Interviewer: Since math isn't your favorite subject, do you like it better when you can learn it through music?

Jason: No.

I loved this media person. She cut Jason's interview from the film.

The program was shown on T.V. and articles about it showed up in a few other local education-related publications. I felt like I was on my way to becoming an independent educator. My program gave me the freedom to teach in a creative way and I wasn't bogged down with data and testing and the many other demands placed on the regular elementary classroom teachers. I also received praise for what I was doing. Praise for teachers was becoming a rare thing in the elementary schools. They were expected to do more and more with less and less appreciation. Again, I believed it was because the administration was also being bogged down with more and more paperwork so they had less and less time to even know what great things the teachers were doing in the classroom. I would never go back to the regular classroom.

The week of the state test was a happy one for me. As I walked across campus, student after student shouted to me.

"Miss Thomas, the area song helped me on my test!"

"Miss Thomas, I was singing the songs in my mind and I knew the answers on the test!"

"Miss Thomas, I remembered how to do coordinates because of the math mat!"

When the test scores came out, the scores in math had improved and the school got bonus funding. I was reassigned to teach *Academics through Music* the following year. I had a lot of work to do that summer.

Tip for New Teachers: In today's world of elementary education, it's hard to find time to implement original ideas. I believe the time will come again when your unique teaching ideas will be given credence. Until that time, write down your ideas and keep them safe. They might be more valuable than you think.

Fifty-Eight

The Truth Is...I Lied

I was taken off guard one day when Mrs. Patterson walked into my classroom with our area superintendant. She wanted her to see my program.

"Have you ever taught this in another school?" Dr. Pfifer, the area superintendant, asked me.

"No, just here," I answered.

After observing the program in action, Dr. Pfifer said, "This is fantastic!" I had hopes that she would spread the word around the county so that I could teach it to other schools.

A month went by and we were called to a special teachers meeting. The teachers sat in the media center and Mrs. Patterson stood in front of us with a solemn look on her face. She obviously wasn't going to give us good news. "Today we got the numbers from the county and our student population has declined. Because we have fewer students, a combined total of nine teachers and aides will have to be cut from the staff."

When this kind of news comes to a school, emotions run high and are mixed. Everyone's first question was, "Who's being cut?"

Mrs. Patterson answered. "The cuts will come according to seniority in the county. Those who are the newest in the county will be cut unless another teacher or aide volunteers to go in their place." I would not be cut from the school. I had seniority over quite a few teachers. Then she said, "We can only keep six of the seven special area classes." I was being cut.

The next question of those being cut was, "Will we be able to find another job?"

Mrs. Patterson quickly answered that question. "The county will not advertise any jobs until all of those being cut from their jobs have been reassigned." In one way this was a relief, but if the jobs weren't posted, I would have no way of knowing about an opening where my program might fit. Somehow I would find a way to teach *Academics through Music*.

After the meeting, I approached Mrs. Patterson. "Is my program being cut?" I already knew the answer, but had to hear her say it. Although the program was a success for the students and their learning, Mrs. Patterson felt that since my program was the newest in the special area category, it should be the one to go. I was extremely thankful that she had taken a chance with my program, but chagrined that she would let it go when it was doing so much good for the students.

"Yes, I'm going to have to let it go."

"I'm not going back to the classroom," I informed her. "I'll find another school where I can teach the program." I would be moving again.

I went online to see if there were any openings for teaching jobs in the county. There were six, but none of them were in my area of certification. I had no way of knowing what schools might welcome my program, so without giving me a choice, the county placed me in first grade.

First grade. Of all the grades I could have been placed in, kindergarten and first were the ones I *never* wanted to teach. High school teachers work well with older students, middle school teachers with middle school students. I liked the upper elementary grades and now, not only was I going back to the classroom, I was going into a territory I knew next to nothing about. I was at the point in my career where I didn't want to start over with new curriculum, new ways of doing things because the students were young, or all of the other things that would be new to me. I was tired from moving, tired from all of the sad changes that had come to elementary education, and tired from the thought of going back to the classroom with all of its record-keeping and test-taking. I wanted to teach my math program full time, but that choice was not given to me.

The school to which I had been assigned was in a beautiful, upper middle class area. Since living in Florida, all of the schools where I had taught were old and had seen lots of wear and tear. The school I was being transferred to was brand new and almost as large as the high school I graduated from in 1971.

I would be leaving for my new school in a few weeks. Meanwhile, open house night came and I sat alone in my portable as the rain beat down on the roof. My portable was the farthest from the main building. It was next to a woodsy area where the police would chase the bad guys as I sat in my locked portable, calling my friends and family to say goodbye in case I never saw them again. Unlike the last school where I taught, the few times a lockdown happened in this school I had no students in the classroom. Being so far from the main building, and being a special area teacher, I didn't expect any visitors that night. When the door opened, I turned around in surprise, and was even more surprised to see a soaked Mrs. Patterson standing in my room.

"Well, hello, Mrs. Patterson!" Not only was I surprised by her visit, I was curious. "What are you doing out here in this weather?"

"I came to see how you were doing." Really? Was she reverting back to the woman who had hired me? "How do you feel about your new assignment?" She sounded like she sincerely wanted to know.

"Well, if the next time you see me I'm bald, you'll know how I'm doing."

"Yes," she said looking down. "When I saw they had put you in first grade I wondered how you would feel about that." I was truly perplexed about this visit, but I was astonished by her next words. "I made a mistake. I never should have let your program go. Will you come back next year?" I didn't know what had caused the change to come over Mrs. Patterson since I first came to the school, but her humility and sincerity at that moment gave me hope that maybe she would once again be the woman I had met two years previous.

"Yes, I'll come back." I didn't mean to lie, but the moment I said those words I felt a weight on my shoulders. I was exhausted from moving, and although I didn't tell Mrs. Patterson, at that moment I intuitively knew that this next move would be my last.

Tip for New Teachers: There will be turning points in your career, and in your life, when it's time to move on. Even if you think you want to stay in a certain place or at a specific task, life will sometimes pull the rug out from under you and force you to go in a direction you might not otherwise go. Trust that those times, no matter how painful, are often when you will grow and learn the most — and that's what education is all about.

Fifty-Nine

The Truth Is...I Didn't Want

to Move Forward

I had now taught twenty-three years and had moved eighteen times. I was tired and in some ways I was feeling a little beat up. Between the moves, the meetings, difficult student situations, the expectations placed upon teachers in this technology-driven world, the accountability issues and the paperwork that accompanied them, and all of the time, energy, and passion I put into my program that had come and gone so quickly, it was hard to feel enthused about starting over.

It was my last week teaching at Mrs. Patterson's school. After a day of teaching math songs, dances, and activities, I drove to my new school to meet the principal, Mr. Smith. Just as I wasn't given a choice as to whether I wanted to work at his school, he wasn't given a choice about hiring me. He was a serious, but reasonable man, and he seemed overwhelmed. He was opening a new school with over one thousand elementary students and the population was growing every day. We had a pleasant conversation and I told him about my math program. He said that he'd wished he'd known about it earlier because he would have hired me to teach it as a special area class. It was too late for that now, but it did give me hope that maybe, at a near future date, he would have me teach my *Academics through*

Music class. I was to report for my first day at the new school the following Monday.

Monday came, and before going to my new school I stopped at my previous school to take care of a few odds and ends. As I walked down the sidewalk, I met up with a teacher friend and we talked for a few minutes. As we talked, Josh, one of the solo performers in the state test rally, walked up to us and waited for a break in our conversation. When it came, he put his arms around me and said, "Goodbye, Miss Thomas. I don't want you to go." He held me tight and I could feel my eyes tearing up.

Behind him came Vincent, another student who also wanted to say goodbye. And then, one by one, student after student got in line, more somber than I knew they could be, each waiting his turn to hug me goodbye and ask me to stay. The line snaked down the sidewalk and my friend said, "The county administrators need to see this." The days of the county, or the state, or the country having time to see moments like these were becoming rare. It seemed that there was no time to find what made students happy as they learned. In my experience, we had become too busy studying data and giving tests to be concerned with happiness. Without knowing it, the students were saying goodbye to more than just me.

When I arrived at my new school, I, along with two other new teachers, was introduced to Mr. Smith's secretary, Angie Clemens. She walked us around the school, showing us where the teachers' mailroom and lunchroom were, giving us a quick overview of the protocol for getting classroom copies made, and explained other miscellaneous routine procedures. She then took one teacher to her room and dropped the other teacher and me off in an empty classroom where we would stay until our room assignments were made.

After Angie left, I called the county office and asked to speak with someone in hiring. My emotions of having to say goodbye to the children that morning had taken over. By the time I was connected with someone who could help me, the person on the other end of the line probably thought I needed more help than she could give me.

"I am so frustrated," I told her. "I taught a math program in the school where I was and the principal decided to let it go. I didn't want to go back to the regular classroom and I tried to find a school where I could teach my program, but the county gave no names of elementary schools where there were openings. I was assigned to first grade in a school twenty-three miles from my home. Why was I put in first grade? In the regular classroom, I've always taught the older children."

As I look back on this conversation, I can see that the person I was talking with must have wondered about me teaching any grade. She didn't know who I was and what I was about. She didn't know I was feeling like a caged animal that needed its freedom to function at its best. She just knew that I was certified to teach elementary school and that included first grade.

"You are certified for first grade," she said. "That means you can be placed in first grade or any other grade for which you are certified." I knew that was true, but I had always been given a choice about the grade and subjects I taught.

"I was teaching an *Academics through Music* program at my other school and it really helped the students in math. I wanted to continue to teach the program." I was sounding like a whining child. I was sad and I wanted someone to make everything better.

"I'm sorry, but your principal made her decision. There's nothing we can do about it." Of course they couldn't help me. She was right. I was certified to teach grades one through six and I had decided not to go back to the regular classroom in the school I had just left. This was not how I had pictured my future in education.

When I got off the phone, I mulled over my situation and then resigned myself to the idea that for the time, this would be my new home. The teacher sharing the room with me listened as I complained. I knew that she and I were in very different places in our lives. She was much younger than I. In fact, I was one of the oldest teachers at the school. How did that happen? I knew that I really couldn't expect another person to understand where I was coming from. I wanted to share my feelings, my frustrations, and my successes with this teacher, but how could she relate? She probably couldn't, but I told her anyway.

Tip for New Teachers: If you feel that you're sometimes misunderstood as a teacher, get used to it.

Sixty

The Truth Is...I Knew Better than to Assume

espite my frustrations with my new assignment, there was one happy surprise — I loved teaching first grade! With every grade I taught there was a trade-off. Fifth graders were independent, but first graders were funny. They took everything literally and gave me at least one good laugh a day. For instance, one day there were hurricane warnings and to help the first graders I was now teaching understand what this meant, we talked about hurricanes, the eye of the storm, the high winds and rain that accompany a hurricane, and how to prepare for this kind of weather. Later that afternoon, Mr. Smith instructed those of us in the portables to come to the main building before the weather became threatening. As I lined up my first graders, one of the students began to cry. I assured him that we would be in no danger as we walked to the building. He couldn't be comforted and the more I tried, the worse he became. Firmly I asked, "Jackson, what are you afraid of?"

With a trembling voice he said, "When we go outside, the eye of the hurricane will see me and then the hurricane will come after me." This was my introduction to the mind of a first grader.

Another day I told the students that the Chief of Police was coming to talk to our class.

"What is the Chief of Police?" Craig asked.

"He's the head of the police department," I answered. The students looked at each other as though they were going to be sick.

"Eewww," a few students responded.

My brain could not grasp why they would react this way. "What's wrong?" I really didn't know.

"There's a head in the police department?!" The interesting thing to me about this misunderstanding was that the entire class thought the same thing. First graders must have a "literal meaning" section in their brain that evolves into a "first think about it" section as they grow older. The day of the plastic knife, I wished I had used the "first think about it" section of my brain before giving two students instructions that literally caused my class to run for their lives.

I had a lemon tree by my house and when the lemons were ripe, I used them in my teaching. That year, I picked one lemon for each child and for one day was able to weave all of my lessons around lemons. The grand finale of the day was to make lemonade. I brought in a white, plastic, serrated knife to cut the lemons, and after I cut them, I let each child squeeze his own lemon and add sugar. The kids were a sticky mess and having a great time.

Before we left for the day, we cleaned up and I washed off the plastic knife and put it in my purse. The students lined up at the door and with my purse on my shoulder, I led the class to the buses.

It was a long walk to the bus area. We were the farthest portable from the main building and the bus pickup and drop off area was on the back side of the main building, making it an even longer walk. Not only was it a long walk, it was a long way to keep a straight and orderly line. We were just making our way down the sidewalk when I heard two students at the end of the line call my name.

"Miss Thomas!"

I looked back and saw Sarah and Patrick standing in the grass by a portable, looking down.

I called to them, "What's going on?"

Sarah looked up at me. "There's a knife in the grass."

I don't know if what happened to me at that moment is common for the human brain, but my brain automatically transferred the word *knife* to the white plastic knife I had cleaned and put in my purse. I assumed it had fallen out into the grass and so I called, "Okay. Pick it up and bring it to me and I'll throw it away."

"All right!" Patrick called back in an overly-excited voice. He reached down into the grass and when his arm came back up, he was holding a three foot machete. The glee in the faces of Sarah and Patrick at finding such a treasure didn't come close to the panic on my face when I saw them standing holding a knife almost as tall as they were.

"Don't move!" I yelled as I sprinted towards them. I had visions of missing arms and legs. The rest of the class ran behind me, wanting to get a closer look at the weapon.

"Boys and Girls," I sternly warned them, "stay away from the knife!" I took the machete by the handle and suddenly had no idea what to do with it. I needed to get my class to the buses, and I was pretty sure there was something in the school handbook about no machetes in the bus area. I didn't know who it was, but someone in my class screamed as I stood there holding the machete in my hand. That's all it took. My class broke into an uproar, running willy nilly down the sidewalk towards the bus area, screaming at the tops of their lungs. If my class showed up in the bus area with no supervision, running and screaming like maniacs, I would be called to the office.

I yelled at the top of my voice, "Class! Class!" Impulsively, I raised the machete into the air and shouted, "STOP!" Every child stopped on a dime, and slowly turned their heads in my direction. They stood frozen for one moment, saw me with the machete raised into the air, and again broke loose into a crazy, screaming frenzy.

That was the last I saw of my class that day. Sometimes things get so out of hand they reach the point of no return. There were teachers and other adults at the bus area. I knew the students would be safe. My job on the other hand...

As I walked alone across the playground area, I felt very strange in my heels and dress carrying my purse and a machete. The sound of voices broke into my thoughts and I noticed that sitting on the grass in a field not too far from the playground were some workers taking a break from laying sod.

"Laying sod," I thought. I knew where the machete had come from.

I switched directions and walked towards the men, feeling like the hero of the day. I was sure the machete was theirs and I knew they'd be happy to see its safe return. My Spanish isn't very good - *Mi espanol no es muy bueno* - but I decided to speak to them in their native tongue. When I finished telling them about the knife, they looked really mad. I could've gotten a word or two wrong, or maybe all of them. I translated my Spanish into English. With a scowl on his face, the owner of the machete took it from me. I didn't feel a morsel of gratitude from him.

"You're lucky none of the students got hurt!" I said in English. He grumbled something back to me in Spanish and I walked away, wondering if these men had any idea how lucky they were that no one got hurt. I hoped to have that same luck keeping my job when Mr. Smith heard about my unsupervised students running into the bus area screaming about their teacher with a machete.

I felt it best to tell Mr. Smith about the machete. I thought he'd appreciate my judgment in not taking it to the bus area, and then my cleverness in figuring out where it had come from and returning it to its owner. I could never read Mr. Smith. This time, after I told him the story, he rolled his eyes and walked away. That was two people I didn't feel a morsel of gratitude from that day. The next time I was going to keep the machete.

Tip for New Teachers: When you hear the word *knife* (or gun, grenade, torpedo, bomb...) from a student, think *danger* until you've checked out why he's using that word. It's probably just boy talk, but then again, you never know.

Sixty-One

The Truth Is...I'm a Wreck When It Comes to Blood

I NEVER entertained the idea of becoming a doctor, a nurse, or anyone who has to deal with blood. Seeing my own blood streaming out of a cut doesn't bother me. However, seeing someone else's blood, or broken arm, or dangling loose tooth makes me weak. I consider myself to be a pretty strong person in most areas, but when it comes to someone else's injury, I'm pathetic. While blood is my biggest weakness, I'm not much stronger when it comes to other bodily fluids. In many ways, being an elementary teacher is like being a mother. The children you teach need nurturing, discipline, understanding, and many times, a tissue.

I'll never forget the day, although I wish I could, when I was teaching my first grade class and asked a question. I called on one of my boys who had raised his hand to answer, and just before he could speak, he sneezed and I began to gag at the sight of what was hanging out of both nostrils. The poor child ran to the restroom as I stood at the front of the class unable to control my reaction. I felt bad, but I'm a highly visual person and no sooner would I get the picture of the two, thick, green waterfalls out of my mind than it would unexpectedly pop up and trigger my gag reflex. When the child came out of the restroom, the mere sight of him once again started me gagging and although it had nothing to do with him as an individual, he was on the verge of tears because his teacher couldn't look at him without feeling sick.

At times I teased my first graders, telling them I was going to grab that loose tooth and yank it out, but in reality I could never do that. I can't count the number of times I was deep in thought, teaching a child, or working on something for the class when a student would tap me on the shoulder, say, "Look, Miss Thomas!" and without thinking, I would turn and find a bloody tooth hanging by a thread from the child's gums. It never failed that I would give out a little scream and quickly turn away, telling the child not to show me his tooth again. The student loved it, chuckling as he walked back to his seat, knowing that in some way he had power over Miss Thomas.

A vision that will forever be with me is that of my first graders' Mother's Day presentation. The children had put hours of practice into two Mother's Day songs I had written. One was upbeat and fun, the other was serious and sentimental. The latter was always the mothers' favorite. The children also made a special book for their mothers, and we compiled a slide presentation of pictures that had been taken throughout the year. I baked pies for the occasion and we were ready for the mothers to come.

When the mothers arrived, the students wanted to show them everything at once. I asked everyone to be seated, welcomed the mothers, and a few toddlers who had come along, and started the presentation. The students left the room and stood outside the door until they heard the programmed beat from my keyboard. On cue, they boogied into the classroom, keeping beat with their snapping fingers — for those who could snap. When the music started, they turned to their mothers and sang:

I have a mother and she is great!
She gets up early and stays up late,
Trying to get through all that she must do.
I guess that's just a mother's fate.

The class continued to sing, doing a stellar job of describing a mother's life through song. It was now time for our serious song. Surprisingly, the children also loved this song. A mother's relationship with her child is special and this song spoke to that unique bond. The orchestration for this song was on a CD, so I directed as the children sang. They looked like angels.

I'm just a child, so how do you know
All I will need to help me to grow
Into the person that I want to be?
Are you an angel sent to love me?

I smiled at them and felt tears welling up in my eyes. I knew that the mothers were also touched and could hear sniffing as eyes were dabbed. I then heard another sound, unpleasantly familiar, that was followed by commotion. One of the toddlers, whose head was resting on his mother's shoulder, suddenly threw up everything he had eaten that day, and maybe the day before, and this mixture of food was spraying the mothers behind him, streaming down the back of his mother and forming large pools on the floor. The mothers in the line of fire did their best to dodge the projectile. The children kept singing:

God surely knew that I'd go astray,

The children were no longer smiling.

So He sent you to show me the way.

They were watching their mothers clean up the floor. And although they were still singing, no one, except for one boy, was watching me. That boy rolled his eyes to the back of his head, stuck out his tongue, and hugged his stomach with his arms as he doubled over gagging. I began to laugh as I watched our sweet Mother's Day presentation turn into a typical day for a mother. I was in the back and no one was paying attention to me so no one saw my reaction to the scenario. I was just glad it wasn't blood.

For me, one of the worst experiences dealing with a student and things not for the faint-hearted happened when I taught fifth grade at Karen Wallace's school. The students were assigned to give a class presentation and to bring in an object to go along with it. By fifth grade, students knew what was and wasn't allowed at school. At least they were supposed to know.

I was at the board teaching when James's object for his presentation fell out of his desk. Unbeknownst to me, he had brought fishhooks.

"Miss Thomas, I think something's wrong with James." Stephie's words were full of concern.

I turned around and noticed that James was bent over in his chair, his right hand on the floor and his left hand doing something I couldn't make out. "James," I said, "what are you doing?" He didn't answer, but he looked up at me with fear in his eyes. It was then that I was able to see a fishhook coming out of the carpet, going through his hand between his thumb and his index finger, and the point and barb sticking through the top of his hand. He was hooked to the carpet and the only way to set him free was to get the hook out of his hand. He couldn't move and neither could I.

"Stephie, buzz the office!" She ran to the button on the wall and pressed it.

"Yes?" came the secretary's voice.

"We need help right away!" I shouted. "Please send someone!" Within minutes, Mrs. Wallace was in my room and she immediately called for the custodian. My principal was a fisherwoman and she knew fishhooks.

"Bring carpet scissors," she ordered the janitor. The custodian soon arrived and used the scissors to carefully cut a hole in the carpet so that James could raise his hand from the floor. As he sat with his hooked hand on the desk, the custodian cut the carpet off of the hook and the principal called James's parents. James was taken to the hospital where they cut off the barb and the point and were able to pull the hook through his hand without performing surgery.

Growing up in a family of seven children meant many visits to the doctor and hospital for various and sundry mini-disasters. You would think that my childhood years would have prepared me for teaching children and all that comes with it. Maybe it did. Maybe I would have been carried off on a stretcher if I hadn't experienced what I did growing up. Being an elementary school teacher, you deal with a lot more than teaching. Just please don't let it be blood.

Tip for New Teachers: Teaching elementary students is not for the faint-hearted. If you want to be truly prepared for your occupation, take some human anatomy and dissecting classes — and watch a lot of horror movies. THAT will make you a master teacher!

Sixty-Two

The Truth Is...Underwear Was the Last
Present I Expected

M y years in education were adding up and things were progressively getting harder. The students where I taught were great, but the policies we had to live by were suffocating me, and from what I could observe, other teachers as well. Each year there were new requirements in multiple areas of the elementary teacher's profession. There were more issues involving accountability, more testing, more record-keeping, and more classes and workshops we were required to attend. The most unrealistic part of this picture was that nothing from the already staggering workload was being taken away. It seemed that the policymakers didn't think about elementary school teachers as human, with only so much energy, time, and ability to perform the miracles that were being expected of them. There were new teachers questioning their decision to become elementary school teachers, and I saw more than one new teacher break down or get physically sick over the impossible requirements they were to keep up with.

At the beginning of my elementary teaching career, a teacher's professional judgment was respected in all matters pertaining to the classroom and the students he taught. Then the state test came to Florida and took away the teacher's responsibility and power to decide whether or not a student should be promoted to the next grade.

As a teacher, it had been my job to identify any needs a student might have that went beyond my expertise in teaching. Once a need was identified, the child was referred for testing. The testing was done quickly and if the child qualified for help, he was put in a program that zeroed in on his needs. Teachers who had been trained specifically to teach children with learning disabilities or emotional handicaps taught these programs. Now a system called Response to Intervention, RTI, was being implemented, and this system decided if a child could even be tested to diagnose a learning problem. As a teacher, I was no longer allowed to immediately refer a child for testing if I suspected she needed help beyond what I could give her. The RTI procedure had to be followed and it involved more paperwork, more classroom one-on-one time with the student having difficulties, more testing and monitoring, more conferences, and more record-keeping. One of the biggest flaws with this new program was that the teacher still had the rest of the class to plan for and teach, and what was he supposed to do with the other students while he was working one-on-one with the child going through the RTI process?

One year I had four children in the RTI process, students in pull-out programs, as well as a student who had been identified as autistic and other children who eventually would be. I watched with guilt, the students who needed academic challenges, knowing I had no time or energy left to give them what they needed. They were often used as peer tutors, put on the computers, or told to read a book. The creative lessons I once taught had been geared to the brightest students and had much to offer every other student in the class so that the entire class progressed. The systems now being implemented spoke to the struggling students and left the others with little or no challenge. As teachers, we were to meet the needs of every child at every level. The question was, when did teachers have time to plan, develop, and implement the creative and level-appropriate lessons they were to be teaching each student? Was there an RTI process for a logic disability? A few policymakers needed to be tested.

In the mix of students with learning disabilities, autism, ADHD, and emotional handicaps were the students who just wanted attention.

In my class, Franklin was that student who just wanted attention. He was very smart and lovable, but at times his need for attention got in the way of his lovableness. He was having some difficult days in class, fighting with other students over petty things which resulted in emotional outbursts and disruptions to the students' learning. I wrote a note to his parents explaining Franklin's behavior and said that I would have him visit with the assistant principal if things didn't get better. The next day Franklin came into the classroom and the first thing he told me was that he needed to see Mrs. Iglesia, our assistant principal.

"Why do you need to see Mrs. Iglesia?" I asked.

"Because it says so in my planner." I opened his planner and could only find the note that I had written to his parents. "See," he said pointing to the note, "it says so right there."

"Franklin, I wrote that note to your parents and told them you would have to see Mrs. Iglesia only if you didn't behave." Little did I know that Franklin *wanted* to see pretty Mrs. Iglesia and so he did everything he could to be sent to the office.

First, he stood on his desk and howled. "Franklin," I said in surprise, "what are you doing? Get down from there before you get hurt." I then had the students move their desks in preparation for a math test. Franklin moved his onto the tile part of the floor and scraped the legs back and forth, making a loud screeching sound.

"Franklin, please stop that!" I scolded him.

He looked directly at me and continued. *Eeeee! Eeeee! Eeeee! Eeeee!* Push, pull, push, pull.

"What is going on with you? Please stop that!" It was finally quiet in the classroom and I handed out the math tests. I read the test to the children, one problem at a time, and after reading a problem, I gave the students time to work it out. While walking around the room monitoring the students, Franklin called out to me.

"Miss Thomas, I need help!"

I quickly turned in his direction and gave him my "Don't you dare talk out!" look.

"I need your help!" he said in a loud voice.

I went to him and said, "Franklin, if you need help you are to raise your hand. You know that. Now, how can I help you?"

He threw his head back, opened his mouth, and wagged his tongue back and forth, making loud noises while he did so. "Ahhhhhhhhhhh!"

I walked away, and no sooner had I gotten across the room than he called out, "Miss Thomas, I need your help!"

"Franklin," I said in a loud whisper, "raise your hand!"

He ignored my words. "I need your help." I again walked to him and he again threw his head back, opened his mouth, and made the same noises as before while he wagged his tongue.

I looked at him through slits in my eyes and said, "Well, Franklin, I hope you really don't need help because you're not going to get it," and I walked away. Again I made it across the room when Franklin called out. But this time he said something different.

"Miss Thomas, I itch." I ignored him. "I itch." he said louder. I ignored him. "Miss Thomas, I itch!"

I turned around and there was Franklin sitting in his chair with his slacks down around his ankles, scratching his thighs. Barely covering his bottom, and the rest of what needed to be covered, was a cobalt blue, spandex speedo. The class was busily working on their tests and hadn't yet noticed Franklin's new outfit. I quickly got to him, stood at the side of his chair facing the class, and pulled my full skirt out trying to hide him.

"Put your pants on," I whispered.

"I itch!"

The students' concentration had now been broken and the girls squealed, "Eewww! Franklin! Put your pants on!"

I lectured them, "Girls, don't look at him. Keep your eyes on your tests!" How could they help but look at him? Those brilliant blue speedos demanded attention.

It was time for lunch and I took Franklin to the office. He was smiling away, happy that he was finally going to get his time with Mrs. Iglesia.

"Excuse me, Mrs. Iglesia, do you have a moment to speak with Franklin?" She welcomed us into her office and had Franklin sit down.

"How can I help you, Franklin?" she asked.

It was obvious that he loved sitting in the office of the young, pretty Mrs. Iglesia. "I don't know," he said.

I helped remind him. "What about standing on your desk?"

"Oh, that."

"And what about scraping your desk across the tile over and over?"

He scrunched up his face. "And what about taking your clothes off in class and sitting in your underwear?"

He suddenly came to life. "I didn't take my clothes off. I still had my socks and shoes on." Mrs. Iglesia sucked in her cheeks, trying her best not to laugh. First graders are extremely literal.

Another day the students were giving oral book reports. I was listening to a report when I felt a tap on my shoulder. Before I turned around, Franklin whispered in my ear, "I don't know whose these belong to so I thought you might want them." He then handed me a pair of Calvin Klein briefs and walked back to his seat.

I don't know about anyone else, but I sure don't remember students bringing underwear to the teacher when I was in elementary school. I hoped they had updated the college methods classes. The old methods were no longer going to work.

Tip for New Teachers: Be prepared for anything.

Sixty-Three

The Truth Is...I Felt Picked On

Because I was teaching in a portable far away from the main building, it was not easy to haul my teaching materials to and from the parking lot each day. My style of teaching has always involved lots of hands-on activities. If you have hands-on activities, you need something to put your hands on, so I was constantly lugging something from home to use in my lessons. We teachers were told that we were not to park by the portables because it was a fire safety hazard. We were allowed to unload our cars by the portables, but then we were to move them to the parking area.

It was *Polar Express* day for the first-graders, and on this day the students and teachers wore pajamas, drank hot chocolate, and did numerous activities that related to the book *The Polar Express* that we had read in class. I had lots of goodies to bring that day, so I drove my VW bug to my portable and unloaded it. When I finished unloading the goods, it was almost time for the students to be in class, so I quickly got into my car and attempted to drive to the parking lot. My timing was bad. School buses blocked the entrance to the lot and I knew that if I waited for the buses to clear out, my students would be standing outside the portable with no supervision. I decided the best thing to do would be to drive back to the portable and move my car to the parking lot during the morning specials. I parked beside the portable and let the students into the classroom.

The students were excited and so was I. Most elementary school teachers enjoy the special days as much as the students do. I had my nightgown on over my clothes and the students giggled when they saw me, thrilled that their teacher had gotten into the spirit of the day. The students were dressed in a variety of PJ's, some decorated with princesses, some with Hot Wheels cars — none with Barney. They insisted that they were way too grown up for Barney.

It was soon special area time and the students left through the portable door that opened onto the playground. My class split for special areas, groups of three and four going to five different classes. Once I saw that the students were where they needed to be, I went back into the portable to get things set up for our *Polar Express* party.

When the class returned, I served the students hot chocolate and taught them a song from the movie *The Polar Express*. In the middle of our singing, one of my students glanced out the window through the blinds and said, "Miss Thomas, there's an ambulance and a fire truck out there."

"Real funny, James." James was known for his tall tales so I dismissed what he said.

"No, I'm serious," he said. "There really is a fire truck and an ambulance next to our portable." He looked sincere, so I went to the window and sure enough, there was a fire truck and an ambulance next to our portable. Then it dawned on me.

"My car! Oh no, my car is parked out there!" What were the chances that on the one day I parked my car by my portable and then completely forgot about it, a fire truck and ambulance would park by my portable?

I walked out onto our little ramp platform and yelled to the nearest fireman, "Is my car in your way?"

"No, it's not a problem," he said, and then he stared at me. I couldn't imagine why he was staring and then it dawned on me — I was in my nightgown.

"Sometimes I get really tired at work," I said with a smile as I went back inside the portable.

Although the fireman told me that my car had not been a problem, for some reason I felt it was my duty to explain to Mr. Smith why my car was parked by my portable. After school I went to his office.

"I'm sorry my car was by the portable when the fire truck came today." Mr. Smith gave me a puzzled look. "Today when the fire truck and ambulance were at the portable, my car was back there because I got trapped by the school buses after unloading my *Polar Express* things this morning."

"I didn't notice it," Mr. Smith responded and I wished I hadn't mentioned it to him.

Two months later I drove to school with a trunk full of bagged holiday candy. A friend of mine worked for a local grocery store and they were getting rid of the candy. "The students and teachers will love this!" I told her as she helped me load my trunk. It took me longer to unload the loot than I had anticipated, so by the time I drove my car to the parking lot, the buses were blocking the way and I again made the decision to park my car by the portable and then move it, and I again forgot to move it. This time was different, though. There was no fire truck or ambulance, but there was a call to my room telling me to report to the office when the students went to special area.

Did Mr. Smith want to talk with me about my math program? He had been asking the staff to let him know if they had any ideas to help raise our math scores, and I had reminded Mr. Smith about my program. I had also shown him my coordinate grid math mat and demonstrated how I used it with the children. At the time, he didn't say anything either positive or negative about it. Maybe he had been thinking it over and wanted to give it a try.

My students were dismissed to special area classes and I happily went to the office where I was given a directive for parking my car by the portable. Directives are given when a teacher or staff member willfully goes against school policy. It wasn't in my nature to willfully go against school policy (unless I got a cute pencil sharpener in the mail). Now I was receiving a directive for forgetting I had parked my car by my portable — and it was only there because I had brought in treats for EVERYONE!

In the directive it said that what I had done showed that I was not considerate of the children's psychological state. What?! I knew the students were being driven crazy by the tests and nonstop work they were being given. That's why I was bringing them candy!

The day after being given my directive for parking by the portable, the teachers were told to park by the portables. The second graders were putting on a special program and parents needed to park in the parking lot. I didn't know what the difference would be in the students' psychological state when *I* parked by the portable as compared to when the whole staff parked by the portables, but I did know that my psychological state was being challenged. It was a good thing I had bags of chocolate candy in my room. That would get me through anything!

Tip for New Teachers: Don't try to make sense out of school policies that don't make sense, just keep a drawer full of chocolate.

Sixty-Four

The Truth Is...I Hadn't Read

the Fine Print

In most places of business and learning, there are absurdities — like being written up for parking your car by your portable and then being told the next day to park your car by your portable. The days went on and it was getting harder for me to be me. Throughout my teaching career I was taught that children have different learning styles, so as a teacher, it was important that my lessons addressed these styles. The modern day problem with that philosophy is that the way the teachers are now being made to teach is a "one size fits all" method. How could those in power not understand that this way of teaching will not address the students' different learning styles? And just as individual students have their own style of learning, individual teachers have their own style of teaching. All teachers were once children who learned in different ways and were encouraged to express themselves as unique individuals. So it stands to reason that when these teachers become adults, they will have their own unique teaching styles. Making all teachers fit into the same teaching mold is no different than trying to make every child learn the same way, despite the differences in how they learn. To be told how to teach, and then to be held accountable for a teaching method forced upon us teachers was another absurdity in twenty-first century public education.

This was my twenty-eighth year in the public schools and the absurdities that now existed in the schools were stressing even the youngest of teachers. There was the unrealistic No Child Left Behind Act, the ambiguous RTI system, the expectations for regular classroom teachers to take care of student health problems that would normally require a nurse's training, the state test that was in many ways necessary but inconsistent and cryptic in its expectations, and too powerful in its ability to decide a student's fate from year to year, the Race to the Top federal government program that awarded money to schools based on strict rules of compliance, while at the same time generating more paperwork for the teachers and administrators, and the unrelenting pace at which computer technology had taken our society.

As I stated earlier, I believed that those who were coming up with ideas to improve the public education system meant well. However, like the soldiers who are in the trenches actually fighting the battles, only the teachers implementing the commands of those above them knew the truth about whether the system was working and if they would survive it. Even as a highly driven person with no family to take care of, the task of keeping up with the demands placed upon me as an elementary school teacher was overwhelming. My last year in teaching would prove too much for me as I, along with all the other elementary teachers I knew, were told there would be more added to what we were already doing and nothing taken away.

A new evaluation system was being implemented in many schools across the country. Teachers would now receive a rating of *Beginning, Developing, Applying,* or *Innovative* as their lessons were observed. We were told about the new evaluation system at a meeting, where we were also told that only 10% of the entire district teacher population would get *Innovative* as their evaluation rating, so the chances of receiving a top rating were very slim. I sat in that meeting and felt my drive to do my best at my job seeping out of me. What the new evaluation system called an innovative teacher had very little to do with personal creativity or innovation, or the way a teacher related to her students. It was more about a specific system all teachers were to follow that spelled out for us how to teach, when to teach what, and how to relate to the students — even if the way we were told to relate to them wasn't the most effective way for each individual teacher to relate to his own students. Every day I felt more and more like I was part of a mass production education system.

Our pay structure was also changing. Florida teachers would now receive merit pay. Part of this pay would come from the teacher evaluation. Printed in the Orlando Sentinel on July 17, 2012 were the following words: *Steve Fannin was honored in Washington, D.C. as one of the nation's best math and science educators. Despite this honor, he was identified as a "beginning" teacher by a mid-year evaluation because he erased the day's "learning goal" from his board while teaching a chemistry lesson. Some teachers who spoke to the paper (Orlando Sentinel) said they felt they were being judged (evaluated) primarily on whether their students used hand gestures to indicate how well they had learned something and on whether they wrote "learning goals" on the board every day. "It's been humiliating for a lot of extremely accomplished people," said Mary Louise Wells, who was one of five finalists for the state teacher of the year award in 2002.*

The other part of our pay would come from student test scores. Because I had taught so many different children with such diverse backgrounds, I knew this system would never work. The school where I was now employed could in no way be compared to the school where my students fought all day. The classroom teachers who were given the most behaviorally difficult students could not be compared with the teachers with students who focused and listened and did their work. Teachers who had administrators who were supportive could not be compared with teachers who had little to no support from their administrators. And what about parent involvement? Teaching in a school where I saw parents only when they needed paperwork filled out for government welfare, as opposed to a school where parents were keenly involved in their children's education, told me again that the merit pay system would not work.

Teacher friends who I had known over the years often talked about how things had changed in the public elementary schools since we first began our careers. Testing, data, and record-keeping were now all-important and one of my principals even told me in a meeting, "Don't even think of saying anything about this because it's set in stone and you can't change it."

So I quit thinking about the creative ways I used to teach. I now rarely used my math songs with the children, and the math mat that had helped many children who had difficulty in math was now used as a place to sit when I needed the children to gather in one spot.

We had a mural of a town on our classroom wall and it was time to change the season. It was fall and Halloween was getting close. In first grade we talked about neighborhoods and communities and I was able to connect an activity to our learning goal that I thought would enable us to sneak in a little fun for the day. We would divide the class into "neighborhoods" of four students each and trick-or-treat through the "neighborhoods" in the classroom. I had done this the year before and the students loved it. Each student was to bring in some sort of treat for each of the other students and I would bring in fake jack 'o lanterns with battery-operated lights to create a fall mood. Despite being fifty-eight, I still loved these activities.

I had been working late at school almost every night since school started. Staying late at school wasn't a new thing for me, but staying late to work on data and common boards was. I was happy to work on interesting lessons for the students, and staying late for that was something I chose to do. There was no joy for me as I worked on the common board, one of our new requirements, wrote detailed lesson plans, and studied the new elements of our revised evaluation. The only real joy I felt in my job came from being with my students. I loved them and *no* one could take that away from me.

We would have our trick-or-treat day on Monday—Halloween—so when the candy came in I piled it on top of the bookshelf by my desk.

I lined the students up for lunch and walked them to the cafeteria. After getting them through the lunch line and situated at their table, I went to the teachers' lunchroom and joined other teachers in light conversation about the beautiful fall weather and other things unrelated to our evaluations. Lunch was over too soon and I left the teachers' lounge to pick up my students and take them to recess.

As the students escaped the confinement of the school, and were greeted by the intoxicating October weather, they yelled with elation. It was a glorious day, and it was also the day that would set a new course for me. It was the day I "passed out" and was taken to the hospital.

I came back to school the following Monday and the candy was still sitting on top of the bookshelf. Mrs. Rodriguez, who had been with me at recess right before I passed out, told me that when the students saw me taken away in the ambulance, they thought I was going to die. She went back to the room with my class and promised the students that I would be okay. She relayed to me that the students were upset and crying, all except Franklin, the speedo underwear kid. He assured the class, "It's okay! We have candy!"

I stood alone in my room, in some ways feeling strange that I was back. It would take a week or more for me to feel "normal" after a syncope episode such as the one I had had. When the students arrived that day, I immediately felt better. As was true in all of my days of teaching, despite the workload and ever increasing demands, being with my students always made me a better, and 99.9% of the time, happier person. I never ceased to laugh at the antics of my first graders, nor ceased to marvel at their abilities. I would miss having frequent contact with such wonderful people.

The rest of the school year was bittersweet. I always equated the holidays and traditional vacations with school, for in my life, the school calendar was the one I lived by. Soon my calendar would change. What would it be like in the fall when green leaves became golden, orange, and crimson, not to have a class of eager students with whom I could share the wonders of nature? How would I feel around the special days of the year without being energized by the happy feelings the children exuded? The traditional books I read to my class every year would soon be sitting on my bookshelves at home, and I knew they would rarely be touched. How could silently reading a child's book to myself take the place of dramatically reading it in front of a captive audience who traveled with me to lands created by words and imagination? And what would my life be like without the unconditional love given me every day by my students?

As my last year was coming to an end, I met with financial advisors about my retirement account. I was informed that if I retired before I was fifty-nine and a half, I would lose the money I would otherwise be given for my accrued sick days. I would be returning to school in August for six weeks. So much for nostalgia.

Tip for New Teachers: Find out about your retirement NOW!

Sixty-Five

The Truth Is...I Just Wanted Cake

How does one feel when they think they've retired but find out they haven't? In my case, thankful, but tired. I was thankful that I could come back for the needed six weeks, but those last six weeks almost did me in.

When I arrived at school on the first day back after summer vacation, I was handed the key to Mrs. Rossi's portable and was told that I'd be setting up for, and teaching, her second grade class until my six weeks were up. Mrs. Rossi was pregnant and had opened only a few boxes of her materials before she went into early labor. I would substitute for her class until the actual sub came six weeks later. Why end the last six weeks of my career on a light, stress-free note? I felt bad for Mrs. Rossi, for myself, and for the students. I felt bad for Mrs. Rossi because I knew that she would want her room set up in a specific way and I was pretty certain I wouldn't be setting it up the way she wanted it. I felt bad for myself because I would have to figure out the second grade curriculum on my own time, and would be spending most of my in-class time testing the students. This meant that I would have to spend the waking hours I wasn't learning the curriculum, getting worksheets and centers ready for the students who would need something to do while I was testing individuals. And I felt bad for the students because, just as they would get used to me and begin to bond with me, I would leave them.

Mrs. Rossi had worked hard over the summer getting things ready for the substitute who would take over her class on the date originally scheduled for her maternity leave. I was using what I thought were the materials Mrs. Rossi had copied for the sub to use for the second graders. The first week of school I gave the class their spelling words. The words were typed on the weekly homework sheet Mrs. Rossi had prepared. I was surprised, not only at the amount of homework the second graders had, but also at the difficulty of the work. Compared to the first grade words, the second grade spelling words were very difficult. The list contained words such as *auditorium, genealogy,* and *speculation.* A few parents called me, upset by the workload and I assured them that their children would get used to it. In actuality, I wasn't sure how they were going to handle the workload. Some of them could barely read.

Because of the situation I was thrust into, I didn't have time to look at all of the homework papers and workbook assignments I was giving the students. Spelling was pretty routine, so I assigned workbook pages and on Thursday, allowed the students to grade their own books using the teacher's manual for the answers. I was testing and under a strict deadline, so I had to do what I could to get the testing done while keeping the rest of the class busy.

Friday came and it was time for the weekly spelling test. The students wrote their names and the date on their sheets of notebook paper while I got my spelling book. I felt a little guilty that I hadn't opened the spelling book until that moment. But better that I felt a tinge of guilt than to get a reprimanding scowl for my testing not being completed before retiring.

I looked at the first week's list and saw word number one — *flat.* "What?" I thought. I flipped through the pages looking for the list I had given the students that week. Throughout the whole book, none of the weekly lists compared in difficulty to the words I had given them. The second word on the workbook spelling list was *flap.* I obviously had given the students the wrong list. No wonder the parents were upset. Since the students had studied the difficult list, those were the words I gave them. I began, "*Auditorium*. There was an assembly in the *auditorium*." The students quietly wrote. "Number two," I continued, "*genealogy*. Philip was working on his family's *genealogy*." Unlike my first graders, not one student complained, told me to wait because I was going too fast, or cried. "Number three..." I went on until I had given them all ten words. I then said, "I'm going to try a little experiment. I'm going to give you a few more words that I know you haven't studied. I won't take a grade on these words unless you do really well." I made a mental note that I also wouldn't take a grade on the hard list I had given them unless they did really well. I began to dictate the actual spelling words for the week. "*Flat*," I said, "the tire was *flat*." Some of the students looked up at me and smiled.

"That's easy," said Florence.

"I'll bet it is," I thought, "after spelling the word association, lots of words will seem easy." I continued to dictate the "easy" words and collected the papers. When I graded them I found that every child in the room had passed the actual spelling test for the week. Most of them got a one hundred percent — and they hadn't even studied the words. I think I had discovered a new way to teach spelling!

I called Mrs. Rossi about the homework sheet and the words I had given the students that first week.

"I taught the gifted third grade class last year," she said. "Those homework sheets were for them. I didn't know until a few weeks before school started that I was being switched to second grade." I knew the parents were going to be extremely happy with the next spelling list their children brought home.

The weeks of testing were grueling. I was exhausted, the students were exhausted, and it didn't seem fair that we couldn't start out the school year with exciting, motivating lessons. In the middle of testing, tropical storms made their appearance, which meant everyone in the portables had to go to the main building. Classes had to double up, and because there was too much movement going on in the room for students who were testing to concentrate, I couldn't test them. On top of having to double up, the air conditioning quit working in large sections of the building which, due to hair and clothes soaked with perspiration, gave the students another reason to not be able to concentrate.

Progress reports would be going home just about the time I'd be retiring. I had stacks of papers I had graded, but no time and no password to get into Mrs. Rossi's data entry system to enter the grades. I had asked the administration for the password, but like me, they were swamped with beginning of the year paperwork and procedures and hadn't gotten the chance to give it to me. My final six weeks were passing quickly and I felt more stress than ever trying to accomplish all that I had been given to do before leaving.

Over the twenty-eight years I taught, I attended many retirement festivities. A few times, I even provided the musical entertainment. As a result, I had always wondered what my retirement get-together would be like when my teaching days were through. There weren't too many days left before I'd be leaving. I hadn't heard even a hint of a retirement celebration. I did receive a card from the staff the first time I thought I was retiring, but because I had six more weeks to go, there was no cake. I was appreciative of the card and the goodbye messages, and I'm not one that needs a big fanfare, but I do like cake. All I wanted was to share cake with my colleagues before I said goodbye.

It was Wednesday, a week and a half before my last day. The staff was given notice that there would be a meeting in the media center after student dismissal. I tried not to show my excitement, but I knew this had to be the cake and punch get-together. I was assigned car duty that week, the worst duty of them all. Despite the sticky ninety-degree temperatures mixed with the hot exhaust fumes burning my legs as parents drove up to the curb, I loaded the children into their cars with a smile on my face. When duty was over, I, with the other teachers, made my way to the media center and cake. When I walked into the meeting room, the place was already filled with teachers and other staff members and there on the large screen that had been lowered from the wall were the words *RTI*.

"What?" I thought. "This meeting is about *RTI*?" Response to Intervention — my least favorite program of twenty-first century education.

Mrs. Rodriguez, my fellow first grade teacher, was giving the presentation. When she saw me she quietly said with a smile, "You know you don't have to be here. You'll soon be free!"

There really *wasn't* going to be any cake. No, I *wanted* to stay. I sat down and as my feelings of disappointment about no cake and my frustration about *RTI* mixed, I became angrier by the minute. Upstaged by *RTI*! The meeting began and Mrs. Rodriguez said, "Before I get started, does anyone have anything they'd like to say about *RTI*?"

"Oh yeah," I thought, "I have something to say." I didn't want to be disrespectful to my colleague giving the presentation, but what I had to say had nothing to do with her. Because I was retiring and couldn't be fired, for the first time in years I felt free to express my true feelings about something I disagreed with in education.

"I don't know who thought this system was a good idea," I started, "but what I have seen in the past three years is that it has kept my students who need special help from getting it, and prevented my academically high students from getting the challenges they need because I spend most of my time helping the struggling students. I want to help the students who have difficulties in school, but I feel like the rest of my class is suffering because they aren't getting the attention they need. We're supposed to teach every student on his level and according to his learning style — with a system that doesn't allow us to do that, have dynamic lessons prepared for every level of learning, and yet we are given no time to prepare or teach these lessons. Who is coming up with these ideas, anyway?" I saw a few shocked looks, a few teachers shifting in their chairs, some teachers looking down, and the rest sitting in silence. "I don't know if anyone else feels the way I do about *RTI*, but that's how I feel."

Mrs. Blake, a young, vibrant teacher, broke the silence. "Well we do, but unlike you, we're not retiring anytime soon." The teachers broke out in laughter and the tension in the room lifted. All we needed was cake to make the moment perfect.

After the meeting, a group of young teachers came to me and one of them said, "Do you know how much we love you? We're so glad you said what you did." It felt good to say what I did, but I knew that what I said wasn't going to change anything. I was leaving and the teachers still in the system had little to no power to change what they were being required to do. I didn't know how they would keep up with the demands placed on them, but because of their love for the children, I did know that if they could, they would try to survive the system.

It was my last day of teaching and I had completed all of the testing. The scores were recorded on the data sheet and my final task, before going home that night, would be to enter all of the worksheet and test grades into the report card data system. I had received the password a few days previous, but between the daily common board requirements, lesson plans, beginning of the year parent forms, paper grading, testing, oh — and teaching — there had been no time to input the grades for progress reports.

It was Friday and the students would take their weekly tests. However, I had decided that for my last day we would also have some fun. I planned to show a *Magic School Bus* movie about energy and then do some energy-related science activities. Oral reading time would be longer today because I wanted to finish the *Little House on the Prairie* book I had been reading to the class. Later in the day we would go outside so the students could share their talents in a spur-of-the-moment talent show I would announce that morning. And, for the final fanfare, the class and I would eat ice-cream bars that I had brought in.

The students had their spelling test papers out and I began the dictation. "*Mine.* That hat is *mine.*"

Bringggg! Bringggg! I answered the phone on my desk.

"This is Miss Thomas. May I help you?"

The person on the other end didn't identify herself. "Hello, Miss Thomas. Today is your last day (*Was she calling to tell me about cake and punch in the media center?*) and we've noticed you have not inputted your grades for the upcoming progress report. We need these before you leave today."

In all of my years of teaching, I, like most teachers I knew, not only did what we were required to do, but went hours and hours a week beyond the call of duty. The last six weeks of my teaching career had been no different in that respect and now, six hours before my last official teaching day would be over, I was being questioned about finishing my work?

"You'll get them!" I fumed, hung up the phone, and then continued with the test. The portable door opened and in walked Angie, Mr. Smith's secretary, with a woman I had never seen. Angie was cordial and apologetic about interrupting my teaching.

"Miss Thomas, this is Mrs. Nadeem," Angie said. "She will be the substitute when you leave and is here to shadow you today so that she will know the routine."

I don't swear, but wanted to. I do cry, and wanted to, but didn't. I didn't want to smile at the substitute, but did. After all, I knew that this wasn't her fault. How could I carry out the day I had planned with the students when the substitute needed to know the regular routine, and I was sure, had many questions about the numberless classroom procedures? Even if I hadn't planned a special day with the students, because up until that point all we had done was test, no official regular routine had been established. Angie left and Mrs. Nadeem stayed.

Sometimes parents can be very demanding with teachers, even unreasonable, until the teacher is so upset with those parents, it takes all of her will not to take her frustration out on the child of those parents. That's how I was now feeling. In this case, though, I was upset with the administration and I was doing everything I could not to take my frustration out on the substitute. Why hadn't anyone told me about this, and hadn't it occurred to anyone that I just might not be having a regular school day with my kids on the last day of my twenty-eight year career?

I did my best to help Mrs. Nadeem, but I felt that I spent more time explaining why I didn't have the answers to all of her questions due to the intense testing we had just finished, than I spent giving her helpful information. The time I thought I might have to input grades while the students were watching the movie, I instead spent with Mrs. Nadeem. My planning time I spent with Mrs. Nadeem. Any time I wasn't working with the children I was working with Mrs. Nadeem, and yet I knew that she still had many, many questions.

It was time for lunch and as the children ate, I spent my last twenty-minute school lunch with Mrs. Nadeem and a few other teachers sitting in the teachers' room. What a day. I wanted to cry about so many things, but before I had the chance, Mrs. Maxwell, a wonderful kindergarten teacher who I was just getting to know, walked into the room with a large bakery box in her hands.

"Miss Thomas," she said, "this is for you."

In the box was a large cake. I had mixed emotions about finally getting my cake. I was truly touched and began to get misty-eyed, but I was also embarrassed, figuring someone had spread the word that I was hurt about not getting a cake and so the teachers took up a collection to buy this at the last minute.

"Oh, thank you," I smiled as I took the box from her. "Did the teachers do this?"

"No," Mrs. Maxwell said, "a parent brought it in for my class and it has so much food coloring in the frosting I didn't want the kids to have it. I knew they'd end up with it all over their clothes."

"Thanks, Natalie," I said and Mrs. Maxwell left the room.

I sat at the table with a large blue and red frosted cake sitting in front of me. The other teachers looked at me, waiting for me to say something. I tried to explain the saga of my illusive retirement cake, but I began to laugh so hard, I couldn't get out what I was trying to say. I didn't know if Mrs. Maxwell knew about me wanting a retirement cake, or if she just happened to give it to me because it was my last day. It didn't matter — I loved Mrs. Maxwell.

The day was almost at its end with twenty minutes left to do our talent show. Mrs. Nadeem and I took the class outside, and one by one the students sang, danced, threw footballs and baseballs, and shared other talents with us. As the last student showed us some pictures he had drawn, the sound of feedback from the PA system caught our attention.

"Good afternoon Boys and Girls," came the voice over the PA system. It was afternoon announcements and then it would be dismissal. I ran to the teachers' lounge and got the ice-cream bars from the freezer. While the students ate their treats, the announcements continued. I was unable to make out anything being said except the words "Miss Thomas." I hoped that whatever they were saying about me had nothing to do with testing, progress reports, or common boards.

Lines of students began to make their way across the playground blacktop to the dismissal areas. I still had car duty that week and was glad it was the last day in my life for that. I shouted orders at my students, telling them to get where they needed to be for dismissal and hated that I had to become a sergeant my last moments with them.

As classes of children passed me in their lines, many stopped and quickly hugged me. "They said on the announcements that today's your last day and to say goodbye," students told me as they put their arms around me. Were they kidding? There wasn't time to hug the students goodbye. I had car duty and if I wasn't there on time, someone would be complaining. As different students reached out for a hug, I quickly walked past them, explaining that I needed to be at my post.

As was usual for the end of September in Florida, it was hot and humid and the car exhaust made the unbearable weather conditions even worse. In staff meetings we were often reminded that we had to "keep the cars moving in the car rider line" which meant there was no time to socialize with the parents. There were parents and students who wanted to say goodbye to me. I didn't want to be reprimanded on my last day of teaching, so when I could, I snuck quick hugs as students were being loaded into their cars and then waved goodbye to the parents.

I said goodbye to the few teachers at duty and then made my way back to the portable to input grades. When I opened the door, I was surprised to find Mr. Smith and Mrs. Nadeem at my desk, rummaging through things.

"Hello," I started, "did you need something?"

Mr. Smith stopped for a second and said, "We're looking for next week's lesson plans."

While teaching, my students rarely saw me at my breaking point, but at that moment I had reached it. My lips quivered and my face felt hot as I hung onto the last bit of self control I possessed. "This has been the worst day in my teaching career!" The words rapidly spewed out of my mouth. Mr. Smith looked more nervous than I had ever seen him. His eyes instantly showed fear; fear that I was going to say something that would send Mrs. Nadeem running. Before I could say another word, Mr. Smith spoke.

"That's okay," he said. "We'll worry about the lesson plans later."

They left the room and I began inputting grades for progress reports. While I worked at my desk, a few teachers called and a few teachers came to say goodbye, but I never got to say goodbye to the majority of people I had worked with my last five years. When the custodian came to clean the room, he listened as I shared my sad tale about getting no retirement cake. He then shared a similar story about his birthday and how he wanted cake but his wife didn't get it for him either, so he understood how I felt.

It was 8:15 when I left that evening. Other than the custodians', there were no other cars in the parking lot. Over the years, as I had imagined my retirement day, this scene never came to mind. It was probably good that my teaching career ended this way — it would keep me from wondering if I had made the right decision to leave.

Despite the frustration and stress of my last weeks of teaching, I never regretted becoming an elementary school teacher. Reflecting back over my years of teaching, myriads of faces come to mind. Some names I remember, more names I don't. But I remember the faces, and the stories that go with those faces. I remember the laughter and tears and teacher looks, and the wonderful children who made me a much better person than the person I was before I became an elementary school teacher. And to all elementary students I want to say, "If you don't remember anything else you learn in school, remember this one thing. You are unique and have special gifts to give the world. Find those gifts and share them. There is an elementary school teacher waiting to hear all about your discoveries!"

Tip for New Teachers: The world of teaching is a world I no longer recognize. I don't know what is ahead for the public school system,

but one thing I do know is that as educators, we must never forget that teaching is not about numbers and tests, but about the unique personality and soul of every student who enters our classrooms. Teaching is also about the gifts we can bring to those students by way of our own unique personalities and different styles of teaching. It is teaching to the heart that makes a great student-teacher relationship and opens the way for learning, not teaching to the numbers. Of course, if you're an elementary school teacher you already know that. After all, teaching to the heart is what an elementary school teacher does and no one can take that away from you!

Do You Have a Story?

If you're a teacher, you have a story. If you'd like to share a story that you feel should be a part of *The Truth Is...Confessions and Tips from an Elementary School Teacher Part II,* please send it by way of attachment to rebecca@msthomaspresents.com

Please include your full name, an email address, and a phone number where you can be reached. To protect yourself and the people in your story, please change the names of the characters and any school involved.

If your story is chosen to be in the book, you will be contacted. You will also be acknowledged in the book.

We look forward to reading about you and your life as a teacher!

Workshops, Speaking Engagements, and Singing with the Students

If you are interested in finding out more about Rebecca paying a visit to your school, please contact her at rebecca@msthomaspresents.com

Made in the USA
Charleston, SC
14 April 2016